THE SERIOUS DECISIVE BUSINESS START-UP GUIDE

How to Set Up Your Business in 4 Easy-to-Follow Steps:

For High-Achievers Who Are Serious About Developing

Multiple Sources of Income, Maintaining Financial Stability

and Love Being Their Own BOSS!

Amina Chitembo

- ✓ The Corporate and Executive's High-Performance Coaching Expert
- ✓ Keynote Speaker on **'Financial Stability and Mental Health in Leadership'**
- ✓ Author and Trainer

© 2017 Copyright Amina Chitembo International, All Rights Reserved.

For details of our coaching, consultancy and training services and for information about how to apply for permission to reuse the copyright material in this book or any other of our publications, please contact Amina Chitembo International at *STRATEGIES@AMINACHITEMBO.COM* .

Please note that no part of this book may be reproduced or transmitted in any form whatsoever, electronic or mechanical, including photocopying, recording, or by any informational storage or retrieval system without the permission of the author and copyright holder. The right of the author to be identified as the author of this work has been asserted by the United Kingdom Copyright, Designs and Patents Act 1988, Copyright, Designs and Patents Act 1988, without the prior permission of the author.

London Borough of Redbridge	
30108032965175	
Askews & Holts	
650	£10.97
5579731	REDILF

Inspiring you, executives and business leaders to perform consistently at high levels and to achieve greater balance in your professional and personal life.

Disclaimer

This self-help publication with all its information and ideas are provided in good faith or in the opinion of me, the author who believes the information is true and honest to the best of my knowledge and experience. All opinions expressed in this publication represent only my views and opinions at the time of writing.

I, the author reserve the right to vary or change any such opinions subsequently. It is impossible to provide comprehensive information and advice tailored to each situation within a publication such as this, and it should not be regarded as any substitute for appropriate and personalised professional advice. Nothing in this publication can be used as a promise or guarantee. Adoption, implementation or trial of any of the information, ideas, methods or systems mention in this publication and on the associated website are entirely at the reader's own risk. You, the reader is totally responsible for the choices and decisions you make, and for all consequences of those decisions.

Apologies for any errors, omissions or inaccuracies that may be found in this publication.

My aim is to produce books and other publications that will empower and encourage high-achievement and professional development for all people regardless of race, creed, colour, sexual orientation or religion. I hope you find it useful and empowering, and I hope it helps towards reaching your highest level of achievement and handle all goals you with a purpose and dynamism!

ISBN: Number: 978-0-9957396-2-8 (Paperback)

Dedication and Special Thanks

To my husband Ali Abdoul and our daughters, Ngosa, Razina, Naila and Iman, for the love, support and unfailing inspiration. I love you, family!

To the Peter Thomson International Team, Leamington Spa, UK and the 100+ Club for the support.

To Brendon Burchard, Mama Christiane Burchard, and the Certified High Performance Coach™ Team for the Mentorship and Comradery.

Amina Chitembo

Honour the Struggle and Bring the Joy!

~ Brendon Burchard.

Inspiring you, executives and business leaders to perform consistently at high levels and to achieve greater balance in your professional and personal life.

FINANCIAL STABILITY is at the Core of Life.

You need to work and earn to maintain FINANCIAL STABILITY. As a LEADER, you need have good MENTAL HEALTH and WELL-BEING to work, think and act responsibly and make CRITICAL DECISIONS.

Other people's lives depend on the DECISIONS you make both in your PROFESSIONAL and PERSONAL life.

When your MENTAL HEALTH suffers, you start making the WRONG DECISIONS. The WRONG DECISIONS you make can cost you your job and EARNINGS ABILITIES.

The loss of EARNING ABILITIES will consequently lead to loss of FINANCIAL STABILITY.

When your FINANCIAL STABILITY (professional or personal) is IMPACTED, your HEALTH and WELL-BEING will suffer, and you risk problems such as DEPRESSION, ANXIETY or worse still suicide.

EXECUTIVES and BUSINESS LEADERS are at risk of MENTAL HEALTH ILNESS, too.

DON'T IGNORE feeling low. TALK TO AMINA; She is a comrade and confidant, not a shrink!

~ Amina Chitembo, Author, Trainer, Speaker, High-Performance Coaching Expert for Corporates and Executives.

Inspiring you, executives and business leaders to perform consistently at high levels and to achieve greater balance in your professional and personal life.

> We strongly pledge to lead the way in raising awareness and improving the Health and Well-being of people in leadership. We donate two per cent of all our profits to Mental Health and Domestic Abuse charitable NGOs.

This Guide is for Serious Players Only!

Inspiring you, executives and business leaders to perform consistently at high levels and to achieve greater balance in your professional and personal life.

Hello High Achiever,

THANK YOU! It is clear you are serious about seeing your vision becoming a reality.

Do you have a burning desire to start your own business, but you don't know where to start?

Have you been procrastinating about it and wishing someone would hold your hand and help you?

Yes, we have all been there. The beginning is always the hardest part. It is why I wrote this guide. It will get you and your business up and running in no time! Starting your own business is exciting for a lot of people but usually just ends up as an idea.

If you are committed to going all in and working hard, here is the starting point: making sure you a have checklist to guide you.

If you'd like extra support and motivation, so you don't feel like you are moving alone, I invite you to join my **Business Start-ups Turnaround Monthly**. You will get the benefit of receiving my monthly webcast, live or recorded. I will answer all your questions, and you can join other people just like you, as well as myself, in my **Private Facebook group**. For details, you can complete the form at the back of this book or visit www.aminachitembo.com.

So here we go, answer the questions as honestly as you can. Nothing is set in stone. You can move dates, add and remove activities as you go along. Please note that this is a self-help tool. It doesn't negate the need for you to seek appropriate legal, financial, or other advice necessary for your compliance with the law. FTA,

Inspiring you, executives and business leaders to perform consistently at high levels and to achieve greater balance in your professional and personal life.

DCTC and Amina Chitembo accept no responsibility for any omissions to compliance with the law on your part.

Enjoy, see you on the other side and best wishes.

STEP ONE:

FIRST, NO STRESS HERE

TURNING THE IDEA INTO REALITY

Inspiring you, executives and business leaders to perform consistently at high levels and to achieve greater balance in your professional and personal life.

A good business idea must be a good fit for you personally, for your target audience and for where you want to operate. Running a business is more than a short-term project, so it should be something that you enjoy and believe in and can see yourself still enjoying for at least five years. It is not some quick win profit making scheme. With that cleared up, let's get started. Write the answers in the spaces as you go. This is your manual; there's no need to keep it clean, write in it.

1. Do you already have a good business idea?

Yes? Describe your business	No? No problem, think of what you enjoy doing. Write down three ideas and see if there is one that makes more sense.

Inspiring you, executives and business leaders to perform consistently at high levels and to achieve greater balance in your professional and personal life.

If your answer to question one was **no;** of the three ideas, you wrote down, which one comes to you more naturally?

2. Define your offer in a fewer than 25 words (Think of how you can explain what you do to other people. These words will become your strapline; you can tweak it, but make sure it is as accurate as possible. You might want to get a separate piece of paper and refine it as much as you can. Ask someone before you write it here, as you will run out of space for corrections, trust me!

I help

Do/Develop/Understand

Inspiring you, executives and business leaders to perform consistently at high levels and to achieve greater balance in your professional and personal life.

So, that they can

```
┌─────────────────────────────────────────┐
│                                         │
│                                         │
│                                         │
│                                         │
└─────────────────────────────────────────┘
```

3. Identify and list your strengths and opportunities that will help you turn your idea into an actual business. For example, maybe you are a marketing professional, and your business idea is about helping people like me market their business. A **strength** might be your qualifications or networking skills. An **opportunity** is that you already know where to find customers. These are just examples, so think of some good ones.

	Strengths	Opportunities
1.		
2.		
3.		
4.		

Inspiring you, executives and business leaders to perform consistently at high levels and to achieve greater balance in your professional and personal life.

	Strengths	Opportunities
5.		
6.		
7.		
8.		
9.		
10.		

4. List any skills you will need to develop; these can be skills you don't have or where you do not perform as well. For example: for me, it was marketing and selling skills. (These will help you understand what external help or training you may need.)

5. List any fears you have about developing and running your business. For example fear of being judged.

6. Now thinking ahead to the future, your business is running. Think of what success will look like to you. List FIVE things that will be in place for you when are successful, and the business is running as you envisioned it. In other words, how will you know you have achieved your goal?

a.	
b.	
c.	
d.	
e.	

7. List the TOP 3 possible business names and test them out by asking people around you. Again, I would suggest starting with a blank piece of paper and then list the shortlisted three names here. I would even make it fun, run a contest with loved ones! Why not?

a.	
b.	
c.	

Inspiring you, executives and business leaders to perform consistently at high levels and to achieve greater balance in your professional and personal life.

The Chosen Business Name is?

Inspiring you, executives and business leaders to perform consistently at high levels and to achieve greater balance in your professional and personal life.

Celebrate the Milestone and stick this on the wall so you can see this great achievement.

You are already better than millions of people who are still thinking about it!

8. List FIVE advantages your offer will have over your competitors (Unique Selling Points or USP). What makes you different from the other people offering the same product? Let's be fair, whatever you think of, someone is selling it somewhere, it could even be your next-door neighbour, but what sets you apart or what extra value are you adding? For example ASDA Tesco, Sainsbury's, Waitrose. We all have reasons why we choose one over the other. This section is likely to be where you will get your tag line, but don't worry about that right now.

a.	
b.	
c.	
d.	
e.	

Decide when you are going to launch the business. Put the DATE on the calendar and a **WALL** so you can see it all the time as a reminder. It will help you have a goal to work towards and keep you motivated. (Remember to give yourself enough planning time).

Business Launch Date:	

9. Tying up loose ends.

Now it's time to go back through points 1 to 8 and make sure they are as complete as possible and that you are happy with everything you have written down. **If you have any extra notes, doubts, questions,** etc., write them down in the space below so you can ask for help later.

_____

_____

_____

_____

_____

_____

_____

_____

_____

_____

_____

Inspiring you, executives and business leaders to **perform** consistently at high levels and to achieve greater balance in your professional and personal life.

STEP TWO:

TEST YOUR BUSINESS IDEA, MAP OUT BUSINESS MILESTONES AND WHEN YOU PLAN TO ACHIEVE THEM.

WHAT YOU NEED TO ACHIEVE BY THE LAUNCH DATE

Action plan

This action plan is where you will write all the tasks you need to accomplish. Think of realistic completions dates, and because I know you are competitive, I have added a deadline and an actual completion date. It will just help you to see where you are and make you feel great when you smash your deadline. If you are likely to miss the deadline, which by the way is OK, just write comments or a reason and set a new deadline. There is even enough space for you to add extra notes if required.

Activity	Enter the Completion Deadline	Enter Actual Date Completed	Only complete if you miss the deadline, Indicate reasons
1. Talk to 5 people who know or understand your business area/industry			
2. Find a mentor or accountable partner (this person is not someone who will be a business partner but someone who can help keep you in check. It can be			
10.			

Activity	Enter the Completion Deadline	Enter Actual Date Completed	Only complete if you miss the deadline, indicate reasons
10. a family member or friend you respect and trust, or a professional mentor or coach)			
3. Carry out some market research (Google is best, but feel free to use other platforms.)			
4. Who is your ideal customer?			
5. What is your target market?			
6. What problem do they face? (define the problem or pain point your business intends to solve)			

Inspiring you, executives and business leaders to perform consistently at high levels and to achieve greater balance in your professional and personal life.

Activity	Enter the Completion Deadline	Enter Actual Date Completed	Only complete if you miss the deadline, indicate reasons
7. What will your business offer to solve their problem? (Describe solution your business will offer)			
8. How do you know if what is you are selling is urgently needed? A survey maybe?			
9. How big is your market size?			
10. Find the price points for at least FIVE similar products.			
11. List at least THREE items you will sell in order of			

Inspiring you, executives and business leaders to perform consistently at high levels and to achieve greater balance in your professional and personal life.

Activity	Enter the Completion Deadline	Enter Actual Date Completed	Only complete if you miss the deadline, indicate reasons
10. basic, mid-level, and premium.			
12. List at least three affiliates. These are people you can partner with to market your business even more. Remember, you can only go so far on your own.			
13. List where you will you run your business, e.g., online, home, or rent an office/shop.			
14. List the forms of communication you will use for your business.			

inspiring you, executives and business leaders to perform consistently at high levels and to achieve greater balance in your professional and personal life.

Note that the list is not conclusive, feel free to add more activities to this list, depending on your business.

Activity	Enter the Completion Deadline	Enter Actual Date Completed	Only complete if you miss the deadline, indicate reasons
10.			
15. Other (add as appropriate)			

STEP THREE:
TURNING THE IDEA INTO THE BUSINESS

THE DOING

Activity	List	Date Completed	Only complete if you miss the deadline. Indicate reasons and set new deadline
1. Outline sources for the team that will help you execute your idea decide if you need a business partner or not. At the beginning of every business, I strongly recommend you do not employ staff right away. You can use contractors or freelancers. A site like FIVERR has all sorts of people with just about every skill you will need, though if it is physical, you might need to look elsewhere. I am not endorsing any sites, but I have mentioned FIVERR as it has served me well so far.			
2. **Investment** Will you need upfront investment? If so, complete **a financial plan or projection** to help you understand how much you need. If you are going to seek external funding, you may need			

Activity	List	Date Completed	Only complete if you miss the deadline. Indicate reasons and set new deadline
to develop **a business plan.** Lenders like banks may ask for one. *I cover this in detail in **my seminars** and Business Start-ups Turnaround Monthly **3. Expenses** Estimate your basic expenses and forecast sales to ensure that you can make a profit with your business. Do not forget travel, lunch, and printing expenses. It will show you the true picture of expenditure so you can work out a near enough return on investment			

Inspiring you, executives and business leaders to perform consistently at high levels and to achieve greater balance in your professional and personal life.

Activity	List	Date Completed	Only complete if you miss the deadline. Indicate reasons and set new deadline
4. **Business Structure** What business structure will you use? e.g. Limited Company, Sole Trader. The structure you choose will depend on a number of circumstances. The merits are different; this is not a topic I cover here but will in my live events and Google will help you understand the differences if you don't already know. *I cover this in detail in my seminars and Business Start-ups Turnaround Monthly*			
5. **Get the right advice** Find an accountant, a tax advisor, and legal representation. You may not need these right away, but you will require them			

Activity	List	Date Completed	Only complete if you miss the deadline. Indicate reasons and set new deadline
6. Registration of your Business Name *I cover this in detail in my seminars and Business Start-ups Turnaround Monthly* at some point, and it is a best practice, in my opinion. Checking that your name is unique to you. If there is one that is the same as yours, is there something you could add or remove to make yours different? Registering Trademarks, Intellectual Properties, etc. It is important to check these because you might end up in trouble if you use someone else's name and they take legal action against you.			

Inspiring you, executives and business leaders to perform consistently at high levels and to achieve greater balance in your professional and personal life.

35

Activity	List	Date Completed	Only complete if you miss the deadline. Indicate reasons and set new deadline
I cover this in detail in my seminars and Business Start-ups *Turnaround Monthly* **7.** Domain name registration (even before you get a website. There are some listings where you can just list yourself as using a domain name.) If you can, you might want to invest in both the .com and .co.uk or whatever the equivalent is in your country. In most cases, you can redirect as many domain names as you wish to the same website. It will stop bad people from taking advantage or stealing your domain, only sell it to you at a very high price.			

Inspiring you, executives and business leaders to perform consistently at high levels and to achieve greater balance in your professional and personal life.

Activity	List	Date Completed	Only complete if you miss the deadline. Indicate reasons and set new deadline
8. **Business Bank** Yes, you need to get a business bank account. The one where the money will go when you sell stuff! If you are a limited company, it is a legal requirement to have a business account. Even if you choose to go as self-employed, it's still a best practice to separate the money coming for your business from your salary.			
9. **Branding** Decide what you want your brand to look and feel like – at a minimum: colour scheme, fonts, and logo. It doesn't have to stop there. Branding a can include a lot of things. It's all up to you. E.G., I like bright colours, so I go for bright red, golden			

Inspiring you, executives and business leaders to perform consistently at high levels and to achieve greater balance in your professional and personal life.

Activity	List	Date Completed	Only complete if you miss the deadline. Indicate reasons and set new deadline
	yellow and green. The brand becomes your business identity.		
10.	Other (add as appropriate)		

Note that the list is not conclusive, feel free to add more activities to this list, depending on your business.

Congratulations, celebrate!

You have earned it.

I applaud you for coming this far; you are now in the top 20 per cent of people that don't wait for life to happen!

Inspiring you, executives and business leaders to perform consistently at high levels and to achieve greater balance in your professional and personal life.

STEP 4:

OTHER CONSIDERATIONS

SELLING AND COMPLIANCE

THE OFFER

It's worth thinking carefully about what you're offering. For physical products, you might want to look at regulations that govern the product you are going to sell. If its information or advice, you might want to consider what licences, accreditations and insurance you may need. This list is endless, but at least you can see that it has already gotten you from just an idea to having something on paper.

The list below covers further items you may wish to consider. You will need them at some point. It also elaborates further on some of the items in the lists above. If you want to learn more, I cover them in my seminars and webcasts, or you can Google most of them!

1. **The Pitch:** Pitching your business is one of the most nerve-racking things you will do, but also the most important. Writing the pitch, even if it doesn't sound real, is a starting point. You will perfect it over time. It shouldn't stop you from launching

2. **How to Brand for your Business:** A strong brand is crucial to your business presence in the marketplace. If people can identify with your brand, they are likely to buy more from you. Branding is also about values, mission and vision.

   1. Develop a tagline
   2. Define what your brand looks like

3. **How you are going to market your business:** So, you have your products ready, how do you get them to your customers?

Inspiring you, executives and business leaders to perform consistently at high levels and to achieve greater balance in your professional and personal life.

How do you let people know what they can buy from you and not what you are selling to them? You might benefit from having a s**ocial media marketing strategy and plan.** Get used to it, start loving social media and you will start making more money from your business.

4. **Compliance with the law:** Before you can open shop and comfortably start doing business, you will need to make sure you have compliance, depending on the business and the clients you will serve. Some of the top things to consider are:

1. Employer Registration (in the UK, this is HMRC for example)
2. Payroll system (in the UK, you can start with PAYE Tools by HMRC)
3. Licences (if applicable)
4. VAT/Tax Registration
5. File for trademark protection
6. Intellectual property
7. Solicitor or Attorney (if you need one)
8. An accounting system
9. Know your exit strategy
10. Insurance types may include professional liability, employer liability, public liability or equivalent, depending on your country.

5. **Networking:** You can start spreading the word by networking, joining some local groups or online communities. It is here where you might find your next collaborator and make new friends.

6. **Contracts:** You will need contracts for certain aspects of your business, depending on what it is.

7. **The Launch:** How to start with your current contacts and not get overwhelmed by requests for free help.

FINAL WORDS

I am very sure there is a lot more you can add to this list, but at least you have the basic structure. I cannot personalise information in this guide because each one of us is different. If you require one on one support, you can apply for my coaching programme, or you can join the **Business Start-ups Turnaround Monthly,** where you can ask as many questions as you want and you can be part of a community of like-minded people.

Let me end by honouring you for taking this step. For all comments on this guide, please contact me at *STRATEGIES@AMINACHITEMBO.COM* .

You can also visit my brands at:

WWW.AMINACHITEMBO.COM

WWW.DIVERSE-CULTURES.COM

You can write to me at P O Box 1369, Peterborough, PE2 2RG

NOTES

Inspiring you, executives and business leaders to perform consistently at high levels and to achieve greater balance in your professional and personal life.

Inspiring you, executives and business leaders to perform consistently at high levels and to achieve greater balance in your professional and personal life.

Inspiring you, executives and business leaders to perform consistently at high levels and to achieve greater balance in your professional and personal life.

TESTIMONIALS

Hanna Moore, CEO, FuturePerfect / Realtor, Jacksonville, Florida, USA.

I have been working with Amina for over five years now. She has not only changed my way of thinking, but my attitude towards life, too. I had set up and grown my Real Estate Business from the ground. Her "High Performance Coaching" is life changing. She is a great trainer and coach; she is a high performer herself, so she works for you and makes you feel appreciated. Her unique tools helped me track my progress all the way through. I have continued to get coached by her, and this is helping my business grow to another level. Her courses are laid out in such an easy to follow way, but offer great depth. I recommend you try Amina.

Mr. and Mrs. Chowdhury, Owners of Little Magna Restaurant, West Sussex, UK

As business owners, we were juggling work and three girls. It was all getting tiring, managing time and staff were not easy, and the business was starting to suffer. Amina came in and helped us develop an easy plan than that helped us to turn things around. She helped us look to the future and think of growing our business. At first, we were sceptical about this "High-Performance Coaching". But just by the third week, we could see our performance improve. She helped us develop clear plans for our business and our life in general. We no longer work long hours.

We are now enjoying a good balance, and we manage stress better in the family. She is a great trainer and coach. She also has a very supportive and responsive team. We now tell everyone that FTA is the go-to place for high performance training. Give Financial Turnaround Academy a go and let the results speak for themselves. You won't regret it!

Pamela M., Occupational Therapist, West Midlands, UK

I started working with Amina in 2007 when my confidence level was at its lowest. She took me under her wing and took the time to teach and mould me into the person I am today. Through her mentorship and coaching, I learnt to believe in myself and that it is only me who can shape my future and my destiny. She taught me and gave me the opportunity to lead, coordinate, manage projects and apply for funding for projects. Since then, I have gone on to achieve what other people may perceive as impossible. I have now obtained a Master's Degree in Development Studies and a B.S. Honours in Occupational Therapy. Amina has taught me how to aim high and achieve my dreams. I am a manager at my job, something I never thought was possible. She still mentors, coaches and motivates me, reminding me that only I can stop myself from progressing in my career. If you are stuck and need someone who can give you the confidence and tools to move forward, give Amina and Financial Turnaround Academy a try. FTA has been my number one resource for learning leadership and management. You get everything you need to start from the basics and transition into a high performing leader. The best part for me was learning how to delegate and persuade so that I get the best out of my team. Amina is very professional, and I would certainly recommend working with her.

ABOUT AMINA

Amina Chitembo is an Internationally **certified corporate and executive High-Performance Coaching expert and trainer.** She helps **executives, senior leaders, and business owners** achieve and maintain f **inancial stability, achieve profitability and balance by teaching them to how gain CLARITY, ENERGY, COURAGE, PRODUCTIVITY, AND INFLUENCE** in their professional and personal lives. As they develop **mastery in these five key areas, they start to feel more PURPOSEFUL AND FULFILLED. They experience a paradigm shift in that they start working harder and leaner, NOT longer hours, which leads to** high productivity and a happier life. Being happy helps maintain better mental health.

Amina is an avid learner and entrepreneur, she is the founder and CEO of Financial Turnaround Academy for Executives, Business Leaders, and Entrepreneurs, and Diverse Cultures Training and Consultancy for non-profit managers and leaders. She spent ten years as the founder/CEO and later chair of BME (Black and Ethnic Minority) Community Services, a charitable company that successfully changed thousands of lives by helping disadvantaged people access better services through pioneering new services and handing them over to mainstream organisations.

Inspiring you, executives and business leaders to perform consistently at high levels and to achieve greater balance in your professional and personal life.

She has a great track record of helping others achieve their goals through her Early Financial Turnarounds Strategies Framework, which she has perfected over the years.

Born in in in the Mtendere shanty compound of Lusaka, Zambia, Amina is living proof that your origins do not define you. Amina was born the youngest of 10 children and was raised by a single mum and sisters after her parents split up when she was three years old. She became a teenage mum at 19 and lost both her parents and six of her siblings by age 30.

Amina defied the odds achieved a total Turnaround through hard work and moved to England in 2001 where she joined the Health Service. After experiencing difficulties accessing services as an immigrant ethnic minority, and seeing first-hand the needs of disadvantaged ethnic minority people, she committed her life to helping other migrants gain better services in the UK and later started helping women and children in her native Zambia.

She and her team fearlessly advocated for better services through working with lawmakers to change policies and make services inclusive. Amina earned a master's degree in Leadership and Management in 2010, making her the only one of her siblings to complete a university education.

Amina enjoys strong family values with her loving husband and four daughters and has managed to achieve a healthy work-life balance. Through her experience, she has become a strong keynote speaker to raise awareness of the strong link between financial stability and mental health, and domestic violence issues in leadership.

CREDENTIALS

Certified High-Performance Coach, High-Performance Academy, USA

Certified Corporate and Executive Coach, The Coaching Academy, UK

Master of Science Leadership and Management, University of Southampton, UK

City and Guilds Qualified Further Education Teacher

Fellow of the Institute of Leadership and Management

Member Institute of Interim Managers

Experts Academy Graduate, California, USA

World's Greatest Speaker Training Graduate, California, USA

OTHER BOOKS FROM AMINA

Co-Author of Madam CEO: How to Think and Act like a Chief Executive (Chapter 3: Face the fear and do it anyway: Handling Transition and Change)

Co-Author of What's the Difference? Embracing Diversity & Inclusivity (Chapter 15: Succeeding in a World with Diverse Cultures)

Inspiring you, executives and business leaders to perform consistently at high levels and to achieve greater balance in your professional and personal life.

Co-Author of How to Break the Glass Ceiling Without Using a Hammer (Chapter 20: Home Away from Home: Embracing Change and Breaking the Glass Ceiling as an Expatriate)

FEATURED COURSES AND PROGRAMS

1. CERTIFIED HIGH-PERFORMANCE COACHING FOR LEADERS (DELUXE)

Amina offers <u>one to one</u> coaching for a small number of carefully selected high-achieving Executives, Directors, Senior Managers and Business Owners. **Certified High Performance Coaching is a 12 session Programme created to explore all the ways you can reach heightened and sustained levels of performance and potential in both your professional and personal life.** Her job is to help you to:

a. gain **CLARITY** on where you are, your strengths and gaps in life right now, works through the gaps which will give you absolute strength to perform better
b. understand how much **ENERGY** you have each day and how to amplify it to higher levels so that you have the vibrancy and stamina needed to achieve your goals
c. Explore where you are regarding **COURAGE,** how confident and courageous you feel your life right now. Any stereotypes, imperfections, anxieties or fears stopping you from achieving the success you deserve and ultimately turn those in into drives to your goal.
d. Explore the areas where there are gaps in your **PRODUCTIVITY,** together you review how effective you feel in your life and work, and give you a set of tools and

Inspiring you, executives and business leaders to perform consistently at high levels and to achieve greater balance in your professional and personal life.

concepts to help you accomplish tasks leaner and faster in your day and not work unnecessarily long hours which could lead to burnout

e. gauge the level of **INFLUENCE** you've felt in your relationships and career, work out where you are right now and give you a few tools and concepts that will dramatically raise your game even higher to lead and inspire your work colleagues, customers, family and all those you serve.

The aim is to help you develop mastery in these five areas so you can feel more **purposeful and fulfilled**. The process typically explores how you feel about your overall life and goals; whether you have the physical energy and mental stamina to perform your best; how confidently and boldly you are showing up in the world.

In High Performance Coaching, Amina often asks some tough questions, those that your 'buddies' will be too afraid to ask. **The main goal is to help you find your emotional truths and life transformations** .

Ultimately, this is a process where you get out as much as you put in. You need to bring your **'A' Game** *to the process and be willing to be challenged and encouraged.*

Because of high demand, she only opens her list for short periods of time. To apply for a free strategy session and find out more, visit *WWW.AMINACHITEMBO.COM*.

2. CERTIFIED HIGH PERFORMANCE GROUP COACHING: LEADERSHIP TURNAROUND MONTHLY WEBCAST (VIP)

Amina offers **group coaching** via the Leadership Turnaround Monthly: A Live webcast featuring Q&A for high-achieving clients of any level.

Certified High Performance Group Coaching is a 12-Sessons Rolling Programme (over 6 Six Months) to explore all the ways you can reach heightened and sustained levels of performance and potential in both your professional and personal life. Each month, Amina takes one topic out of the 12 sessions High Performance Coaching Programme she offers her one on one coaching clients and coaches the group for 40 minutes, and then answers pre-filed questions for 20. She works with the group through FIVE different areas: **CLARITY, ENERGY, COURAGE, PRODUCTIVITY, AND INFLUENCE.**

The aim is to help you develop mastery in these five areas so you can feel more **purposeful and fulfilled**. The process typically explores how you feel about your overall life and goals; whether you have the physical energy and mental stamina to perform your best; how confidently and boldly you are showing up in the world.

It also looks at distractions or poor habits that cause you to fall off course on your performance and what routines can keep you on track and, finally, what you can do to better influence, lead and inspire your work colleagues, customers, family and all those you serve. You develop self-mastery in this process and discover new beliefs, habits and tools that help you join the world's most successful people.

In High Performance Coaching, Amina often asks some tough questions, those that you 'buddies' will be too afraid to ask. **The main goal is to help you find your emotional truths and life transformations** .

*Ultimately, this is a process where you get out as much as you put in. You need to bring your '**A' Game** to the process and be willing to be challenged and encouraged.*

To be able to manage the group and commit time to all group member, there is a limit to the number of people she can work with at a time. To apply for a free strategy session to find out more visit *WWW.AMINACHITEMBO.COM*.

3. DIVERSE CULTURES MENTORSHIP PROGRAMME: BUSINESS START-UPS TURNAROUND MONTHLY (STANDARD)

Amina offers this exclusive <u>Business Start-ups Turnaround Monthly Webinar Series</u>. Is it a recorded webinar series, so you can start at any time and go back to any sessions you would like to repeat. You work at your own pace, so you don't have to worry about time. It is based on her book, **The Serious Player's Decisive Business Start-up Guide: How to Set Up Your Business in 4 Easy to Follow Steps.**

Inspiring you, executives and business leaders to perform consistently at high levels and to achieve greater balance in your professional and personal life.

It is aimed at you if you are struggling with starting a new business whether are as an extra source of income to ensure financial stability for yourself and loved ones or as a first business for what ever reason. Even if you are just thinking about it, and even if you just don't know what to do with your life next!

She takes students to a deeper level of development to help them turn their business ideas into a business. She teaches for 40 minutes and answers pre-filed questions throughout the business development process. She also features industry experts to talk about aspects of intellectual property, finance, tax compliance, pitching and presentation skills. You have all the tools you need for your business startup. The aim is to have more people running their businesses and achieving high levels of financial stability and loving being their own BOSS.

Ultimately, this is a process where you get out as much as you put in. You need to bring your '**A 'Game** *to the process and be willing to be challenged and encouraged .*

Learn more at *WWW.DIVERSE-CULTURES.COM*

4. DIVERSE CULTURES AUTHORS

Do you want to credibility for your business as a published author?

Do you wish to share your story and empower others through writing but find the idea of writing a whole book daunting?

We are looking for **co-authors** for books in various titles. All you need to do is write 10 to 15 pages per chapter, including any original pictures or/and illustrations. Submit them to us, and we will do the rest. You will be a published author, and you will receive royalties from your book. You will also can purchase copies at a reduced price from us.

It does not matter where in you are in the world; you can join the exclusive list of authors. Register your Chapter at *DIVERSE CULTURES AUTHORS*

5. LEADERSHIP TURNAROUND AND RECHARGE RETREAT LIVE: A PRESTIGIOUS TWO-DAY MASTERY AND NETWORKING EVENT

The Retreat is a gathering of executives and senior managers, as well as upcoming leaders from private, public and voluntary sectors in the UK and from around the world. It gives you an opportunity to meet other highly-experienced people who will become future clients, business associates as you get the opportunity to build professional relationships. Amina teaches her best tools and techniques to help you gain clarity and influence and become a leading force in your professional life. She also invites a specially chosen expert guest or two.

A learning and networking event and not one filled with sales pitches.

The weekend starts with registration on Saturday at 7:30 a.m., though guests who arrive on Friday can register between 8 and 9

Inspiring you, executives and business leaders to perform consistently at high levels and to achieve greater balance in your professional and personal life.

p.m. on Friday. The sessions run from 9:00 a.m. and finish at 5:30 p.m. on Saturday, and on Sunday the session starts at 9:00 a.m. and finishes at 1:00 p.m. to allow for those travelling to be on their way.

The weekend is held in Gorgeous Hotels with calm surroundings approximately one hour from London by train and with great road networks and four other nearby airports.

All our events are designed to equip you to live and maintain the career and business life you want, as well as to maintain good mental health and financial stability so you can create balance in your professional and personal life.

Learn more at *WWW.FINANCIAL-TURNAROUND-ACADEMY.COM* .

6. AFFILIATE PROGRAMME

Register to become an affiliate and earn up to 50 per cent of all your referrals who purchase from us.

It's easy money for you! If you are interested in becoming one of our affiliates, just register your details. It's completely free to sign up, and there are no strings attached at *WWW.AMINACHITEMBO.COM*.

As an affiliate, we will send you a unique link to product campaigns we are running. You can then send the link to your connections on social media or email list. Tell them about the product and encourage them to buy (no hard sales please, we don't force people to buy, we do it ethically). If any of your referrals purchase from us, you will receive the following depending on your level:

Standard affiliates receive 35 per cent of the price of the product after we pay 'Value Added Tax' to the government.

VIP Affiliates 50 per cent of the price after we pay VAT. When you reach your 50th sale, you become a VIP affiliate. VIPs receive extra bonuses.

Sounds fair, right?

Register your interest at *WWW.AMINACHITEMBO.COM*!

MONEY BACK GUARANTEES

All our products have a 30-day money back guarantee. If for any reason you are not happy with your purchase, we will be happy to refund you. No hard feelings, after the 30 days your account will be locked, and you can cancel anytime, but your payment will cover you until your next billing cycle. Any cancellation requests after the initial 30 days must be sent at least five days before your billing date. All cancellations and refund requests must be emailed to *STRATEGIES@AMINACHITEMBO.COM* provided you follow the simple guidelines below:

VARIATIONS

Physical Products

Email us for a refund form and send the product back in its original packaging within 14 days from the date you receive the refund form. We will refund you within seven working days.

Online Products

Email us for a refund form. Return it to us with seven days from the date you receive the form. We will refund you within seven working days.

Live events

If you are not happy, you can <u>quietly</u> leave before the tea break, notify a team member on the day to complete a refund form, leave your badge and vacate the conference area. You can stay in the hotel if you like, but you will not be re-admitted to our conference area.

PRIVACY STATEMENT

We will not share your details with anyone else.

EARNINGS DISCLAIMER

The results of any of our products will be proportionate to the amount of effort you put in. We do not operate 'get rich quick' schemes. We are unable to guarantee your success because we do not know your circumstances, but we will aim to support you 100 per cent to help you achieve the best results

Your level of success in attaining results from using our products and information depends on the time you devote to the program, ideas and techniques used, your finances, knowledge and various skills.

Since these factors differ among each of us, we cannot guarantee your success or income level, nor are we responsible for any of your actions.

All forward-looking statements on any of our websites and products are intended to express our opinion of the earnings potential that some people may achieve.

But many factors will be important in determining your actual results, and we make no guarantees that you will achieve results like ours or anyone else's. In fact, we make no guarantees that you will achieve any results from the ideas and techniques contained on our website or in our products.

In fact, as with any product or service, we know that some people will purchase our products but never use them at all, and therefore will get no results whatsoever. You should, therefore, assume that you will obtain no results with this program.

Even though we make no guarantees that our product will produce any particular result for you, you can still take advantage of our return policy if you are not completely satisfied. In such instances, you can return the product for a refund according to the terms and timelines indicated in our refund policy described in the Terms and Conditions section on our websites.

YOU FULLY AGREE AND UNDERSTAND THAT AMINA CHITEMBO, HER TEAM AND ASSOCIATES ARE NOT RESPONSIBLE FOR YOUR SUCCESS OR FAILURE AND MAKES NO REPRESENTATIONS OR WARRANTIES OF ANY KIND WHATSOEVER THAT OUR PRODUCTS OR SERVICES WILL PRODUCE ANY PARTICULAR RESULT FOR YOU

Printed in Great Britain
by Amazon

CHARITIES, GOVERNANCE AND THE LAW: THE WAY FORWARD

Editors

Debra Morris and Jean Warburton

Contributors

Karen Atkinson, Research Assistant, Charity Law Unit, University of Liverpool
Michael Carpenter, Retired Executive Legal Charity Commissioner
Robin Currie, Chief Executive of PSS
Dorothy Dalton, Director of Voluntary Sector Development, Howarth Clark Whitehill
Valerie James, Partner, Wrigleys Solicitors
Gregory Jobome, Lecturer in Economics, University of Liverpool
John Marshall, NHS Regional Appointments Commissioner
Robert Meakin, Partner, Stone King, Solicitors
Debra Morris, Lecturer, Cayman Island Law School
David Mullins, Reader in Housing Studies, University of Birmingham
David Nussbaum, Managing Director, Transparency International
Roger Singleton CBE, Chief Executive, Barnardo's
Jean Warburton, Professor of Law, Charity Law Unit, University of Liverpool

Published by Key Haven Publications PLC
Unit 6, Hurlingham Business Park, Sulivan Road
London SW6 3DU
Telephone + 44 (0) 20 7731 7700 Facsimile +44 (0) 20 7731 6622
Website Address: www.khpplc.com

Disclaimer

DISCLAIMER

The views contained herein are put forward for further consideration only and are not to be acted upon without independent and professional advice.

Neither the Publisher nor the Authors or the Contributors can accept any responsibility for any loss occasioned to any person no matter howsoever caused or arising as a result of or in consequence of action taken or refrained from in reliance on the contents hereof.

ISBN 1-901614 19-0

©2003 KEY HAVEN PUBLICATION PLC
Moral rights of the authors have been asserted.

Conditions of Sale

All rights strictly reserved. No part of this publication may be reproduced, stored in a retrieval system, or transmitted, in any form or any means, electronic, mechanical, photocopying, recording or otherwise, without prior written permission of the publisher.

Any person infringing the publisher's copyright will be liable to criminal and/or civil proceedings.

Printed in England by Pims Digital

Preface

PREFACE

At the turn of the century, we became aware that there was much discussion of governance issues as they affected charities but that little of the discussion had any reference to the law. As charity lawyers this concerned us and we became of the view that there was a need for debate focussed on the extent to which the present law inhibited good governance of charities and what changes were desirable.

Our concerns were shared by the Advisory Committee to the Charity Law Unit who encouraged us to set up a series of seminars bringing together charity lawyers, charity trustees and employees, accountants and consultants advising charities and charity researchers to discuss charity governance problems. We were fortunate that the P.H. Holt Charitable Trust also shared our views and kindly made a grant to support the seminars. The grant not only allowed the seminars to take place, with the papers which form this book, but also allowed wider participation in the seminars than would otherwise have been possible.

We are very grateful to all those who took part in the seminars, especially those who contributed papers. Individual participants were very open to views from those with different backgrounds from themselves leading to lively debate and, we think, valuable contribution to the future of the law as it affects charity governance. The reader will judge if we are right by perusing the chapters that follow and, in particular, the short papers setting out the points arising from each seminar.

No book of papers produces itself and we have benefited from the assistance of colleagues in the Charity Law Unit. Particular thanks must go to Karen Atkinson, research assistant, who not only efficiently organised the seminars but who also provided invaluable assistance in the preparation of the papers for publication.

Our final thanks must go to the publishers for showing faith in this project from the beginning.

Debra Morris   Jean Warburton

Table of Contents

TABLE OF CONTENTS

Preface iii
Table of Cases xi
Table of Statutes xiii
Summary 1 71
Summary 2 119
Summary 3 191
Summary 4 253
Index 275

**Chapter 1 -   Introduction: Governance and Charity Law –
                The Context and the Issues**

The Importance Of Governance 1.1
Methodology 1.2
Four Aspects Of Governance 1.3
Recruiting and Retaining an Effective Body Of Trustees 1.4
Involvement of Users in Governance 1.5
Strategy or Management by Trustees 1.6
Influence of Funders 1.7

**Chapter 2 -   The Law as it Affects the Recruitment and Retention
                of Trustees**

Introduction 2.1
Disqualification 2.2
Motivation 2.3
Trustee Liability 2.4
Relief from Liability 2.5
Contractual Liability 2.6
Trustees to Act Without Payment 2.7
Retention of Trustees 2.8

Chapter 3 - The Recruitment and Retention of Trustees: A Perspective from the Voluntary Sector

Background	3.1
A Dearth of Suitable People	3.1.1
Competition from the Public Sector	3.1.2
Diversity	3.1.3
2002 "Who's Who in Charities"	3.1.4
Trustee Support and Training	3.1.5
Recruitment	3.2
Due Diligence	3.2.1
Nomination Committees and Skills Audit	3.2.2
Identifying Potential Trustees	3.2.3
Induction, Support and Training	3.2.4
Planning and Reporting Cycles, Agendas and Information Needs for Good Governance	3.2.5
The Retention of Trustees	3.3
Reasons for Leaving	3.3.1
Powers to Remove Trustees	3.3.2
Attracting, Motivating and Retaining	3.3.3
The Future	3.4
An Unresolved Issue	3.4.1
An Institute for Charity Governance	3.4.2

Chapter 4 - Recruitment, Training and Retention of Trustees

Introduction	4.1
The Role of Boards	4.2
Scrutiny by Local Government	4.3
Recruitment, Training & Development, Mentoring & Appraisal	4.4
Contractual Arrangements	4.5
Status	4.6
Succession Planning	4.7
Politics and Financial Pressures	4.8
Equal Opportunities	4.9
Conclusion	4.10

Chapter 5 - The Legal Aspects of User Trusteeship

Introduction	5.1
Why Have User Involvement?	5.2
Why is The Concept of User Trusteeship Potentially Problematic From a Legal Perspective?	5.3
What is The Charity Commission View of User Trusteeship?	5.4
Defining User Trustees and Related Terms	5.5
Capacity to Act as a Charity Trustee	5.6
Age	5.7
Mental Capacity	5.8
Disqualification under the Charities Act 1993	5.9
Providing For User Trustees In The Governing Instrument	5.10
The Duty of Care	5.11
Conflicts of Interest	5.12
Directly Affecting a Trustee	5.13
Indirectly Affecting A Trustee	5.14
The No Benefits Rule	5.15
The Self-Dealing and the Fair Dealing Rules	5.16
The Duty not to make a Secret Profit	5.17
Confidentiality	5.18
Alternatives	5.19
Increasing the Level of Communication	5.20
Advisory Members of the Board	5.21
Representation?	5.22
Conclusion	5.23

Chapter 6 - Involvement of Users in Governance: Some Experiences from the Non-Profit Housing Sector

Introduction	6.1
Tenant Involvement in Governance	6.2
Regulatory and Constitutional Issues and Interaction with Charity Law	6.2.1
Housing Sector Case Studies	6.3
Case Study 1: Housing Association Group Structures	6.3.1
Case Study 2: Tenant Management Organisations	6.3.2
Conclusion: Some Emerging Issues	6.4
Organisational Issues	6.4.1
Convergence of Governance Models?	6.4.1.1
Transparency and Accountability	6.4.1.2
Incentives for Users to Participate	6.4.1.3

Legal and Constitutional Issues ... 6.4.2

Chapter 7 - Strategy or Management by Trustees?

Introduction ... 7.1
The Governing Instrument ... 7.2
Liability of Trustees ... 7.3
Do Trustees Need to Take Notice of Commission Guidance? ... 7.4
Can Poor Decisions Be Set Aside? ... 7.5
Was the decision within the powers of the trustees? ... 7.5.1
Was the decision made by the trustees one which a reasonable body of trustees could have made (or was the decision perverse or irrational)? ... 7.5.2
Did the trustees act in good faith? ... 7.5.3
Did the trustees take into account any factors which it was not proper for them to take into account? ... 7.5.4
Did the trustees fail to take into account any factors which they should have taken into account? ... 7.5.5
Did the trustees adequately inform themselves in order to make the decision in question? ... 7.5.6
What Does all this Amount to? ... 7.6
Conclusion ... 7.7

Chapter 8 - Strategy or Management by Trustees: Corporate Governance

Determining the Vision and Purpose ... 8.1
The Strategic Plan ... 8.2
The Major Policies ... 8.3
Resource Deployment ... 8.4
Risk Management ... 8.5
Public Image ... 8.6
Delegation And Reporting ... 8.7

Chapter 9 - Corporate Governance and Performance in Large UK Nonprofits

Introduction ... 9.1
Nonprofits and Agency Problems ... 9.2
Donor Motivation and Nonprofit Fundraising ... 9.3
Assessing the Performance of Nonprofits ... 9.4

Donations Functions ... 9.4.1
Passthrough Functions ... 9.4.2
Empirical Models and Estimation Procedure ... 9.5
The Dataset and some Stylised Facts ... 9.6
Sources and nature of data ... 9.6.1
Stylised Facts ... 9.6.2
Empirical Results ... 9.7
Summary and Conclusion ... 9.8

Chapter 10 -   Charities Biting the Hand that Feeds: Relationships with their Funders

Introduction ... 10.1
Independence ... 10.2
Legal Principles ... 10.3
Charity Trustees Must Stay Within Their Objects ... 10.3.1
Charity Trustees Must Exercise Discretion Appropriately ... 10.3.2
Who Exercises Discretion ... 10.3.2.1
How Discretion is Exercised ... 10.3.2.2
Particular Problems of Funder-Appointed Trustees ... 10.3.3
Influence Over Other Matters ... 10.3.4
Keep Accounting Records ... 10.3.4.1
Prepare Statements of Accounts ... 10.3.4.2
Ensure Independent Examination / Audit of Accounts ... 10.3.4.3
Prepare and Submit Annual Reports ... 10.3.4.4
Enable Public Inspection of Annual Reports and Accounts ... 10.3.4.5
Submit Annual Returns ... 10.3.4.6
Conclusion ... 10.4

Chapter 11 -   Influence of Funders

Introduction ... 11.1
Background ... 11.2
The Influence of Government Funding ... 11.3
Case Study ... 11.4
Conclusion ... 11.5

Chapter 12 - Money or Cause: How much Influence should Funders have on Charities?

Introduction	12.1
Generic Income Types	12.2
The Oxfam Experience	12.3
Trends	12.3.1
Implications for Governance	12.3.2
Trends	12.4
Relationships with funders have become more formal and complex	12.4.1
Levels of funding are linked to public perception of need and political priorities	12.4.2
Increased competition and increasingly tough compliance standards are increasing costs and challenging ways of working and human resources	12.4.3
There is pressure for fewer but larger programmes, and a focus on those outcomes which are easier to measure	12.4.4
Implications of Trends for Governance	12.5
Corporate strategies need to be developed to respond to changes	12.5.1
Independence and Innovation Need Sustaining	12.5.2
Organisational Culture Needs to Change	12.5.3
Reporting and Accounting Issues Need Clarifying	12.5.4
Reforming Charity Governance?	12.6
The "Charity Accountability Triangle"	12.6.1
Conclusion	12.7

Chapter 13 - Charities and Governance: The Role of the Law

Introduction	13.1
Transparency	13.2
Clarity	13.3
Legal Reforms	13.4
Background Values	13.5
Potential Solutions	13.6
Potential Reforms to Charity Governance Practice	13.7
The Role of the Law	13.8
Conclusion	13.9

TABLE OF CASES

Armitage v Nurse [1998] Ch 241 .... 2.5, 7.4, 7.5.3
Attorney General v Brandeth (1842) 1 Y & C Cas 200 .... 10.3.1
Attorney General v Duke of Northumberland (1889) 5 TLR 237 .... 13.3
Attorney General v Glegg (1738) Amb 584 .... 10.3.2.2
Attorney General v Governors of Harrow School (1754) 2 Ves Sen 551 .. 10.3.2.2

Bahin v Hughes (1886) 31 Ch 390 .... 2.8
Baker v Lee (1860) 8 HLC 495 .... 2.2
Baldry v Feinstuck [1972] 1 WLR 552 .... 10.3.1
Bartlett v Barclays Bank Trusts Co Ltd [1980] Ch 515 .... 2.4, 5.11
Beddoes, Re [1893] 1 Ch 547 .... 2.4
Beloved Wilkes' Charity, Re (1851) 3 Mac & G 440 .... 10.3.2.2
Boardman v Phipps [1967] 2 AC 67 .... 10.3.1
Bray v Ford [1896] AC 44 5.12, ... 10.3.3, 13.2, 13.3

Crawford v Forshaw [1891] 2 Ch 261 .... 10.3.2.1

Dundee General Hospitals Board of Management v Walker and Another [1952] 1
    All ER 896 7.5.4, ... 10.3.2.2

Edge v Pensions Ombudsman [1999] 4 All ER 546 .... 7.5.5

Firbank's Executors v Humphreys (1886) 18 QBD 54 .... 10.3.1
Fulham Football Club Ltd v Cabra Estates plc [1994] 1 BCLC 363 .... 10.3.2.2

Gee, Re [1948] Ch 284 .... 5.17
Grove v Young Men's Christian Association (1903) 4 TC 613 .... 10.3.1

Hastings-Bass, Re [1975] Ch 25 7.5.1, ... 10.3.2.2
Hayes' Will Trusts, Pattinson v Hayes, Re [1971] 2 All ER 241 .... 10.3.2.1
Hay's Settlement Trusts, Re [1981] 3 All ER 786 .... 10.3.1

IRC v Oldham Training and Enterprise Council [1996] ATC 1218 .... 13.3
IRC v Schroder [1983] STC 480 .... 13.2

Keech v Sandford (1726) Sel Cas Ch 61 ....5.17

Macadam, Re [1946] Ch 73 ....5.17
Mettoy Pension Trustees Ltd v Evans [1991] 2 All ER 513 ....7.5.5, 7.5.6
Migrant Advisory Service v Chaudri (EAT/1400/97), 28 July 1998 ....13.3
Monds v Stackhouse (1948) 77 CLR 232 ....13.3

Nestle v National Westminster Bank plc [1994] 1 All ER 118 7.5.2, ...13.8
Newen, Re [1894] 2 Ch 297 ....13.2
Norfolk's Settlement Trust, Re Duke of [1982] Ch 61 ....5.15

Perrons v Spackham [1981] STC 739 ....13.3
Prison Charities, Re (1873) LR 16 Eq 129 ....13.3
Public Trustee v Cooper (2001) 2 WTLR 901 ....7.5.6

Queensland Mines Ltd v Hudson (1978) 18 ALR 2 PC 5.17

R (on the application of Heather) v Leonard Cheshire Foundation [2002] 2 All
   ER 936 ....12.1
Regal [Hastings] Ltd v Gulliver [1967] 2 AC 134 5.17, ...10.3.1
Rosemary Simmons Memorial Housing Association Ltd v United Dominions
   Trust Ltd [1987] 1 All ER 281 ....10.3.1

Sargent v National Westminster Bank plc (1991) 61 P&CR 518 ....5.17
Scargill v Charity Commissioners and Attorney General, 4 September 1998,
   unreported 7.4, 13.8
Scott v National Trust [1998] 2 All ER 705 ....7.5.6, 10.3.2.2, 13.8
Skeat's Settlement, Re (1889) 42 Ch 522 ....10.3.3, 13.2
Smallpiece v Attorney-General [1990] Ch. Com. Rep. 5.15
Smith, Eastick v Smith, Re [1904] 1 Ch 139 ....10.3.2.1
Speight v Gaunt (1883) 9 App Cas 1 ....2.4
Stafford Charities, Re (1857) 25 Beav 28 ....2.2
Stannard v Fisons Pension Trust [1992] 1 RLR 27 ....7.5.4, 7.5.6

Thorby v Goldberg (1964) 112 CLR 597 ....10.3.2.2
Tito v Waddell (No 2) [1977] 3 All ER 29 ....5.16

Walker v Stones [2001] QB 902 ....2.5, 7.4
Wallis v Solicitor General for New Zealand [1983] AC 173 ....7.4
Whiteley, Re [1910] 1 Ch 600 ....10.3.2.1
Whitely, Re [1886] 33 Ch 347 ....5.11
Wight v Olswang [2001] WTLR 291 ....7.5.2
Williams' Trustees v IRC [1947] AC 447 ....10.3.1

TABLE OF STATUTES

Charities Act 1993

s.1	1.1
s.1(3)	7.4
s.1(4)	1.1, 7.4
s.3(5)	10.3.4.6
s.8	1.1, 1.3
s.18	5.8, 7.4, 13.8
s.18(3)	5.7
s.18(4)(c)	13.4
s.29	7.4
s.30	13.4
s.32	7.5.6
s.36	5.16
s.41	10.3.4.1
s.42	10.3.4.2
s.43	10.3.4.3
s.45	10.3.4.4, 10.3.4.6, 13.8
s.46(1)	10.3.4.6
s.46(2)	10.3.4.6
s.46(3)	10.3.4.6
s.47	10.3.4.5
s.48	10.3.4.6
s.72	5.9
s.72(1)	2.2
s.72(4)	2.2
s.72(6)	2.2
s.72(7)	2.2
s.97	7.2, 13.2
s.97(1)	1.1, 2.3

Companies Act 1985

s.310(1)	2.6

Employment Rights Act 1996

s.50	13.4

Family Law Reform Act 1969

s.1	5.7
s.2	5.7

Housing Associations Act 1985

s.15	6.2.1

Income and Corporation Taxes Act 1988

s.505(1)(e)	10.3.1
s.505(3)	10.3.1
s.506(1)	10.3.1

Insolvency Act 1986

s.213	2.6
s.214(2)(b)	2.6
s.214(3)	2.6

Law of Property Act 1925

s.20	2.2, 5.7

Local Government Housing Act

s.18	13.4

Mental Health Act 1959

Sch.7 .... 5.8

Mental Health Act 1983

s.148 .... 5.8
Sch.6 .... 5.8

Pluralities Act 1838

s.29 .... 2.2
s.30 .... 2.2

Road Traffic Act 1988

s.38(7) 13.8

School Standards and Framework Act 1998

s.36 .... 2.8
Sch.9 .... 2.8

Trade Union and Labour Relations (Consolidation) Act 1992

s.207(2) 13.8

Trustee Act 1925

s.39 .... 2.8
s.61 .... 2.5

Trustee Act 2000

s.1 .... 1.5, 5.11, 13.2, 13.8
s.1(1) 2.4
s.2 .... 2.4
s.3 .... 1.6
s.5 .... 2.4
s.11(3) 10.3.2.1
s.30(3)(a) 13.5
s.31 .... 2.4, 2.7, 13.3
Sch.1 .... 2.4, 13.2
Sch.1 para.7 .... 2.4
Sch.1(1)(a) 13.8

Chapter 1

INTRODUCTION: GOVERNANCE AND CHARITY LAW – THE CONTEXT AND THE ISSUES
Debra Morris[1]

This collection of essays is intended to provide a critical forward look at the governance of charities. It is based on a series of four seminars that the Charity Law Unit held during 2002. The seminars were designed to focus on the restrictions that the law places on effective charity governance and the lessons that charities can learn from both each other and from other areas or disciplines. The aim of the seminars was to raise debate. This book will also aim to raise debate in a number of specific areas. It does not seek to provide a comprehensive analysis of the legal issues in these areas[2]. Rather, it aims to bring together a thought-provoking collection of essays under four broad headings which reflect the focus of the seminars.

The aspects of charity governance under discussion at the seminars were:

- Recruiting and retaining an effective body of trustees;

- The involvement of users in governance;

- Strategy or management by trustees; and

- The influence of funders.

---

[1] Debra Morris is currently lecturing at Cayman Islands Law School. She was previously Senior Lecturer at Liverpool Law School, and the Director of the Charity Law Unit from 1996-2001.

[2] For a practical look at Charity Law, see e.g. Cairns E. *Charity Law and Practice* 3rd ed. Sweet & Maxwell (1997).

This chapter sets the scene by, first, examining why it was considered important to focus on governance and the place of Charity Law. It then discusses the four aspects of governance that were chosen for examination and the methodological approach taken to tackling these areas. It concludes by introducing each chapter and highlighting some of its main points.

The seminars upon which this collection is based took place during an eventful year for charities. September 2002, when the final seminar took place, saw the publication of both the Treasury's Cross Cutting Review of the Role of the Voluntary and Community Sector in Service Delivery[3], and the Strategy Unit Review of Charities and the Wider Not-For-Profit Sector[4]. The Cross Cutting Review examined what impedes the voluntary and community sector from providing public services and made proposals for reform of the relationship between the government and the sector. The Strategy Unit Review proposed wide ranging changes in the law and regulation of charities and the wider not-for-profit sector. With the exception of this introduction and the concluding essay, the writing of these essays largely precedes, but generally pre-empts, the publication of these reports.

1.1 The Importance of Governance

Governance issues are currently very much on the agenda for the charity sector. In days gone by, charity trustees may have been able to rely on their good intentions and the "good cause" that they represented as a way of excusing any deficiencies in their governance. This is no longer the case. The greater burdens being placed on charities together with increased professionalism and, some would say increased commercialism, have brought into focus the governance of charities. It is likely that the enhanced role for charities, heralded by the introduction of a "contract culture[5]", may well increase in the future. Paul Boateng, Chief Secretary to the Treasury and lead minister for its Cross Cutting Review, wrote, upon introducing the review[6]:

---

[3] HM Treasury *The Role of the Voluntary and Community Sector in Service Delivery. A Cross Cutting Review* (2002).

[4] Strategy Unit, Cabinet Office *Private Action, Public Benefit. A Review of Charities and the Wider Not-For-Profit Sector* (2002).

[5] See e.g. Morris D. *Charities and the Contract Culture: Partners or Contractors? Law and Practice in Conflict* Charity Law Unit (1999).

[6] HM Treasury *The Role of the Voluntary and Community Sector in Service Delivery. A Cross Cutting Review* (2002) p.3.

> "We believe that voluntary and community sector organisations have a crucial role to play in the reform of public services and reinvigoration of civic life. We in government cannot do this on our own."

Now charity trustees are facing more pressure than ever before, both to make their organisations effective in a demanding and changing environment and to make themselves accountable for their charities' activities. Good governance is an essential component.

By statute[7], the Charity Commission has a responsibility to promote the effective use of charitable resources by encouraging the development of better methods of administration and to make effective the work of the charity in meeting the needs designated by its trusts. Recently, the Commission has been turning itself into a modern regulator within its current statutory powers[8] and has given increasing emphasis to its compliance role, devoting new resources to developing its investigations capability[9]. Using the Internet[10], the Charity Commission has greatly expanded the range and quality of information publicly available, created an on-line Register of Charities and published its internal guidance. All these developments help to encourage and enforce good governance. Nevertheless, the Charity Commission does not have the power to act in the administration of a charity[11]. Trustees, however they came to that position, or whatever they are called[12], bear the ultimate responsibility for the proper administration of their charity and must exercise proper oversight and scrutiny. Though much may be delegated by trustees[13], there must be clear lines of authority, with ultimate responsibility with the trustees.

Whilst the Charity Commission seeks to ensure that trustees understand their

---

[7] Charities Act 1993, s.1.

[8] See Strategy Unit, Cabinet Office *Private Action, Public Benefit. A Review of Charities and the Wider Not-For-Profit Sector* (2002), ch 7 of which proposes various changes to the Commission's powers.

[9] Strategy Unit, Cabinet Office *Private Action, Public Benefit. A Review of Charities and the Wider Not-For-Profit Sector* (2002) para.7.3.

[10] The Charity Commission website url is: www.charity-commission.gov.uk

[11] Charities Act 1993, s.1(4).

[12] See Charities Act 1993, s.97(1) where "charity trustees" are defined as "the persons having the general control and management of the administration of a charity". See also para 2.3

[13] See e.g. para 7.2

legal responsibilities and how these are carried through by charity staff or volunteers, an increasing number of Charity Commission enquiries into individual charities are revealing failings on the part of charity trustees in their governance[14]. In more than 40% of the investigation cases that the Charity Commission closed in 2000/01, mismanagement or maladministration was a factor[15]. Poor governance, including poor understanding or performance of trustee responsibilities, was a frequent feature in these cases.

The recent Strategy Unit report acknowledged that good governance is crucial to ensuring that organisations are operating effectively[16]:

> *"Governance problems can have a profound impact, especially when organisations are forced to dedicate considerable resources to resolving internal disputes."*

Similarly, the Cross Cutting Review, referring to research by the Voluntary Sector National Training Organisation[17], which found significant skills gaps in the sector – specific skills of fundraising, volunteer management and trusteeship, recognised that the voluntary and community sector requires support to develop leadership and management skills[18].

The governance of charities is influenced by a unique range of factors, one of which is Charity Law. There has been much discussion of governance issues[19] but little has been with specific reference to the influence of the law on governance. Four particular areas where governance concerns may be raised were chosen for examination. These were areas of current concern to trustees, where it was considered that the law might create problems but also has the potential for having a positive influence on the governance of charities. One basic problem

---

[14] See the Charity Commission website for the details of reports on Charity Commission enquiries carried out in accordance with Charities Act 1993, s.8.

[15] RS1 *Trustee Recruitment, Selection and Induction* Charity Commission (2002) p.7.

[16] Strategy Unit, Cabinet Office *Private Action, Public Benefit. A Review of Charities and the Wider Not-For-Profit Sector* (2002) para.6.41.

[17] VSNTO *Skills Matter: A skills foresight for the voluntary sector across England, Scotland and Wales* (2000).

[18] HM Treasury *The Role of the Voluntary and Community Sector in Service Delivery. A Cross Cutting Review* (2002) para.4.16.

[19] See e.g. Cornforth C. *Recent Trends in Charity Governance and Trusteeship* NCVO (2001).

with the relevant law is that it may not be sufficiently transparent to those whom it affects. Either there is general ignorance of the relevant legal principles and their impact upon governance by trustees or the law in these areas may well be unclear. There are also concerns that good practice does not always fit with the law in these areas. It will be seen[20] that all these concerns were borne out by the seminars, with participants raising the need for both transparency and clarity in a number of specific areas.

1.2 Methodology

Governance of charities is a constantly moving debate[21] and a series of seminars bringing together charity lawyers, charity personnel (both trustees and paid staff) and charity researchers was held as a way of analysing present problems and showing the way forward. The seminars were also used as an opportunity to share good practice. The need to learn from others and to recognise the diversity of the charitable sector, was acknowledged by seminar participants who welcomed the opportunity to be open with each other and to increase their understanding of how others are coping with governance issues. The forum provided an occasion for participants to learn from other charities, from practitioners and from academics with both interests in Charity Law and other related areas.

The pattern of each seminar, with invited participants, was a paper on the law, a case study from a particular charity and a paper on another area or discipline, with opportunity to discuss each paper and to draw lessons for the sector. The inter-disciplinary approach was taken in order to learn from other areas. After the seminars, bullet points were drawn up to reflect the main points arising from the discussion and these are also included in this collection. The format of this book mirrors the pattern of the seminars, and concludes with a final chapter drawing together some threads.

1.3 Four Aspects of Governance

The first aspect of governance chosen for examination is recruiting and retaining an effective body of trustees. Whilst there may be some evidence to the

---

[20] See both the Summary points noting the items of discussion at each seminar, and, in particular, the final chapter, where Warburton draws together the main concerns raised during the seminar series.

[21] Note, for example, the publication during 2002 of the Strategy Unit report whose recommendations, if implemented, will impact on trustees' governance role.

contrary[22], there is a widespread view that in general, good trustees are hard to find[23]. This clearly has a knock-on effect upon trustees' ability to govern their charity. Trustee recruitment, retention and training are therefore crucially important. The Strategy Unit report recognised[24] that where charity trustees lack the necessary skills, knowledge and expertise, this can lead to governance problems. It can mean that trustees are less enterprising and less focussed on quality improvement than they might be. The better a charity handles the selection, recruitment and induction of new trustees at the outset, the greater the immediate contribution that they will be able to make to the quality of its governance and its work[25]. This is likely to produce, not only better results for those that the charity is there to help, but also greater confidence and fulfilment for the new trustees themselves.

This is an extremely topical subject. In March 2002, the Charity Commission published the first of a new series of regulatory reports on issues considered important for regulating the propriety and effectiveness with which charities are governed. The subject chosen was trustee recruitment, selection and induction[26]. The findings are based on the Commission's own experience – which is perhaps too often of trustee problems – and a postal survey. The report takes a fairly robust view – that trustee recruitment is less of a problem in reality than is generally thought. Recruitment methods are blamed for charities' difficulties in finding good trustees[27]:

---

[22] RS1 *Trustee Recruitment, Selection and Induction* Charity Commission (2002) p.11.

[23] See e.g. para 3.1.1

[24] Strategy Unit, Cabinet Office *Private Action, Public Benefit. A Review of Charities and the Wider Not-For-Profit Sector* (2002) para.6.41.

[25] RS1 *Trustee Recruitment, Selection and Induction* Charity Commission (2002) p.7.

[26] RS1 *Trustee Recruitment, Selection and Induction* Charity Commission (2002).

[27] Ibid. p.1.

> *"Too many charities are relying too much on recruitment methods that are narrower and more passive than they could and should be. If more charities used the full range of options more imaginatively, our work suggests that the common impression that potential trustees are scarce would be less widespread."*

The report also recommends that charities should use trustee job descriptions or similar guidance to provide prospective trustees with a balanced account of what the role of trustee entails, including their duties and responsibilities as a trustee. Once recruited, they should be trained appropriately in their role. The report concludes with a substantial list of other sources of help in recruiting and adequately equipping trustees for their tasks.

The second aspect of governance under consideration is involvement of users in governance. A growing number of charities, particularly those concerned with health and disability, are seeking to recruit more of their service users as trustees. Reasons for this growth include external pressure from funders and internal pressure as a result of the growing confidence of many users themselves. Involving service users in the decision-making of charities can bring major benefits, but as well as involving a significant cultural shift, it can also throw up challenges. It can be a complex process and, if allegations of tokenism are to be avoided, one that must be carefully thought through and supported by the non-user trustees and the charity staff and volunteers.

One practical challenge charities must tackle is ensuring that user trustees' participation in decision-making is meaningful. Another problem is possible confrontations between user trustees and other trustees, such as medical specialists, who may have different priorities for the charity's development.

The main legal challenge is the requirement for trustees to avoid conflicts of interest. Trustees should put the interests of their charity before any other personal or professional interests. With users as trustees, there are nevertheless situations where conflicts of interest are unavoidable and charities must take great care in the management of these[28]. Examples of conflicts of interest (and of the action taken as a result) occur with some frequency in the inquiry reports published by the Charity Commission[29]. If a transaction affected by a conflict of interest is challenged, there is a risk that it will be declared invalid unless it has been properly authorised. If the Commission believes that a charity is being run

---

[28] See in general, CC24 *Users on Board: Beneficiaries who become Trustees* (2000).

[29] See the Charity Commission website for details of reports on Charity Commission inquiries carried out in accordance with Charities Act 1993, s.8.

for self-interest, it has powers to correct the situation and, where a trustee has benefited without authorisation, to pursue the issue of restitution[30].

The third aspect of governance to be examined is strategy or management. Strategy, policy matters and monitoring of efficiency and effectiveness are often quoted as functions of trustees. Operational details are to be left to paid staff and volunteers. So, the trustees' role in governance is not necessarily about doing things; it is about making sure that things are done[31]. However, in practice, it is not always easy to draw such clear distinctions[32]. For example, in smaller organisations trustees may be closely involved in the work of the charity, possibly acting as service volunteers as well as trustees. In this situation they make decisions as trustees and then, as service volunteers, implement them. The two roles should not be confused. Similarly, in larger organisations, paid staff may well be making important decisions. This is appropriate provided that they are line with policy frameworks set by the trustees. In this situation, trustees and senior management (especially the chief executive) need to review regularly their respective roles and consider how they are contributing to carrying them out. There is a fine line to be drawn between the trustees' governance role and undue interference with the operational aspects of the running of a charity[33].

The final aspect of governance under investigation is influence of funders. Charity trustees have a responsibility to exercise their independence. Whilst funders do have legitimate interests when funding charities, there are concerns that they may well interfere with trustees' independence when funders have a role in the governance of a charity. For example, if funders have a role in the appointment of charity trustees, this must be carried out in the best interests of the charity (not the funder) and the funders' appointees must equally act in the best interests of the charity. Problems of independence have been exacerbated through the contract culture, in which funders may seek to deprive the trustees of the responsibility to select the charity's beneficiaries[34]. Alternatively, funders

---

30 See e.g. the Charity Commission inquiry into the Redstone Trust & Somerset Care Trust, dated 2nd October 2000, which resulted in money being repaid to the charity by a solicitor trustee who had received unauthorised payment for his services to the charity.

31 See e.g. Adirondack S. *The Good Governance Action Plan for Voluntary Organisations* NCVO (2002).

32 See also, in the context of the governance of housing associations, Mullins' reference on para 6.4.1.1 to "*reverse delegation*".

33 See e.g. ACEVO *Leading the Organisation: The Relationship between Chair and Chief Executive* (2002).

34 See e.g. Morris D. *Charities and the Contract Culture: Partners or Contractors? Law and Practice in Conflict* Charity Law Unit (1999).

sometimes ask charities to provide excessive information in the name of accountability, which can divert resources away from the charity's main function.

The Charity Commission emphasises that independence is an important characteristic of a charity[35] and has recently warned that:

> "*[trustee] boards should work to avoid situations where knowledge, or an excessive degree of influence, is held in the hands of a select few (who may not be trustees themselves)* [36]*.*"

It will be seen that each aspect of governance, whilst considered separately, is very much intertwined. In each of the four areas, for example, we see a discussion of the fiduciary nature of trusteeship, which is the legal underpinning of a trustee's obligations. We also see that in each area, prevention is better than cure[37]. It therefore seemed logical to start the seminar series on the subject of the recruitment of trustees – if charities do not get that right, there is not much chance of good governance being the end product. In the words of the Charity Commission[38]:

> "*An effective induction programme can equip a board to fulfil its role. In our experience, boards that do not have an appropriate induction programme are less able to 'hold their own' when faced with a challenge to their authority. These boards often run into difficulties that may lead to our intervention.*"

1.4 Recruiting and Retaining an Effective Body of Trustees

Valerie James opens this section by examining whether the law encourages the recruitment and retention of an effective body of trustees. It is interesting that she begins her discussion by looking at the law relating to disqualification from acting as a trustee. This is an important issue; in a NOP survey commissioned by the Charity Commission in the summer of 2001, only 33% of the charities surveyed

---

[35] RR1 *The Review of the Register of Charities* Charity Commission (2001).

[36] RS1 *Trustee Recruitment, Selection and Induction* Charity Commission (2002) p.21.

[37] This is in line with the Charity Commission's approach. See Charity Commission *Annual Report 2001-2002* (2002) p.13.

[38] RS1 *Trustee Recruitment, Selection and Induction* Charity Commission (2002) p.21.

had carried out formal checks on prospective trustees[39]. The current position is unacceptable, as it puts both charities and individuals at risk. James then turns to the issue of potential personal liability for trustees, which, understandably, may well act as a deterrent to recruitment and retention. She refers to a number of possible ways of avoiding personal liability or its consequences, including: statutory relief from liability; exclusion clauses; trustee indemnity insurance; and, incorporation of the charity as a charitable company. Each solution brings its own problems and uncertainties. Juxtaposing the potential problems of personal liability and the general principle that trustees are to act voluntarily, as James does, brings to mind the possibility that the latter, when linked with the former, may well discourage the recruitment and retention of an effective body of trustees. Nevertheless, the voluntary principle of trusteeship has been debated many times in recent years and is generally upheld. The discussion of payment of trustees in the Strategy Unit report, when considering measures to encourage trusteeship, is typical[40]. During consultations with charities, a good deal of continuing support was shown for maintaining the principle of voluntary trusteeship as the basis of charity governance. The report concludes that the present position should be maintained so that, in general, payments to trustees which are made purely in their capacity as trustees, should not be allowed. The report also notes that consultation provides little evidence to suggest that the promise of payment is an effective general incentive to take on trusteeship.

Against the background of the law, Dorothy Dalton looks at strategies used by charities to gain a more effective and representative body of trustees. Her approach is very much based upon the provision of adequate information to both prospective and current trustees; how can one complain about the inadequacies of trustees' performance if they have never been told what is expected of them in the first place? Similarly, trustee meetings will run more effectively if trustees are sufficiently armed with appropriate information. In this respect, trustees are very much reliant on the charity's paid staff, especially the chief executive. Dalton's message can be summed up in the words: *"you get out what you put in"*. In this regard, an interesting suggestion to charity funders is that they should ensure that a proportion of their funding is spent on developing governance[41]. For its part,

---

[39] Ibid. p.15.

[40] Strategy Unit, Cabinet Office *Private Action, Public Benefit. A Review of Charities and the Wider Not-For-Profit Sector* (2002) paras.6.43 – 6.46. The principle of unpaid trusteeship was also generally endorsed by respondents to a Charity Commission public consultation on the payment of trustees in late 1999 – see, now, CC11 *Payment of Trustees* (2000).

[41] Kumar and Nunan have also recently recommended that funders should consider specific grants to strengthen governance. Kumar S. and Nunan K. *A Lighter Touch. An Evaluaton of the Governance Project* YPS for Joseph Rowntree Foundation (2002).

the Government, in its Code of Good Practice on Funding[42] recognises that, as a funder, government should help to meet the core costs of charities, which are acknowledged as including *"governance – support of the trustee structure[43]"*.

Interesting light is shed on the subject of recruitment, training and retention of trustees through John Marshall's contribution in which he examines lessons to be learned from the National Health Service (NHS) Appointments Commission. The Commission was established in 2001 to take over from health ministers the appointment of chairs and non-executives to the boards of health authorities, NHS trusts and primary care trusts. Other duties of the Commission include recruitment, appraisal and support of non-executives through mentoring and training programmes. Whilst the Commission has only been established for a short time and is still in the process of developing some of its procedures, we learn of the contrasts in this field: recruitment and training is formalised; appointments are fixed term with an expectation that appointees will move on to make way for new blood after a second term of office; and payment for appointees is the norm, and is in accordance with a fixed rate of remuneration[44].

1.5 Involvement of Users in Governance

Robert Meakin launches this section by looking at the law, which may appear to stand in the way of charity users acting as trustees. His overall message is that most of the obstacles can be removed by careful drafting of governing documents[45]. Ideally, these issues will have been dealt with at the inception of the charity, but if not, then governing documents can be amended, with Charity Commission consent where appropriate. Meakin refers to the new statutory duty of care for trustees, in section 1 of the Trustee Act 2000, and suggests that this may relieve to some extent the legal obligations of user trustees as it allows for a modified duty of care according to the circumstances. This may well tolerate a

---

[42] Active Community Unit, Home Office *Funding: A Code of Good Practice. Compact on Relations between Government and the Voluntary and Community Sector in England* (2000).

[43] Ibid. Appendix 1.

[44] For example, NHS trusts are allocated to bands according to their turnover in the latest year for which audited accounts are available and rates of remuneration for chairs are set for each band.

[45] That is the trust deed, constitution, memorandum and articles of association, Scheme of the Charity Commission, conveyance, will or other document describing the charity's purposes and, usually, how it is to be administered.

lower standard of care from user trustees who lack specific knowledge or experience.

At the seminar, Mike Locke spoke about the sorts of strategies to be adopted to involve users in governance[46]. Whilst the general view is that user involvement is a good thing, he noted that it is proving very difficult to implement in practice. It is not necessarily the case that appointing some users as trustees is the best way to involve users in the governance of a charity. One size does not fit all when it comes to getting users involved in governance.

By comparison, using two case studies where very different governance forms have been adopted, David Mullins considers the history of tenant involvement in the non-profit housing sector and provides some lessons to be learnt from the experience of involving tenants in governance. Here again, whilst there may be universal support for the principle of user involvement, there is a great variety in the arrangements that are put into place to put this principle into practice. It is interesting that in the context of registered social landlords, the Charity Commission, together with the Housing Corporation, has published a model clause for managing potential conflicts of interest. In this one respect, Meakin's "*pressing need*[47]", for the Charity Commission to draft or approve model governing instruments which can be universally used by charities wishing to have user trustees, has been met.

1.6   Strategy or Management by Trustees

Michael Carpenter begins by considering the legal issues which govern a trustee's approach to strategy or management. Again, there is focus on the charity's governing documents, which should now reflect the modern approach to trusteeship, which is, according to Carpenter, that the trustee is the "conductor", rather than the player of all the musical instruments. He reports on a new regulatory environment in which charity trustees may well have, constitutionally, all the powers that they need to govern their charity[48]. The regulatory question therefore moves away from asking whether the trustees *had the power* to do what they did, to whether the trustees should have *exercised the power* in the way that they did. Again, the fiduciary obligation of charity trustees to act in the best

---

[46] The general themes of his presentation are rehearsed in Locke M., Begum N. and Robson P. 'Service Users and Charity Governance' in Cornforth C. (ed) *The Governance of Public and Non-Profit Organisations: What Do Boards Do?* Routledge (2002).

[47] See para 5.23

[48] See e.g. the new general statutory power to invest trust funds, contained in Trustee Act 2000, s.3.

interests of their charity, is crucial. Carpenter then discusses the status of Charity Commission guidance and good practice statements, and, in particular, whether or not trustees must follow such advice. He concludes that it would usually be "reasonable" for trustees to do so.

Roger Singleton then outlines the route taken by one charity for achieving the balance between strategy and management and the roles of the trustees and the chief executive, advocating a symbiotic partnership approach. He gives a step-by-step account of the way in which the trustees at Barnardo's develop their strategic plan and then go about implementing it. Singleton reminds us of the important role of the trustees as overseeing the deployment of the charity's resources, but he also notes that the trustees are heavily reliant on the paid staff in this task. Taking us back to our first theme, the skills composition of the trustee body as a whole is important here.

Gregory Jobome then examines the correlation between the adoption of key corporate governance mechanisms by large charities and their performance. Performance is defined in two ways to include both fund-raising and effectiveness in channelling such funds to the donor-intended charitable objects. Jobome does this by using a sample of the 100 highest earning UK charities. The findings are encouraging. He concludes that the adoption of corporate governance mechanisms of the type recommended by the Cadbury Committee does have a positive effect upon performance. For example, the adoption of a nominations committee[49] to handle trustee recruitment seems to be a factor in increasing the performance of some charities.

1.7 Influence of Funders

This section begins with Debra Morris and Karen Atkinson looking at the legal issues surrounding the influence of funders upon trustees and their governance.
Particular concerns arise when funder-appointed trustees regard their function as simply to represent the interest of the funders. Once more, the focus is on the fiduciary obligations of trusteeship, and this time it is seen that the law can encourage good governance and act as a shield against any undue pressure being exerted by funders.

Robin Currie then details one charity's experience of balancing the competing requirements of funders with the charity's mission. Whilst PSS's turnover has grown tenfold in the last decade, Currie notes that the trustees were determined

---

[49] See para 3.2.2, which advocates the use of a nominations committee for the appointment of charity trustees.

to resist pressures from funders and to remain in control of the charity's development. Strategies adopted included: ensuring a diversification of funding; saying no to funders who wanted the charity to branch out into other areas of service provision; and, investing in training for both trustees and senior staff. It is interesting here to note that trustees felt more able to say no to subsidising contracts with health or local authorities as a result of the Charity Commission guidance (which explains the law) on this issue. Here the law has helped trustees to govern well[50].

David Nussbaum completes this section with a look at the particular difficulties when dealing with institutional funders and the implications for governance of trends in relationships between charities and funders. For example, he raises the particular concern of whether a charity's campaigning role is compromised by working under contract to the public body whose policies it is publicly campaigning to change[51]. He also raises some issues in relation to the management of institutional funding and its impact on compliance with the SORP reporting requirements[52]. He suggests a reformed governance model finely balanced somewhere around his "charity accountability triangle" which takes into account beneficiaries as well as trustees and donors.

In the final chapter, Jean Warburton reviews the four seminars, paying particular attention to concerns raised by participants, and suggests possible future developments, both legal and extra-legal, to encourage effective governance of charities.

This is the first book of its kind to examine charity governance in the context of Charity Law. It is hoped that the book will help to spread good practice throughout the sector. It highlights charities' good governance achievements, and also seeks to draw attention to the legal underpinnings which charity trustees must bear in mind in their governance activities. In each of the four areas chosen for examination, we find that the law is not necessarily the best instrument for achieving good governance, and it is certainly not the only one. Nevertheless, Charity Law does play a vital role in encouraging good governance. It is hoped that this collection of essays assists in both highlighting the law, identifying problems and suggesting a way forward.

---

50   The guidance may not be sufficiently clear for all charities. Clarity in this area was called for by seminar participants. See para 13.3 below.

51   On this see e.g. Morris D. 'Paying the Piper: The "Contract Culture" As Dependency Culture for Charities?' in Dunn A. (ed) *The Voluntary Sector, The State and The Law* Hart Publishing (2000).

52   See further para 103.4.1 etseq below.

Contributors to this collection range from practising lawyers, to academics from a wide variety of disciplines including law, economics and accounting and housing studies, through to chief executives of national charities. It was felt important largely to retain the original style of each contribution, so that the reader is invited to embrace the diversity of the contributions, which are linked by common themes.

Chapter 2

THE LAW AS IT AFFECTS THE RECRUITMENT AND RETENTION OF TRUSTEES
Valerie James[1]

2.1 Introduction

Figures recently published by the Charity Commission show that the number of registered charities at the end of 2001 was 188,116. These, and other charities not subject to registration, all need to be managed and controlled and sufficient trustees need to be found to do the job. It is said that there are more than a million charity trustees in this country. By their nature, charities operate for the public benefit and it is therefore in society's interest for the law to encourage the recruitment and retention of dedicated trustees. Does it do so?

I intend to look initially at matters which may disqualify an individual from being considered for trusteeship. I shall then look at the two issues which, I believe, are most likely to deter an individual from accepting appointment. These are personal liability, in which context I shall examine a trustee's duty of care, and the obligation to forgo any payment for the trouble involved. I shall conclude with some practical advice on how, having recruited a trustee, a charity may get the most from that person to their mutual benefit.

2.2 Disqualification

Only a minority of people are prohibited by the law from becoming charity trustees. The Charities Act 1993[2] disqualifies anyone:

---

[1] Valerie James became a partner of Wrigleys Solicitors in Leeds in 2002 and now acts for a broad range of charities, particularly on governance and property issues. For some eight years she was a governor and a trustee of an independent school.

[2] Charities Act 1993, s.72(1).

- Convicted of an offence involving dishonesty or deception, unless the conviction is spent within the terms of the Rehabilitation of Offenders Act 1974.

- Who is an undischarged bankrupt or whose estate has been sequestrated.

- Who has made an arrangement or composition with his creditors from which he has not been discharged.

- Who has been removed from office as a charity trustee by the Commissioners or the High Court for misconduct or mismanagement of the charity's administration.

- Who is subject to a disqualification order under the Company Directors Disqualification Act 1986 or an order made under section 429(2)(b) Insolvency Act 1986.

Any person so disqualified may apply to the Commissioners for a waiver of the disqualification, either generally or with regard to a particular charity or class of charities[3]. The Commissioners are only precluded from granting a waiver where a company is involved and the person is prohibited from acting as a director under the Company Directors Disqualification Act 1986[4]. In those cases leave may only be granted under that Act or by the Court which made the relevant Order.

The Commissioners are required to keep a register of persons who have been removed from office[5], either by themselves or by the Court, which is to be open to public inspection[6].

It is generally believed that only adults may become charity trustees. This is true in the case of a charity which is an unincorporated association or a trust[7] but persons under 18 may be company directors provided they are old enough to understand the duties involved.

Conversely, clergymen are apparently not permitted to be company directors by

---

[3] s.72(4).

[4] s.72(4)(a).

[5] Charities Act 1993, s.72(6).

[6] s.72(7).

[7] Law of Property Act 1925, s.20.

virtue of section 29 Pluralities Act 1838. This forbids those holding ecclesiastical office from dealing for gain or profit without a licence from the bishop after consultation with the Parochial Church Council, an exception being made for being a director in *"any benefit society, or fire or life assurance society"*[8]. The modern equivalent would probably be an Industrial and Provident Society rather than a registered charity. The 1838 penalty for breach is suspension or deprivation of office. I think this is one of those laws of which few people are aware and the likelihood of enforcement negligible.

The particular governing document of a charity may impose a positive qualification for trusteeship which needs to be complied with. For example, the trustees of a regeneration charity may need to have a connection, by reason of residence or workplace, with the area of benefit. Independently of any express provision in the governing document, where a charity is established exclusively for the benefit of members of the Church of England, case law supports the view that only members of that church should be appointed trustees[9].

2.3 Motivation

Why would an individual want to become a charity trustee? The highest and best motivation is a real desire to further the charitable objects of the charity and I submit that without a real belief in what the charity is trying to achieve the demands of charity trusteeship may be too onerous. Undoubtedly there are less altruistic motives which may encourage a person to become a trustee: working with a group of people to a common purpose is a good way of getting to know them and can provide useful connections; the management of a charity is likely to bring with it many new challenges providing a valuable learning experience; being a trustee of a respected charity looks good on a C.V. It is possible that a real commitment to the charitable purposes may only come with a greater understanding of what the charity is about after accepting an invitation to become a trustee.

Because the governing document of a charity can be in one of several forms, it is not always completely clear who a charity's trustees are. The principal types of charity are an unincorporated association or society, a charitable company and a charitable trust. In the case of an unincorporated association, its governing document is likely to be a constitution or a set of rules and the usual title given to the charity trustees is the executive or management committee. A charitable

---

[8] Pluralities Act 1838, s.30.

[9] *Baker v Lee* (1860) 8 HLC 495; *Re Stafford Charities* (1857) 25 Beav. 28

company will be governed by a Memorandum and Articles of Association and the charity trustees will be the directors of that company. A charitable trust will usually be established by a Trust Deed or Will and in this case the trustees will often be called trustees or, perhaps, governors. The trustees of a charity are those persons having the general control and management of the administration of the charity[10]. A lot has been done in recent years to educate charity trustees to understand their position and responsibilities but it remains possible that many still do not realise that they are trustees.

With education has come the realisation that by becoming a charity trustee, duties and responsibilities are accepted which can lead to personal liability. In my experience this is of significant concern to many trustees. They are prepared to put their time and expertise at the disposal of the charity but draw the line at exposing their personal assets and the financial well-being of their dependants.

2.4 Trustee Liability

If trustees act prudently, lawfully and in accordance with their governing document then any liabilities they incur as trustees can be met out of the charity's resources[11], but if they act otherwise they may be in breach of trust and personally liable to meet any call on the charity's property arising from their actions, or to make good any loss to the charity. For a few people this can be a real worry but in fact it has been extremely rare for a trustee to be made personally liable in this way.

The fundamental duty of a trustee is to further the purposes of the trust of which he or she has accepted the office of trustee[12]. The measure of this duty at common law is to act with the same diligence and care as men and women of ordinary prudence and vigilance would in the management of their own affairs[13]. This assumes an awareness of financial management and legal issues, although not a detailed and technical knowledge. However, the degree of care expected would increase if an individual is an expert in a particular area[14].

---

[10] Charities Act 1993, s.97(1).

[11] *Re Beddoe* [1893] 1 Ch 547, 558; Trustee Act 2000, s.31.

[12] *Duke on Charitable Uses* (1676) p.116.

[13] *Speight v. Gaunt* (1883) 9 App.Cas. 1

[14] *Bartlett v Barclays Bank Trust Co Ltd* [1980] Ch 515

The Trustee Act 2000 has now introduced a statutory duty of care specifically linked to the exercise of the powers afforded by the Act, which include investment powers and also the power to insure trust property. This duty may, however, be expressly excluded in the trust instrument[15]. You should note that this Act has no application to the corporate property of a charitable company, but directors of charitable companies should nevertheless be aware of the standard required because arguably they should be beyond criticism if this is the standard followed.

The statutory duty of care is to exercise such care and skill as is reasonable in the circumstances, having particular regard to any special knowledge or experience that the trustee has or holds himself out as having and, if the trustee acts in the course of a business or profession, to any special knowledge or experience that it is reasonable to expect of a person acting in the course of that kind of business or profession[16]. In one sense this new statutory duty could be regarded as less onerous for lay trustees than the common law duty of care which measures them against the ordinary prudent businessman. Where it applies[17], the statutory duty replaces the common law duty of care.

The 2000 Act also introduced a requirement that a trustee must obtain and consider proper advice in various circumstances including the way in which a power of investment should be exercised[18]. This applies not only to the general power of investment afforded by the Act but also to any power of investment however arising.[19] The advice must be obtained from a person who is reasonably believed by the trustee to be qualified to give it by reason of his ability and experience of financial and other matters[20]. The only exception to this requirement is where a trustee reasonably concludes that in all the circumstances it is unnecessary or inappropriate to seek advice[21]. Although the duty of care may be less onerous for lay trustees, they should be particularly observant in following the requirement to take advice.

---

15 Trustee Act 2000, s.2; sch 1 para.7.

16 Trustee Act 2000, s.1(1).

17 For application of duty see Trustee Act 2000, sch 1.

18 Trustee Act 2000, s.5.

19 s.5(1).

20 s.5(4).

21 s.5(3).

2.5 Relief from Liability

Some comfort is afforded by the equitable jurisdiction of the High Court to relieve a trustee from personal liability where he has acted honestly and loss has arisen to the charity merely from a mistake. There is also discretionary relief from liability for breach under section 61 Trustee Act 1925 for a trustee who has acted honestly and reasonably and ought fairly to be excused for the breach. A trustee may however lose a lot of sleep over the possible consequences of an innocent mistake before a matter is resolved by the courts in this way. The charity's governing instrument may itself contain an exclusion provision and the interpretation of such a provision was interpreted with enormous sympathy for the trustee in 1998 in *Armitage v Nurse*[22] but more strictly two years later in relation to a solicitor-trustee in *Walker v Stones*[23], which is now on appeal to the House of Lords.

Trustee indemnity insurance is popular with trustees but not so much, apparently, with the Charity Commission. The purchase of trustee indemnity insurance at the expense of the charity is regarded as a trustee benefit for which express authority is required, usually in the governing document. Trustees do not always appreciate this and there are frequent occasions when it is purchased without the necessary authority. The Commission appear to feel, as indeed I do, that it is often a waste of money and I know of no successful claim under such a policy. Nevertheless, the enthusiasm of trustees for the comfort such a policy provides is undiminished.

2.6 Contractual Liability

Little can change the liability a trustee has to the charity in respect of breach of trust, but not all trustees are in exactly the same position when it comes to contractual liability and this is an area where the constitution of the charity can make a difference to the personal exposure of its trustees.

It is a rare charity indeed, which never needs to enter into contracts in order to carry out its work. These may be contracts with suppliers of goods or services: contracts to supply services, for example, to a local authority, or a contract for the purchase or construction of new premises for the charity. Because trusts and associations do not have legal personality, individual trustees need to contract on behalf of an unincorporated charity. Provided the contract is entered into properly in furtherance of the charity's objects, the charity's resources may be

---

[22] [1998] Ch 241

[23] [2001] QB 902

used to meet the obligations arising under it[24]. However, if those funds run out, the liability to meet the obligations remains with the trustees personally unless they have made it a term of the contract that their liability will be limited to the value of the charity's assets. Although sympathetic contracting parties may accept such a term, by no means all would.

Conversely, if the charity is incorporated as a charitable company it has legal personality to enter into contracts in its own name and to meet the liability arising. As a result, the trustees themselves have no personal liability under contract.

If a charitable trust or association finds itself increasingly entering into substantial contracts, it may well be advisable for the trustees to take steps for the charity to become a charitable company for their own protection. A disadvantage of this is that the charity will come within the scope of company law which imposes a range of extra duties and expenses[25] but, if the need is there, these are rarely sufficient to discourage the trustees from making the change.

One matter to watch in regard to companies is that by reason of section 310 Companies Act 1985 any provision purporting to indemnify an officer of the company from liability which would otherwise attach for negligence, default, breach of duty or breach of trust in relation to the company is, with some exceptions, void. A company is authorized by statute to maintain insurance for any officer against such liability in relation to the company but a charitable company must have the necessary power in its memorandum and articles to provide this as a trustee benefit before affording itself of the statutory power[26].

There are limited circumstances in which the directors of a charitable company may incur personal liability for the company's debts under provisions in the Insolvency Act 1986. It is possible for the liquidator of a company to obtain a Court Order to the effect that any persons knowingly party to carrying on the business of the company with an intent to defraud creditors must make a contribution to the company's assets[27]. Similarly liability for wrongful trading arises if, at some time before a company went into insolvent liquidation, a director knew or concluded that there was no reasonable prospect that the

---

[24] See Martin J. *Hanbury & Martin: Modern Equity* 16th ed. (2001) p.503.

[25] For a discussion of Company law requirements in relation to charities see Warburton J. *Tudor on Charities* 8th ed. (1995) p.156. et seq. See also Hill J. 'The Trust versus the Company under the Charities Act 1992 and 1993' (1994) 2 CL&PR 133-147.

[26] Companies Act 1985, s.310(1).

[27] Insolvency Act 1986, s.213.

company would avoid liquidation[28]. In these circumstances, such a director may be liable to contribute to the company's assets unless the Court is satisfied that the director took every possible step to minimise the potential loss to the company's creditors[29].

2.7 Trustees to Act Without Payment

It will have become clear that taking on the trusteeship of a charity is a serious commitment which will demand time and application. In spite of the demands of the role, trustees have a duty to act gratuitously. The current position is that they are not entitled to receive any payment out of the charity's property other than reasonable and necessary out of pocket expenses[30]. They cannot be paid a salary for their work. They cannot benefit personally indirectly from the charity by, for instance, leasing charity property, borrowing charity money, or contracting to do business with the charity. Any infringement of this rule may constitute a breach of trust for which the individual concerned will need either to make good any loss or account to the charity for any profit made as a result of the breach. The one exception to this rule is where there is an express provision in the governing document which allows payment of a trustee or where the Charity Commission have authorised the transaction between the trustees and an individual personally[31].

This may be a disincentive to those potential trustees who need to use all their available time to earn a living. Public consultation on this issue in 1999[32] endorsed the principle of unpaid trusteeship and noted its contribution to public confidence in charities. Having been subject to review, the principle is likely to remain.

2.8 Retention of Trustees

Apart from the situations discussed above where a trustee may become disqualified from continuing as a trustee, the law has little direct effect on the retention of trustees, save that it is not normally possible for a charity trustee to

---

[28] s.214(2)(b).

[29] s.214(3).

[30] Trustee Act 2000, s.31.

[31] See CC11 *Payment of Charity Trustees* (2000).

[32] *Trustee Remuneration Consultation Document* Charity Commission (1999).

resign if less than two trustees remain as a result[33]. The practicalities of engaging the commitment of a trustee are generally of greater relevance. A person is more likely to continue as a trustee if the experience is enjoyable and he or she feels that his or her contribution makes a difference and is appreciated.

The maximum and minimum number of trustees is likely to be laid down in the governing document. The optimum number will largely depend on the nature of the charity: a simple grant-making trust could manage with three whereas an independent school could justify a dozen or more. My instinct is to recommend as few as are really needed to do the job properly. There is no pleasure in an appointment just to make up the numbers - the rewards come when every trustee has a clear role to play.

The general rule is that trustees take a decision together and are collectively responsible for actions and decisions taken[34]. Trustees should ensure that the trustee body as a whole has the skills and abilities necessary to run the organisation efficiently and effectively. When selecting new trustees, consideration must be given to the contribution they can make to the charity and their ability and willingness to give time to ensure that the charity is effectively administered and that the objects for which it is established are fulfilled[35]. Although trustees with a prominent position in the community or an exalted status are useful, that alone is not enough to justify an appointment.

When an opportunity arises to appoint a new trustee, the current skills of the trustee body should be considered. If you can identify skills which seem to be in short supply, it may be possible to draw up a job description of the ideal new trustee and match up potential invitees against those qualifications. Another factor is equal opportunities. You should look at the current balance of your trustee body and ensure that it is not unhelpfully dominated by a particular section of the community, for example, in terms of age, sex, race or background. If the charity has an equal opportunities policy, that should be followed no less in the appointment of trustees as it does to the appointment of staff.

Traditionally, charities have appointed trustees by word of mouth. Of course, it is helpful if people working together know each other well, but one disadvantage is that recruitment may be restricted to the same type of person. It is not unusual now to see advertisements for trustees in journals such as Third Sector and

---

[33] Trustee Act 1925, s.39.

[34] *Bahin v Hughes* (1886) 31 Ch 390; also Law Reform Commission 23rd Report *The Powers and Duties of Trustees* (1982) Cmnd. 8733, 3.60-3.65 - which recommended no change in the above rule.

[35] See CC3 Responsibilities of Charity Trustees (2002) paras.18-23.

Charity Finance. For a small charity though, advertising is perhaps unjustifiably expensive. The National Council for Voluntary Organisations keeps a list of organisations who can help to find trustees.

The method of appointing the new trustee will be set out in the charity's governing document and this should be strictly followed. Common provisions are that some or all of the trustees are elected at the Annual General Meeting of the charity, with additional provisions which allow for interim co-options or for trustees to be nominated by particular interested organisations.

Care should be taken in the induction process. It is important that the trustee should know what will be expected before signing up to accept appointment. He or she should be provided with: -

- A copy of the charity's governing document.

- A copy of the latest annual report.

- Details of the property and investments which belong to the charity.

- A copy of the Charity Commission leaflet "Responsibilities of Charity Trustees[36]."

- A list of the existing trustees and an opportunity to meet them as soon as possible.

In conclusion, I feel the law could do more to encourage the recruitment and retention of trustees. For example, if personal liability is the strongest disincentive to accepting trusteeship, would it not be possible to ensure that all charitable trustees have the same limited liability as those who happen to be directors of charitable companies? Indemnity insurance is so popular with trustees that a statutory provision similar to that provided by the Companies Act for director's liability insurance would be helpful. Surely if these policies became universal and the number of claims remains minimal, this would be reflected in the premium charged - or is this too simplistic?

This paper has tended to focus on the problems associated with trusteeship. I am occasionally asked to advise a potential trustee on whether or not to accept office. I tend to be encouraging as I believe charity trustees provide a valuable public service. My advice tends to focus on establishing that the charity appears to be well managed with good internal controls and adequate training for staff and

---

[36] CC3 *Responsibilities of Charity Trustees* (2002).

trustees, what risks the charity faces in fulfilling its objects and how they may be minimised and finally whether the individual can make time available to fulfill the role properly. We all know that the expectation of "four meetings a year" is no comfort in times of crisis.

Chapter 3

THE RECRUITMENT AND RETENTION OF TRUSTEES: A PERSPECTIVE FROM THE VOLUNTARY SECTOR
Dorothy Dalton[1]

3.1 Background

3.1.1 A Dearth of Suitable People

Today there are very few meetings of charity chief executives at which the conversation does not turn sooner or later to the shortage of skilled staff, trustees and volunteers. In January 2001 one in three charities were reporting difficulties in recruiting staff. By May 2001, this had risen to two out of three charities. For example, United Response, a charity with a turnover of approximately £30m spent over a million pounds last year on agency fees for temporary staff to cover unfilled permanent posts.

Recruitment of volunteers is also causing concern. In 1998 public sector support for volunteering was just under £400m.

---

[1] Dorothy Dalton is currently Director of Voluntary Sector Development at Horwath Clark Whitehill and Charities Consultant to Bircham Dyson Bell. Dorothy was Chief Executive of the Association of Chief Executives of National Voluntary Organisations, (now renamed ACEVO) from 1992 to 2000 and is a trustee of several charities.

Fig.1: Public sector support for volunteering – Summary of data

Source	Funding for volunteering £ million	Funding related to volunteering £ million	Total quantified support £ million
Government departments	53.00	66.00	119.00
Government offices for the regions	0	2.50	2.50
Local authorities	82.50	36.00	118.50
Health authorities	28.00	16.50	44.50
National lottery	35.00	37.00	72.00
Government agencies and NDPBs	1.00	27.00	28.00
Totals	199.50	185.00	384.50

The audit was commissioned by the Home Office in 1998.

Despite an additional £300m investment in volunteering by the Government, most of the major charities that rely heavily on volunteers, such as RSPCA, The Scout Association and the Samaritans, are all currently reporting a worrying drop in the number of volunteers and difficulty in recruiting volunteers in the numbers in which they are needed.

A drop in the number of people volunteering was first detected in a survey carried out in 1997 for the National Centre for Volunteering. The level of volunteering dipped from 51% of the adult population in 1991 to 48% in 1997, although it was noted that existing volunteers were putting more time into their volunteering, up from 2.7 hours per week in 1991 to 4 hours per week in 1997. This meant that despite the loss of perhaps one million volunteers during the period 1991 to 1997 (down from 23 to 22 million), there was a marked increase in the number of hours volunteered, up from 62 million hours of formal volunteering in 1991 to 88 million hours in 1997.

Fig.2: Formal and informal volunteering, 1981-1997

	1981 %	1991 %	1997 %
Proportion undertaking formal voluntary activity in past 12 months	44	51	48
Proportion undertaking informal voluntaryactivity in past 12 months	62	76	74
Base	1808	1488	1486

This survey was carried out by the Institute for Volunteering Research in 1997 for the National Centre for Volunteering

This survey reinforced many of the research findings from earlier studies. I quote:

> "A strong correlation was found between participation and socio-economic group, with those from the highest groups almost twice as likely to take part in a formal voluntary activity as those from the lowest. Those in paid work were found to be more likely to volunteer than those outside the labour market, with a big fall noted among unemployed people, down from 50% in 1991 to 38% in 1997, reinforcing the long held concern that reform of the benefits system has acted as a deterrent to volunteer. In terms of gender, men and women were equally as likely to volunteer (at 48%), with women having seen a slight drop from 1991. As for age the survey confirmed the now well-known finding that volunteering tends to peak in middle age, with a tailing off after the age of retirement. However, it also pointed to two marked trends since 1991: an increase in participation by those in the third age and a sharp decline in involvement by young people, with the rate for the 18-24s down from 55% to 43%. Not only were fewer young people volunteering in 1997 than six years earlier, but the amount of time given was also sharply down, from an average per week of 2.7 hours in 1991, to an average of just 0.7 hours in 1997."

(Quotation taken from the summary report prepared by the Institute for Volunteering Research.)

Despite significant investment by Government and the voluntary sector in the recruitment, support and management of volunteers, the shortage of volunteers continues to grow. Of the estimated 22 million adult volunteers, approximately three quarters of a million are willing to take on the additional duties and responsibilities of being charity trustees. In May 2001 one in three charities reported difficulties in finding suitable trustees.

Fig.3: Distribution of human resources in the voluntary sector

	Less than £10k	£100k - £1m	£1m - £10m	Over £10m
Paid employees	17.2%	29.2%	27.3%	26.2%
Trustees	86.2%	11.6%	1.9%	0.3%
Unpaid workers	59.1%	16.0%	6.6%	18.3%
No. of General charities	90.4%	8.4%	1.1%	0.1%

NCVO Survey

3.1.2 Competition from the Public Sector

A number of charities now advertise for trustees beyond their members and other stakeholders, and the overall satisfaction with response levels and quality of applicants through national advertising is high. However charities are increasingly having to compete with advertisements for public sector appointments, many of which are remunerated. In 2000, the Home Office alone made 1,174 appointments.

Fig.4: Summary of appointments made by the Home Office in 2000

	Chair Appointed	Chair Reappointed	Members Appointed	Members Reappointed
Executive NDPBs	4	1	39	49
Advisory NDPBs	3	1	15	39
Tribunal NDPB's	2	0	96	0
Boards of Visitors to Penal Establishments	0	0	308	617
Total	9	2	458	705
Grand Total	1,174			

3.1.3 Diversity

The identikit picture of a typical trustee appears to have changed little over the years. According to the 2002 "Who's Who in Charities" 77% of trustees in the top 3000 charities are male (as are 73% of chief executives). This is in strong contrast to the gender breakdown of volunteers in general where under half (48 %) of volunteers are male.

An ACENVO (Association of Chief Executives of National Voluntary Organisations) survey in 1997 of 321 national and international charities reflected exactly the same gender split among chairs of trustees.

Fig.5:

	Total income of charity					
	<£100 000	£100k- £1m	£1m - £5m	£5m - £15m	>£15m	*Total*
Number of female chairs	7	46	21	5	4	83
Number of male chairs	16	82	75	29	24	226
Total	23	128	96	34	28	309

ACENVO

The struggle to find younger trustees continues. The 2002 "Who's Who in Charities" survey found that the median age of trustees in the top 3000 charities by income is 61 years.

Fig.6:

	Age Range						
	<30	30 to 39	40 to 49	50 to 59	60 to 69	70 to 79	80 to 89
Trustees	0%	3%	11%	33%	35%	16%	2%

3.1.4 2002 "Who's Who in Charities"

In the 1998 survey carried out by the Institute of Volunteering Research, just over half (53%) of organisations said they believed that their volunteers represented a good cross-section of their local community; with the housing and homelessness sector claiming to be the most representative with 71% saying that they have a good cross-section. Young people and people from ethnic minorities are the two groups that are seen as being under represented, followed by men and people with disabilities. No similar study has been carried out on trustees but anecdotal evidence indicates the situation is significantly worse among trustees. The ACENVO survey also found a direct correlation between size of charity by income, and the level of investment of time and other resources in developing better governance.

3.1.5 Trustee Support and Training

The HLB Kidsons Voluntary Sector Governance Survey 2000 of 755 charities confirmed earlier studies that the majority of trustee boards have between ten and fifteen members although mid range charities (£5m to £10m turnover) were at odds with their larger and smaller counterparts. Most boards of trustees meet every two or three months. Less than half (42%) of the charities in the survey provided some formal induction training and only 13% provided specific training in financial management. 28% of charities had a budget for trustee training. The picture among national and international charities appears to be better. A survey of 563 charities carried out by ACENVO (The Association of Chief Executives of National Voluntary Organisations) in 1997, found that 49% issued an induction pack and 50% provided special induction sessions. Half the charities surveyed held away days for trustees with 85% providing regular briefings. Only one in five provided regular trustee training sessions.

3.2 Recruitment

The publication of the "On Trust" report in the early nineties generated much greater knowledge of the responsibilities shouldered by trustees. The process of educating trustees about their role has helped to develop a greater awareness of the need for good governance. We live, however, in a society that is becoming increasingly more risk averse and increasingly inclined to look for scapegoats in the event of something going wrong. This has resulted in many potential trustees, fearful of quite onerous responsibilities, opting for other forms of voluntary or community involvement rather than taking on the duties of trusteeship.

3.2.1 Due Diligence

Surprisingly, charities still provide very little hard information to potential trustees and, even more surprisingly, potential trustees rarely demand sufficient information i.e. rarely apply "due diligence" prior to accepting an invitation to become a trustee.

At the very least a charity should provide an information pack for prospective trustees containing:

- Statement of the charity's vision, mission and values

- Annual report

- Current strategic plan

- Latest set of audited accounts

- Copy of the most up to date assessment of the charity's performance against its strategic plan

- Person specification *(See Appendix A (page 46) for an example)*

- Job description *(See Appendix B (pages 49))*

- Expected commitment of trustees and the charity's commitment to trustees *(See Appendix C (page 54) for an example)*

- Policy on trustee expenses

- Copy of Charity Commission booklet on *"Responsibilities of Trustees"*

- Details of trustee liability insurance.

Potential trustees should not be reluctant to ask for further information about the charity or to ask challenging questions about the charity's plans, assets and liabilities.

3.2.2 Nomination Committees and Skills Audit

Many trustee boards just add friends, acquaintances and colleagues to the board in the hope that some might turn out to be quite helpful. A growing number of boards now realise that they need to have a mechanism for identifying people who not only have appropriate skills, experience and working styles (board members need to be team players as trustees need to make decisions collectively), but also those who share the vision and values of the charity. Effective boards should try to test the commitment and capabilities of potential trustees prior to them being invited to join the board. Often potential trustees are invited to various charity events and to attend a couple of board meetings prior to a decision being taken by the board as to their suitability to take on the responsibilities of trusteeship.

A strong healthy board is built by having a thorough process for the recruitment and selection of trustees followed by a programme of induction as well as on-going support and development. A driving force in the process of developing a strong and effective board should be the Nominations Committee. The Nominations Committee, perhaps with a few additional responsibilities, is sometimes called the board development committee or governance committee. *(See Appendix D (page 56) for model terms of reference.)*

Skills audits of existing trustees should be carried out annually and trustees need to be asked to reaffirm their commitment to the charity for another year. A skills audit will highlight gaps in the collective experience and expertise of the trustee board as well as being used to identify trustees that may need to be encouraged by the chair of trustees to take a more active part in the governance of the charity or to move on.

Charities can use their annual skills audit form and potential trustees' skills audit form as an opportunity to get trustees to reaffirm (and potential trustees to affirm) their commitment to their role and to the charity. *(See Appendix E (page 60) for possible wording of affirmation.)*

3.2.3   Identifying Potential Trustees

Looking for trustees among one's friends, acquaintances and colleagues is not wrong if it is done as part of a wider strategy. For example, one American not-for-profit organisation identifies suitable board members by inviting twenty well-connected, respected people in fields related to the work of the charity, to join a "One-meeting Committee". At this meeting they are told about the organisation, its current successes and challenges, and the qualities and skills that are needed on the board. Each attendee is asked to nominate an individual who fits the bill.

Within twenty-four hours, meetings are arranged for the twenty people nominated to meet the chief executive and chair. The members of the "One-meeting Committee" leave with a greater knowledge and understanding of the charity, often going on to become supporters and sometimes even trustees.

Other methods of identifying potential trustees include looking among the charity's volunteers, committee members or members of various advisory forums such as user forum or young people's forum. This method allows the charity to see people in action and to test commitment to the charity prior to an approach being made by the Nominations Committee. Other charities identify key organisations that the charity would like to develop stronger links with, and set up mechanisms for assessing their key people as possible trustees.

Trustee vacancies, with the skills and expertise required, can be advertised not just among supporters and members via mailings, newsletters and the website, but more widely such as in local or national newspapers or journals. Advertising in external publications needs to be carefully targeted otherwise it can be costly and bring little response. For example, if a trustee with PR skills is needed it is wise to advertise in a PR journal.

Membership organisations often complain that they cannot develop balanced and diverse boards as they are at the mercy of their members' nominating and voting whims. However, membership organisations can take proactive steps to develop balanced boards that have the skills needed to govern well. Co-option has often been used to obtain trustees with relevant skills and backgrounds. In addition, membership organisations should advertise to their members the skills needed on the board. This should be done both at the time of seeking nominations as well as to voters prior to the election. Some membership charities, such as the Terence Higgins Trust, not only advertise the skills, experience and backgrounds needed on the board but also have a short-listing committee that scrutinises the nominations received and only short-lists for election those who have one or more of the skills needed and who satisfy the nomination criteria or person specification.

Headhunters are occasionally used by charities that can either afford to pay the fees involved or if the headhunter can be persuade to work on a "pro-bono" or reduced fee basis. Methods used by headhunters include search and open competition through advertisements.

3.2.4   Induction, Support and Training

It often helps to ask a more experienced trustee to act as mentor to a new trustee. Arranging an overnight away day for trustees soon after an AGM at which new trustees have been elected, can help new trustees to get to know fellow trustees in a more informal environment, and can help develop the trustees into a team. A one-to one meeting with the chair of trustees after the new trustee has attended a couple of board meetings will enable the trustee and the chair to get to know each other better; it will give the new trustee the opportunity to clarify his/her understanding of the charity and its governance; it can be used to identify any support needs as well as to identify how the new trustee can use his/her skills, interests and experience to become more involved in the charity; and, it gives the new trustee the opportunity to use his/her "fresh eye" to question some of the policies of the board or the charity.

All new trustees need to receive the trustee handbook *(See Appendix F (page 62) for contents of a trustee handbook)* and have briefing sessions on:

- The vision, mission and strategic plans of the charity;

- The charity's big issues and how they are being addressed;

- The roles and responsibilities of trustees;

- The governance structure of the charity and how the structure helps the trustees comply with their legal, regulatory and moral responsibilities;

- Charity finance and how to read the financial information provided to trustees;

- The board's policies and the mechanisms used to review these regularly;

- How the board reflects on its performance, how it assesses the performance of its chief executive and how it measures the performance of the charity.

In addition new trustees need the opportunity to meet members of the senior management team; to walk around the main office and talk to staff and volunteers; as well as visiting some of the service delivery centres if these are not housed in the main building.

As part of the board's annual session on reflecting on the quality of governance, board members need to identify both their individual and collective training needs for the coming twelve months, and to identify what skills or expertise are need either within the board or which need to be made available to the board by the retention of appropriate additional professional advisors.

Governance should appear as a budget heading on the annual budget. This will signal the importance the charity places on good governance and will recognise formally that the charity needs to invest in developing better governance.

It would help governance to move up the charity's agenda if trusts, foundations and other funders insist, when making large grants (in excess of £10,000), that the charity receiving the grant must spend a given percentage (say in the region of 5% to 10%) on developing its governance.

3.2.5 Planning and Reporting Cycles, Agendas and Information Needs for Good Governance

The quality of governance is very dependent on the quality of the board's agendas, the information provided to trustees and to the board's planning and reporting cycles. Most charity trustees show little interest in these, allowing the chief executive a completely free hand in preparing the agenda and providing appropriate papers. This may be acceptable if the chief executive fully understands the nature and importance of governance, and is sensitive to the needs of trustees. For most charities, the chair in partnership with the chief executive needs to ensure that the board receives sufficient (neither excessive quantities nor too little) and timely information in order to make informed decisions; and that any relatively long paper is accompanied by a summary analysing the key issues and policy implications.

The board through the chair needs to hold the chief executive responsible for the quality of the board papers and for ensuring that each paper clearly identifies its purpose, for example "for decision", "for information".

When deciding which items need to appear on the agenda, the chair and chief executive need to follow the agreed planning and reporting cycles. In addition they need to ask whether any item proposed for the board agenda is a fundamental issue for the charity; whether it has policy implications and whether it is a priority for board time.

The chief executive needs to report regularly to the board on progress against the strategic priorities, business and annual plans; and should alert trustees to current and future problems.

3.3 The Retention of Trustees

Governing a charity well is not an easy task. Chait, Holland & Taylor in "Improving Performance of Governing Boards" came to the stark conclusion that:

> *"effective governance by a board of trustees is a relatively rare and unnatural act"*.

They argue that this is because:

> *"the tides of trusteeship carry boards in the wrong direction: from strategy towards operations, from long-term challenges towards immediate concerns, from collective action toward individual initiatives".*

Regrettably they conclude that most boards just drift with the tides and as a result trustees are little more than high-powered, well-intentioned people engaged in low-level activities. Combine this with the legal responsibilities of trustees and it is no wonder that charities have difficultly recruiting and retaining trustees that bring added value to the governance of charities.

In order to identify factors that attract, motivate and retain good trustees, we need first to look at why trustees leave.

3.3.1 Reasons for Leaving

Reasons commonly given by trustees for leaving a charity prior to completing their term of office include:

1. *Trivia*: Issues that come before the board are a mishmash of trivial matters disconnected from each other and from the business strategy. This can be the result of an under-performing chair of trustees, or a chief executive who wants to keep trustees away from the important issues, or a charity that has not articulated or is not focused on its vision, mission, strategic direction or business strategy.

2. *Decision-making*: Decision-making is slow and inconclusive. Decisions are either not made, or trustees and staff do not really know what was decided, or decisions made at one meeting are reconsidered and changed a few meetings later. This can be the result of poor chairing, or a lack of leadership, control and follow through by the chair.

3. *Disengaged*: Decisions are made by sub-committees or individuals (for example the chair and/or the chief executive) and the board is asked to "rubber-stamp". Board meetings can be tightly scripted with decisions predetermined and with trustees having little scope to influence the outcome. Trustees in this situation should articulate their views, should suggest a governance review and rethink how the board delegates its authority.

4   *Lack of Support*: Trustees feel out of their depth or excluded and there is no support or training which will allow them to develop into valuable trustees. They often leave claiming they do not have time to give to the charity. (See para 3.2.4).

5   *Information*: Trustees drown under a deluge of information full of uninterpreted data and facts or meaningless waffle. (See para 3.2.5).

6   *At War*: The board is dysfunctional with large egos and much jostling for power which the chair cannot, or does not wish to address. Trustees who are not involved in the power play, start absenting themselves from unpleasant board meetings and eventually claim "lack of time" when they leave. Instead they need to get together to remove those trustees who are more concerned by their position and authority than they are about achieving the objects and mission of the charity. If necessary they should seek the advice and help of the Charity Commission on the grounds that the assets of the charity may be in danger because of the lack of leadership and accountability by the trustees.

7   *Founder Syndrome*: The board is dominated by the Founder. This occurs when the organisation functions purely according to the personality and wishes of a prominent trustee or the chief executive who is usually, but not always, the founder of the charity. Many founders cannot make the transition from a highly entrepreneurial, reactive, individualistic style to a more pro-active, consensus-managed, forward-planning leadership style. The charity tends to struggle from one crisis to another until eventually the founder is forced out.

8   *Stagnant Membership*: Most of the trustees have been there for decades and have no desire to listen to a different point of view especially from a new trustee who "doesn't know how things are done". The new trustee soon leaves. This can often only be put right when the chair changes and the new chair carries out a governance review bringing in terms of office etc., and perhaps moves long -serving trustees to position that given them status but little authority such as honorary life members or vice presidents.

9   *Breakdown in Trustee / Staff Relationship*: The trustees and staff are locked into a vicious cycle of mutual mistrust and misunderstanding. This is enormously damaging to the charity and often very difficult to put right. Appointing strong external help, such as a professional governance advisor to the board, can help to resolve problems as the outsider can act

as a mediator between trustees and managers, persuade both sides to introduce better practice, and get trustees and senior management to focus on achieving the charity's objects and mission rather than putting all their energies into fighting each other. At times, the situation only changes when there is a change at the top, when either the chair or chief executive leaves, or they both do.

10 *Stormy Waters*: The charity hits a rough patch, for example financial difficulties, and some trustees want to jump ship. If the charity is well governed and trustees feel confident that they have acted reasonably, this situation is less likely to arise. When a charity is poorly governed and poorly managed, trustees may be tempted to hand in their resignation when times get tough but they ought to remember that resigning does not protect them from the consequences of their actions, or lack of actions, when they were trustees.

3.3.2 Powers to Remove Trustees

The governing documents of every charity should be reviewed regularly. Trustees need to be fully cognisant of the objects of the charity (as working outside the objects can mean that trustees are personally liable) and need to be kept fully informed of the powers given to trustees in the governing documents. If the governing documents do not give trustees the power to amend the governing documents, it is important to apply to the Charity Commission to introduce this power. It is also important to have the power to remove a trustee. This power of removal should be supported by a code of conduct for trustees, job descriptions for trustees and staff, terms of reference for board sub-committees and a proper procedure for removing a trustee.

Quite often a trustee needs to be removed not for a misdemeanour but because the trustee rarely attends board meetings or contributes nothing to the governance of the charity. This can be achieved either by term limits, with the trustee not being considered for a further term of office, or by having an attendance policy that could be as simple as a single line in the statement of the commitment of trustees to the charity *(see Appendix C, page 54)*.

Quite often personal intervention by the chair of trustees can resolve the situation without the need for formal processes. Rather than removing a trustee who has served the charity well but who is now a poor attendee, it may be wise for the chair to suggest leave of absence from the board if the trustee has family, health or work problems that prevent him/her temporarily from participating fully as a trustee.

Where the removal of a trustee is necessary for serious reasons such as a trustee who is constantly disruptive, who discloses confidential information, who has been dishonest, or who is unable to accept a democratic board decision etc., it is important that the chair ensures the charity has the power to remove trustees, that the proper procedures for removing a trustee are followed and that advice is obtained from the charity's legal advisers.

3.3.3 Attracting, Motivating and Retaining

In conclusion, in order to attract, motivate and retain good trustees a charity needs to make sure that:

1. The charity has a clear vision, mission, strategic objectives and business strategy, and that there is a common understanding of these by trustees and staff, and that the trustees are focussed on working in partnership with management to achieve these;

2. There is an open and clear process for identifying skills needed on the board, and for identifying and selecting new trustees. Potential trustees should be given sufficient information about the charity, their role and commitment in order that they can make an informed decision as to whether or not they wish to allow their name to go forward for selection/election to the board. Ideally this process should be masterminded by a nominations or governance committee;

3. The charity invests time, money and other resources in the development of better governance;

4. New trustees are provided with initial and on-going support, training and development, and that there are regular board away days;

5. The board reflects regularly on its performance and leads by example in the development of the charity as a learning organisation;

6. The board reviews regularly its governing documents and the governance structure;

7. The board records in writing delegated authority and reporting procedures as well as having clear terms of reference for board committees and job descriptions for honorary officers and trustees, and reviews these regularly; the board develops planning and reporting cycles, ensures that agenda items are pertinent and that trustees receive

timely, accurate and succinct information and advice to allow them to govern well; the board ensures that each trustee plays an active part in the governance of the charity and brings added value;

8   The board and staff recognise that although trustees may not formally benefit from the charity, most trustees gain something from their involvement in the charity and that it is important that they do so;

9   The trustees occasionally have fun!

3.4   The Future

3.4.1   An Unresolved Issue

A couple of years ago the Charity Commission reviewed its policy on the remuneration of trustees. Although the resulting report indicates a more flexible approach to this issue, experience indicates that there has been little change to the Commission's approach. While agreeing whole-heartedly that trusteeship should be a predominantly voluntary activity, I would suggest that the Charity Commission grants permission for exceptional cases on the basis of "net gain" rather than "necessity", as is presently the case. This might be particularly important for chairs of the largest, most complex charities, where the chair is expected to give the charity quite significant amounts of time.

3.4.2   An Institute for Charity Governance

The quality of executive leadership in the voluntary sector has improved significantly in the last decade following the development of professional bodies such as ACEVO (The Association of Chief Executives of Voluntary Organisations). The increasing effectiveness and efficiency of professional managers has left many trustees feeling unsure of their roles; unsure of the level of information they need for good governance; unsure of how they can meet their responsibilities without falling into micro-management; and, unsure of how they can measure the performance of their charity and of their professional managers. In addition the pressure of the immediate, whether it be lack of resources, staffing shortages etc., distracts trustees from keeping their eyes on the long-term and the big picture.

Effective governance is better developed by trustees themselves working together and in partnership with others in the field. This model of increasing effectiveness and quality is best exemplified by the success that chief executives have had in significantly improving the quality of professional management by setting up their own professional association dedicated to increasing the effectiveness of the voluntary sector; as well as their willingness to provide mutual support, to learn from each other and to work together to develop better management practice.

A number of formal and informal networks of trustees or chairs of trustees have been set up. These include the All Saints Group (an informal network of chairs of trustees of the 20 or so largest charities that was fairly active), a network of chairs of hospices, a network of trustees in the West Midlands and, more recently, the Charity Trustee Network that provides support and help to networks of trustees.

Significant improvements are more likely to occur if key people who are in a position to influence change gather together to develop and promote better practice, and to support each other. Chairs of trustees are key to developing better governance. Like the role of the chief executive, the role of a chair of trustees can be a very lonely and difficult one. Chairs of trustees are usually expected to lead their trustee boards in delivering high quality governance with little support and without a professional body to whom they can turn to for advice and help.

Is it therefore not time to set up an Institute for Charity Governance in which chairs of trustees will play the leading role?

The Institute's mission should be:

> *"to increase the effectiveness of the charitable sector through the development, application and delivery of high quality governance."*

APPENDIX A: NCH

Person Specification for Trustees

You will need to demonstrate in your application/ at interview that you possess the essential criteria for the post as detailed below. In addition demonstration of some of the desirable criteria will greatly assist you in your application.

The Nolan Committee identified seven principles to which those in public life should adhere:

1. Selflessness;
2. Integrity;
3. Objectivity;
4. Accountability;
5. Openness;
6. Honesty;
7. Leadership.

Personal qualities	Essential	Desirable
1. Commitment to the ethos and values of NCH	✔	
2. Commitment to equal opportunities and the promotion of diversity	✔	
3. Independence of thought and judgement	✔	
4. Ability to work as part of a team	✔	
5. Willingness to devote time, enthusiasm and effort to the duties and responsibilities of a trustee	✔	
Aptitude and skills	**Essential**	**Desirable**
1. An understanding and acceptance of the legal duties, responsibilities and liabilities of trusteeship	✔	
2. Ability to evaluate and interpret information	✔	
3. An understanding of issues affecting the voluntary sector, especially in respect of children		✔
4. Ability to play a strategic role to successfully effect change and meet objectives of NCH	✔	
Knowledge and experience	**Essential**	**Desirable**
1. Senior management experience in a medium/large public/voluntary sector organisation		✔
2. Specific professional knowledge, experience and skills in at **least one** of the following areas: • social work, especially in relation to children and young people • education • health, especially in relation to children and young people • finance/accountancy	✔	

<ul><li>budget handling/review and financial planning</li><li>legislation, especially in relation to children and young people</li><li>the management of change/business engineering</li><li>monitoring and evaluating performance in commercial and non profit organisations</li><li>information technology</li><li>fundraising</li><li>marketing</li><li>media and PR</li><li>lobbying and campaigning</li><li>recruitment and human resources issues, including employment legislation</li><li>training and staff development</li><li>property and estate management</li><li>pensions issues</li></ul>		
Other requirements	**Essential**	**Desirable**
1. Willingness to attend meetings of Council and other meetings as required, mostly in London	✔	
2. Willingness to undertake visits and other trustee responsibilities as required	✔	
3. Willingness to undertake training and participate in evaluation of NCH Council's work	✔	

Printed with kind permission of Deryk Mead, CE, NCH

APPENDIX B
TRUSTEES: MODEL JOB DESCRIPTION

Key responsibilities:

With other trustees to hold the charity "in trust" for current and future beneficiaries by:

1   Ensuring that the charity has a clear vision, mission and strategic direction and is focused on achieving these;

2   Being responsible for the performance of the charity and for its "corporate" behaviour;

3   Ensuring that the charity complies with all legal and regulatory requirements;

4   Acting as guardians of the charity's assets, both tangible and intangible, taking all due care over their security, deployment and proper application;

5   Ensuring that the charity's governance is of the highest possible standard.

Duties and tasks to fulfil these key responsibilities:

1   Ensuring that the charity has a clear vision, mission and strategic direction and is focused on achieving these;

2   To work in partnership with other trustees, the chief executive and other senior staff to ensure that:

      2.1   The charity has a clear vision, mission and strategic plan that have been agreed by the board, and that there is a common understanding of these by trustees and staff.

2.2 The business, operational and other plans support the vision, mission and strategic priorities.

2.3 The chief executive's annual and longer term objectives and targets support the achievement of the vision, mission & strategic priorities.

2.4 Board policies support the vision, mission and strategic priorities

2.5 There are effective mechanisms:

- To listen to the views of current and future beneficiaries;

- To review the external environment for changes that might effect the charity;

- To re-assess the need for the charity and for the services it provides, or could provide and

- To review regularly its strategic plans and priorities.

3 Being responsible, with the other trustees, for the performance of the charity and for its "corporate" behaviour;

3.1 To agree the method for measuring objectively the progress of the charity in relation to its vision, mission, strategic objectives/priorities, business plans and annual targets, and to receive regularly reports on the performance of the charity.

3.2 To ensure that views of beneficiaries on the performance of the charity are regularly gathered and considered by the board.

3.3 To appoint the chief executive, to set his/her terms and conditions and to ensure that the chief executive and the charity invest in the chief executive's ongoing professional development.

3.4 To receive regular reports from the chief executive on progress towards agreed strategic priorities.

3.5 To hold the chief executive to account for the management and administration of the charity.

3.6 To ensure that the chief executive receives regular, constructive feedback on his/her performance in managing the charity and in meeting his/her annual and longer term targets and objectives.

3.7 To ensure that the chief executive develops a learning organisation and that all staff, both paid and unpaid, review their own performance and regularly receive feedback.

3.8 To articulate the values of the charity.

3.9 To agree board policies.

3.10 To ensure that there are mechanisms for beneficiaries, employees, volunteers, other individuals, groups or organisations to bring to the attention of the trustees any activity that threatens the probity of the charity.

4 Ensuring that the charity complies with all legal and regulatory requirements;

4.1 To be aware of, and to ensure the charity complies with, all legal, regulatory and statutory requirements.

4.2 To maintain familiarity with the rules and constitution that govern the charity, to ensure that the charity complies with its governing instruments and to review the constitution regularly.

4.3 If the charity has powers to delegate, to agree the levels of delegated authority, to ensure that these are recorded in writing by means of minutes, terms of reference for board committees and sub-committees, job descriptions for honorary officers, trustees and key staff, etc., and to ensure that there are clear reporting procedures which are also recorded in writing and complied with.

4.4 To ensure that the responsibilities delegated to the chief executive are clearly expressed and understood, and directions given to him/her come from the board as a whole.

5 Being guardians of all the charities assets, both tangible and intangible, taking all due care over their security, deployment and proper application;

5.1 To ensure that the charity has satisfactory control systems and procedures for holding in trust for the beneficiaries all monies, properties and other assets and to ensure that monies are invested to the maximum benefit of the charity, within the constraints of the law and ethical and other policies laid down by the board.

5.2 To ensure that the major risks to which the charity is exposed are reviewed annually and that systems have been established to mitigate or minimise these risks.

5.3 To ensure that the income and property of the charity is applied for the purposes set out in the governing document and for no other purpose, and with complete fairness between persons who are properly qualified to benefit.

5.4 To act reasonably, prudently and collectively in all matters relating to the charity and always to act in the interests of the charity.

5.5 To be accountable for the solvency and continuing effectiveness of the charity and the preservation of its endowments.

5.6 To exercise effective overall control of the charity's financial affairs and to ensure that the way in which the charity is administered is not open to abuse by unscrupulous associates, employees or volunteers; and that the systems of control are rigorous and constantly maintained through regular evaluation and improvement in the light of experience.

5.7 To ensure that intangible assets such as organisational knowledge and expertise, intellectual property, the charity's good name and reputation etc are properly valued, utilised and safeguarded

5.8 If the charity owns land, to know on a continuing basis what condition it is in, if its boundaries are being encroached upon, what can be done with it and how it is or should be used. In particular, to ensure that any property which is a permanent endowment is preserved and invested in such a way as to produce a good income while at the same time safeguarding the real value of the capital.

5.9 To ensure that all income due to the charity is received and that all tax benefits are obtained and all rating relief due is claimed.

6   Ensuring that the charity's governance is of the highest possible standard.

     6.1   To ensure that the charity has a governance structure that is appropriate to a charity of its size/complexity, stage of development, and its charitable objects, and that enables the trustees to fulfil their responsibilities.

     6.2   To reflect annually on the board's performance and your own performance as a trustee.

     6.3   To ensure that the trustee board has the skills required to govern the charity well, and has access to relevant external professional advice and expertise.

     6.4   To ensure that there is a systematic, open and fair procedure for the recruitment or co-option of trustees.

     6.5   To ensure that there are succession plans for the chair and the chief executive.

     6.6   To participate in individual and collective development and training of trustees.

     6.7   To abide by the code of conduct for trustees.

     6.8   To ensure that major decisions and board policies are made by the trustees acting collectively.

Written by Dorothy Dalton and printed with kind permission of Michael Caudrey, MD, Horwath Consulting

APPENDIX C
INTERNATIONAL STUDENTS HOUSE

Commitment of Governors to the House

- To act solely in the interests of the House.

- To declare all actual or potential conflicts of interest.

- To act collectively.

- To respect confidentiality.

- To make available skills and experience to the House.

- To attend regularly Council and committee meetings having prepared fully for these meetings (Proposed commitment of a minimum of 3 out of 6 Council meetings).

- Ideally to serve on at least one committee.

- To gain a better understanding of the House by attending at least one event each year.

- To support the chief executive and the management of the House.

- Where appropriate, to challenge current thinking, the method of governance and management of the House but always to do so constructively and always acting solely in the best interest of the House.

- To work in partnership with the staff to achieve the mission of the House, understanding and respecting the different but complementary roles of governors and staff.

- To regularly and collectively reflect on how the Council fulfils its responsibilities as governors, trustees and directors of the House and how the Council brings added value to the achievement of the House's objectives.

Commitment of the House to the Governors

- To provide the Council with timely, high quality information in order to allow the Council to govern well.

- To provide the Council with timely advice ensuring that external professional advisors are available as and when needed.

- To work in partnership with the Council to ensure that the Council fulfils all its statutory and legal responsibilities.

- To invest time, money and other resources in order to help develop good governance.

- To ensure that a governors handbook is available and regularly updated *(See Appendix B page 49)*.

- To work in partnership with the honorary officers and the nominations committee to ensure that new governors receive induction and support, and that appropriate briefings and/or training are available to all governors.

- To provide the honorary officers and governors with the necessary administrative and other support that they will need to govern well.

- To reimburse governors' out-of-pocket expenses incurred in the course of their duties as governors, trustees and directors.

Written by Dorothy Dalton and printed with kind permission of
Peter Anwyl, CE. International Students House

APPENDIX D
TERMS OF REFERENCE FOR A NOMINATIONS COMMITTEE

Approved by the Board of Trustees on..200

Composition, Attendees, Quorum and Reporting

(i) The Nominations Committee will consist of not less than....trustees appointed by the Board, and the Chief Executive. The Chair of trustees is normally a member of the Nominations Committee.

> *[Whether the chair of trustees should be the chair of the nominations committee is very much a matter for the individual charity. With a significant growth in the duties and responsibilities of chairs of professionally managed charities, it may be wise to allocate the chairing of this committee to another trustee although the chair of trustees is likely to be an active member of this committee. However, the chair should not be involved in selecting his/her successor. It is important to have people with a range of backgrounds on the Nominations Committee. Committee members also need to be good judges of character.]*

(ii) The Board will appoint the Chair of the Nominations Committee.

> *[The chair of the nominations committee needs to be both fair and impartial, needs to be a skilled board member and knowledgeable about the organisation. If external advertising or external agents (e.g. head-hunters/search agents) are not being used, the chair and members of the committee will need to have access to extensive networks.]*

(iii)   Members of the Nominations Committee may serve for not more than.......years.

(iv)   The Nominations Committee will report back regularly and at least annually to the Board of Trustees.

Overall Responsibility

Take delegated responsibility on behalf of the Board of Trustees for identifying, recruiting and proposing new members of the board, and for their induction, support and development.

Main Duties

1   General

(i)   To carry out regular skills audits of the trustee board and identify the skills, experience, characteristics and backgrounds that are needed to provide high quality effective governance.

> *[Membership organisations that elect trustees at AGMs should inform members of the skills and experience needed on the board and should ask prospective board members to explain briefly in the election literature how they fit the profile.]*

(ii)   To prepare job descriptions, person specifications and an information pack for prospective board members.

> *[It is important to be very open about the time commitments involved and what is expected of each trustee. It is also essential that prospective board members share the charity's mission and values, are team players, can be constructively challenging and independently minded. It is also important to be honest (on a confidential basis) about the challenges facing the charity. Model job descriptions are available from Horwath Consulting and a number of other organisations.]*

(iii)   To prepare a recruitment plan and timetable.

> *[Consideration needs to be given as to whether vacancies should be advertised internally (e.g. through newsletters, the*

intranet etc.), advertised externally (e.g. locally, nationally, in specialist journals if specialist skills are needed such as PR, on the web etc.) and/or whether a recruitment or search agency is used.]

(iv) To identify a list of prospective board members and honorary officers.

[It is important to draw these names from a wide variety of sources. Obtain a written CV. Check CVs against the skills, expertise and experience needed. Produce a short list. (Note: All charities have at least one honorary officer, the chair. Most charities have a number of other honorary officers such as the treasurer, vice chair.)]

(v) To develop the interest of the prospective board members in the work of the charity.

[If at all possible, invite prospective board members to some of the charity's events. This will give other people within the charity an opportunity to meet them informally. It also tests the candidates interest in the work of the charity as well as giving some indication as to whether (s)he has time available to become involved in the charity.]

(vi) To meet the prospective board members and to scrutinise their suitability.

[Ideally arrange for each prospective trustee to meet the chair of the nominations committee, the chair of trustees and the chief executive. This can be formal or informal meeting(s) but either way be clear about what you wish to achieve, what information you need to get and what information you need to give to the prospective trustee. Invite prospective board members to complete the skills audit form or use the skills audit form as a basis of discussion at which the prospective trustee's commitment to the mission and values of the charity should also be assessed. Take up references. Cross check suitability by talking to different people who know the prospective trustee.]

(vii) To invite chosen prospective trustees to allow their names to go forward to the Board and to recommend them to the Board.

[Provide trustees with potted biographies as well as fit with the skills identified through the skills audit. Similarly if trustees are

elected by members at an AGM or by postal votes, provide potted biographies and fit with the skills profile.]

(viii) To inform successful and unsuccessful candidates.

[It is important to confirm that successful candidates still have the time needed to be trustees of the charity. It is also important to debrief unsuccessful candidates and to maintain their interest in the work of the charity in some way.]

(ix) To induct, mentor and involve new board members.

[Ensure that the new trustees also receive an induction pack (Contents of a model induction pack can be found on page ....), list of dates of trustees' meetings, date of the trustee away day, date of AGM as well as other key events in the charity's diary. Organise induction sessions as well as a programme of visits to head office and other offices/centres/branches. If possible after six months as a trustee, the chair of trustees should have a confidential one-to-one chat with the new trustee to see how (s)he is settling in, whether there are any issues that (s)he has spotted and would like to raise, whether (s)he requires any further information, briefings etc.]

(x) To ensure that the board has time to reflect on its own performance, on how it can govern the charity better, future training, support and development needs.

(xi) To ensure that there is an annual programme of board development including technical and other briefing sessions, away day etc.

Written by Dorothy Dalton and printed with kind permission of Michael Caudrey, MD, Horwath Consulting

APPENDIX E

Affirmation:

1. *I continue to be fully supportive of our mission, vision, purposes, goals and values.*

2. *I understand that attendance at, and preparation for, board and committee meetings and board away days will take the equivalent of ....days of my time. I am able to give this time during the coming year and expect to attend all board and committee meetings. If for good reason I am unable to attend a meeting, I will inform the relevant chair in good time.*

3. *I will notify the Chair of trustees if at any time during our discussions and deliberations if I find myself in a conflict of interest position.*

4. *I will abide by the code of conduct for trustees.*

Signature..**Date**..............................

For potential trustees only

Agreement:

1. *I agree to be nominated for election as a trustee.*

2. *I am fully supportive of the mission, vision, purposes, goals and values.*

3. *I understand that attendance at, and preparation for, board and committee meetings and board away days will take the equivalent of.....days of my time. If elected, I am able to give this time during the coming year and expect to attend all board and committee meetings. If for good reason I am unable to attend a meeting, I will inform the relevant chair in good time.*

4. *If elected, I will notify the Chair of trustees if at any time during our discussions and deliberations I find myself in a conflict of interest position.*

5. *If elected, I will abide by the code of conduct for trustees.*

***Signature**...**Date**............................*

APPENDIX F

A **Trustee Handbook or Induction Pack** should include the following:

1   *Introduction to the Charity*

1.1   Vision, Mission and Values

1.2   List of Patrons, President, Vice Presidents etc

1.3   Annual Report

1.4   Calendar of events

2   *Legal Status including:*

2.1   Copy of the Memorandum and Articles of Association

2.2   Copy of Charity Commission booklet on "Responsibilities of Trustees" & "Hallmarks of a Well-Run Charity"

2.3   Companies House booklet on "Directors and Secretaries Guide"

3   *Governance*

3.1   List of current trustees and contact details

3.2   Governance structure diagram and/or list of committees and subcommittees together with details of membership of these

3.3   Terms of reference for committees and sub-committees

3.4   Standing orders if any

3.5   Annual list of board meetings, AGM, board away day etc.

3.6   Details of travelling and subsistence allowances for trustees with a copy of a claims form

3.7   Job descriptions for trustees, chair, treasurer

3.8   Code of conduct for trustees

4   *Management*

4.1   Organisational diagram showing regional or local offices or branches

4.2   Contact details for regional/local centres or offices

4.3   Diagram showing management structure

4.4   List of senior staff and contact details

4.5   Job descriptions of chief executive and members of the senior management team

4.6   Code of conduct for chief executive

5   *Strategy and key policies*

5.1   Strategic plan

5.2   Business plan

5.3   Key policies (For example: employment, crisis/business continuation, health & safety, investment, reserves)

5.4   Risk analysis chart

6   *Finances*

6.1   Audited accounts for last two years

6.2   Current budget

6.3 Financial controls and reporting procedures

Written by Dorothy Dalton and printed with kind permission of Michael Caudrey, MD, Horwath Consulting

Chapter 4

RECRUITMENT, TRAINING AND RETENTION OF TRUSTEES
John Marshall[1]

4.1   Introduction

In the early 1990s the governance of publicly-quoted companies came under the spotlight and eventually led to the setting up of the Cadbury Committee on the Financial Aspects of Corporate Governance in 1992. The Committee published clear guidance notes and these have been embraced by most major organisations in the UK. In particular, the National Health Service, with its vast array of Health Authority Boards (in the 1990s approximately 100) and Hospital, Community, Mental Health & Ambulance Trusts accepted the guidance in order to strengthen accountability, openness and probity in all of these bodies.

During the 1990s the appointment of non-executives to Boards in both the Public & Private Sectors caused concern. The "Old Boys" network, rewards for political services whether fact or rumour led to the Nolan committee's report and to the appointment of a Commissioner for Public Appointments, Dame Rennie Fritchie. One of her early actions, after careful analysis, was to recommend most strongly that appointments to NHS Boards & Trusts should be separated from political influence and that an independent and apolitical organisation, later named the NHS Appointments Commission, should be established. This was approved early in 2001 and the Commission came into existence on July 1st 2001 with Sir William Wells as the First Commissioner, assisted by a team of eight Regional Commissioners covering the whole of England. Much of my lecture today will draw heavily on my experience as the Regional Commissioner for the North East of England but I must also acknowledge the learning process I was privileged to go through during the period when Sir John Harvey Jones was Chairman of ICI and was radically changing the way the Main Board and Divisional Boards functioned in that company. At that time I was a Divisional

---

[1]   John Marshall is Regional Appointments Commissioner for the NHS Northern and Yorkshire Region.

Director in the North of England.

4.2 The Role of Boards

Before recruiting to Boards of Trustees or Directors it is important to understand what the role of the Board is. The London Region of the NHS in conjunction with the Kings Fund, after analysing the recent literature, reduced the role to thirteen main functions:

1   Stating the purpose of the organisation.

2   Creating the "vision".

3   Establishing the climate and culture.

4   Setting strategic direction.

5   Developing partnerships.

6   Resource allocation.

7   Key appointments and remuneration.

8   Delegation of decisions.

9   Overseeing and reviewing performance.

10 Ensuring probity and effective financial stewardship.

11 Being accountable (to Government, to staff, to local people).

12 Promoting quality.

13 Safeguarding rights of staff and users.

Clearly, many other duties can be added to the above but these are the very formal and legal duties that cannot and should not be shirked. I would only mention public relations, links to the media and public-at-large, visiting units on the 'patch', communicating with staff (particularly nursing and operational staff) and with patients for you all to realise that a vast amount is left uncovered by the thirteen. And I cannot move on to my next section without mentioning the handling of complaints and the development of a successful Clinical Governance process as other vital and time-consuming tasks.

4.3 Scrutiny by Local Government

In the NHS we now have the need to communicate effectively with local government via one of their Scrutiny Committees and, in view of the interdependency of Health and Social Services and many Charitable Institutions we know that the NHS cannot do its job properly without effective communication with Local Authorities. As this process becomes better understood by Local Authorities I suspect the meetings will become more exhaustive. I also suspect that where Local Authorities are funding or part-funding Charities or Voluntary Bodies they too will become involved in this or a similar process. I have always felt that the Voluntary Sector is a largely untapped resource for the NHS, we do not nurture it enough financially, not because there is no will, more because NHS staff are almost permanently under pressure financially and time-wise and patients and politics drive the process. The urgent drives out the important!

4.4 Recruitment, Training & Development, Mentoring & Appraisal

I have placed these processes together because, increasingly, the NHS is accepting the importance and value of high quality, well-trained Trustees or NEDs (Non-Executive Directors). We have formalised the recruitment process for the purpose of ensuring a level playing field. This may include advertising posts locally and nationally, providing information packs, ensuring the panel includes a local Chairman, an independent assessor, a third (more distant) expert from within and, if possible, gender balance. We always try to have a manager from the Appointments Team to keep score and ensure processes are followed. Time period for interview, the range of questions and so on are agreed in advance. Some variation must be allowed depending on answers received but, again, this is all part of the level playing field process.

Once appointed we now arrange training and development programmes for all new NEDs and Chairmen, usually spread over two or three days and more detailed, local, training is added as necessary. Increasingly we are using external providers to organise these programmes and they include NHS experts as appropriate.

We invite new non-executives to take on a Mentor from within the system. Some do, some do not, but we do try to give them a suitable name.

Appraisals, for many years absolutely standard in most large private companies where it is linked to the reward structure, is becoming more accepted in the NHS. The Appointment Commission intends to launch a comprehensive scheme for all Chairs and NEDs to start in the new financial year. It will be an annual process with standard forms etc. and the paper-trail will be a vital part of the decision on possible re-appointment.

4.5 Contractual Arrangements

The NHS Appointments Commission has decided that all its appointments will be made for a period of 4 years and successful and effective NEDs and Chairs can look forward to a second term of office of up to the same time period. We are then, with limited exceptions, asking people to move on to make way for new blood, fresh ideas and so on.

Remuneration may be a sore point for most Charities and Voluntary Sector organisations. To a certain extent it is also a sore point within NED circles. However, and ignoring the moans, the system is as follows. Chair appointments are approximately at £16,000, £18,000 or £20,000 per annum for 3 days per week commitments depending on size of the organisation. The three days is a moveable feast and can be very much at the Chair's wishes although there are, of course, set dates such as Board meetings, Board seminars and so on. The PCT Chairs were paid at a lower rate, £10,000 to £12,000, but this was under review by Government and subsequently raised to the same level as other chairs.

At NED level the payment is just over £5,000 per annum. There has been only one inflation-linked increase in recent years but, again, this is under review. However, the time commitment for NEDs has been raised recently to 5 days per month and there is no doubt that many NEDs do far more than this.

It is also useful to mention expenses. Many Trusts cover large areas and to do the job well, NEDs often drive large distances to attend meetings and visit outposts. Mileage allowances are on standard NHS scales and all NEDs are encouraged to enter regular monthly expenses claims which have to be approved by the Chairman. Chairman and CEO are responsible for approving each other's expenses so that the Auditors demands are covered in this respect.

4.6 Status

What are the status aspects of these positions? Until very recently there have been many well-qualified people prepared to tackle Chairmanship posts. Very often early-retired 50+ year olds or people whose partner is working full-time and for whom the salary is a top-up to a lifestyle and not its main ingredient. The status is quite good, with an office in a busy, bustling organisation, secretarial support and plenty of meetings both internally and outside. There are regional functions and occasional National meetings in London or places like Harrogate. For both Chairs and NEDs there are Conferences and training events and the occasional visit from a senior politician to add spice to life.

Most importantly, however, the NHS ranks very high in people's minds as somewhere to "put something back". The interest factor is very high and one will never understand everything that is going on in the NHS organisation. The Magistrates' Bench is seen by many in a similar light but also as something of an ego trip. Being a NED on a NHS Trust is not an ego trip and much more closely aligns to involvement in a Charity or Voluntary Organisation.

4.7 Succession Planning

This subject is now talked about a great deal in the NHS but compared with organisations like the Armed Services, the big oil companies, ICI & Unilever, it is quite limited. At NED level, however, the far-sighted Chair searches for Chair material and, within a given Health Authority recent changes have created anywhere from 4 to 8 new organisations each needing a Chair and 5 NEDs. Thus, helping NEDs develop by attending training programmes, developing chairing skills, changing responsibilities to become more experienced are vital features of succession planning. Good Chairs are also looking outside their Board ranks for new blood and Appointment Commissioners are very conscious that the NHS is weak at seeking out and recruiting high quality NEDs from the outside world.

4.8 Politics and Financial Pressures

The NHS is deeply caught up in the political scene which adds interest and frustration in almost equal measure. One has to accept that politicians will make changes, that sometimes money flows into the NHS and sometimes it doesn't, however brilliant the cause. Increasingly Chairmen and NEDs are being held to account for the performance of their Trust and pretending ignorance or being genuinely ignorant of developing disaster is not acceptable. Monitoring the Executive Team in a £100m+ per year Trust is a tough and challenging exercise, not for the faint-hearted and not for those easily brushed aside by a CEO seeking an easy life. Anxious politicians are always lurking, demanding targets are met and perhaps these are aspects where the NHS differs from the Charities and

Voluntary Sector.

4.9 Equal Opportunities

The NHS Appointments Commission recognizes the importance and value of diversity, and places great emphasis on achieving gender balance, age balance and ethnic minority representation when undertaking the formation of trusts.

4.10 Conclusion

I hope these facets of recruitment, retention and development of NHS non-executives will stimulate debate. Charities are also coming under scrutiny and we are all fishing in the same limited pool for high quality people with skills, knowledge and the commitment we need to make a success of our organisations and deliver high quality services to the public in this increasingly stressful lifestyle.

Summary 1

RECRUITING AND RETAINING AN EFFECTIVE BODY OF TRUSTEES

Trustee Liability: Clarity

- A clear restatement of the law regarding personal liability of trustees is needed, particularly as the Trustee Act 2000 may have lowered the duty of care for some trustees. This restatement needs to reach all trustees and potential trustees.

- Positive marketing of the new SORP risk review requirement is also needed to ensure it is not perceived as a burden by trustees.

Limited Liability: Extension to All Trustees?

- Statutory intervention is needed both to remove concern over personal liability and to create uniform liability for trustees of charities with different legal structures. This will be preferably by enacting the proposal for the new limited liability structure for charities.

Trustee Indemnity Insurance: Education and Alternatives

- The failure of Trustee Indemnity Insurance to provide the protection envisaged needs to be publicised, possibly by the Charity Commission.

- Concurrently, trustees need to be advised on best practice and on alternative methods of protecting both themselves and their organisations, rather than relying on Trustee Indemnity Insurance. Alternative methods include ensuring appropriate legal structure and considering more effective forms of insurance.

Payment of Trustees: Flexibility

- Charities need to be given the *power* to introduce some form of trustee payment, but the power must be flexible enough to reflect the wide variety of trustee needs and circumstances.

- Models such as the 'attendance allowance' schemes used in the magistracy and local authorities should be considered.

- The introduction of statutory time off for trustees should also be looked at.

- Many trustees are of the view that effective induction, support and training is more important than payment. The increase in trustee satisfaction gained through these measures may negate the need for payment in many cases.

- Greater clarity is needed in stating the rules on expenses and payments.

- Reform should consider the concept of 'net benefit' to charities from trustee payment, and the negative implications of trustee payment such as public perception and funding the additional cost.

Minor Role for Law: Emphasis on Education, Training and Best Practice

- The role of the law in ensuring adoption of sound practice should be minor, and limited to the creation of a flexible best practice framework, which can adapt to any future sector changes.

- The focus of the law should be on incentives and rewards rather than penalties.

An Institute of Charity Governance?

- There is a need for a central institute to focus on trustee training and development, which can enable sharing of information and experiences between voluntary organisations.

Role of the Charity Commission

- The important role of the Charity Commission in creating best practice frameworks and guidance should continue and expand. Alternative means of publication should be explored.

- Formulation of best practice and new governance models needs to ensure continued encouragement of diversity by taking into account the needs of under-represented groups.

Trustee Appointments made by Third Parties: Considerations

- Clarification of the responsibilities of third parties appointing trustees is needed, with particular reference to circumstances where bodies are appointing their own members.

- Suggestions for reform of practice include the introduction of formal listing of trustees' possible conflicting interests.

NHS Appointments Committee: Parallels

- The issues identified were explored in the context of NHS Non-Executive Directors (NEDs). The payment of NEDs and their statutory protection from liability currently prevents direct analogies being drawn with the rest of the voluntary sector. However, the approach taken, in particular the emphasis placed on induction, training, appraisal and clearly defined responsibilities, provides useful parallels and can make a positive contribution to the formulation of trustee recruitment and retention policy.

- There was scope for cross-recruitment between NEDs and charity trustees, particularly following the creation of Primary Care Trusts.

Chapter 5

THE LEGAL ASPECTS OF USER TRUSTEESHIP
Robert Meakin[1]

5.1 Introduction

The current law does not support the concept of a user trustee, although it is generally agreed that user trusteeship can be beneficial to charities. This paper looks at how the Charity Commissioners have helped to support the appointment of user trustees and asks what more can be done.

User trustees sitting on governing bodies face a range of potential legal obstacles. It is argued in this paper that these obstacles which may require Charity Commission approval can be overcome through express provision in governing instruments or by specific authorisation by the Charity Commissioners. In approving governing instruments or authorising user trustees, the Charity Commissioners try to apply rules of best practice. This paper concludes with some thoughts on how the Charity Commissioners can draw upon best practice by engaging with the voluntary sector.

5.2 Why Have User Involvement?

In recent years there has been a growing demand from beneficiaries of charities to be represented at Board level. The demand has been particularly strong in the case of disability charities. Charities that advocate equality for their members, if they are to put their message over effectively, need to be able to show that their own beneficiaries are not held back from achieving the highest positions within their own organisation.

---

[1] Robert Meakin is a partner in the Charity Unit at Stone King. He was formerly a lawyer at the Charity Commission and is the author of "*Charity in the NHS: Policy and Practice*" Jordans (1998).

The notion of user trusteeship also accords with modern management practice which advocates the benefits of management from the "bottom up" rather than from the "top down". Policy decisions are more effective if they are informed by the service users.

There is also financial pressure for charities to have users on the Board. The National Lotteries Charities Board, Housing Corporation and many local authority purchasers of charity services expect to see user involvement in the project or service they fund. Even where user involvement is not stipulated by funders, it is an important plus for a charity from a fund-raising perspective to be able to point to user involvement at the highest level.

User trusteeship is also seen as an important method of ensuring that charities are accountable to various interested parties such as beneficiaries, members and other stakeholders. This has been recognised in the Strategy Unit Report: "Private Action, Public Benefit" [2].

In addition, certain charities, as a matter of law, must have user trustees. For example, maintained schools must, by law, have a certain number of parent governors[3]. Most importantly of all, in order for charities to carry out their objects effectively, they must assist their beneficiaries. Certainly, in the case of disability charities, by enabling users to become trustees those charities are setting role models for other beneficiaries to follow.

So for all these reasons it is generally accepted that user trustees can be of benefit to many types of charity. However, the law has lagged behind and, at first sight, there appear to be a number of legal obstacles which need to be addressed before a charity can receive the benefit of user trustees. The aim of this paper is therefore to show why user trusteeship is potentially an awkward fit within the existing law but how ultimately it can be accommodated through the inclusion of express provisions in governing instruments which, in many cases, need Charity Commission authorisation.

5.3 Why is the Concept of User Trusteeship Potentially Problematic From A Legal Perspective?

The concept of user trusteeship is a comparatively recent development. Trustees

---

[2] Strategy Unit, Cabinet Office *Private Action, Public Benefit. A Review of Charities and the Wider Not-For-Profit Sector* (2002).

[3] School Standards and Framework Act 1998, s.36, sch 9.

have a duty to act exclusively in the best interests of their charity and this has traditionally involved gratuitous service and the avoidance of conflicts of interest. The involvement of user trustees does not necessarily conflict with these duties but the user trustee does stray into territory where there would appear to be potential legal difficulties. Why, one may ask, is user trusteeship potentially problematic when it is generally held to be beneficial to many charities?

In the context of charities there are two important points to note. First, the cases upon which the legal principles are founded largely involve private trusts and therefore do not naturally fit with some issues peculiar to the charity sector. Second, which helps to explain the first point, issues involving conflicts of interest are usually dealt with by the Charity Commissioners. As a result Charity Commission interpretation of the legal authorities and Charity Commission practice plays an important part in the way that charity trustees are advised to avoid or manage conflicts of interest. In practice it is the Charity Commissioners, through their agreement of governing instruments and the use of their powers to assist charity trustees that fills the gaps left by charity law.

5.4 What is the Charity Commission View of User Trusteeship?

The Charity Commissioners issued guidance in CC24 "Users on Board: Beneficiaries who become trustees" in the year 2000 which is supportive of the idea of user trustees and points out potential pitfalls and how to avoid them (mainly involving potential conflicts of interest).

5.5 Defining User Trustees and Related Terms

Under the general law there is no legal definition of "user". Nor for that matter are there legal definitions of "beneficiary" or "benefit".

An attempt at defining "users" is made by the Charity Commissioners in CC24. They say:

> "Users in this guidance includes anyone who uses or benefits from a charity's services or facilities, whether provided by the charity on a voluntary basis or as a contractual service, perhaps on behalf of a body like a Local Authority".

Helpful though this definition is it cannot possibly cover every circumstance involving "users" or "benefits". The Charity Commissioners acknowledge this by going on to say that "user" will mean different things to different charities.

They give an example which illustrates the multi-dimensional nature of the term. In the context of a charity which undertakes research into a particular medical condition, a user could be a person with that condition, his or her carers, medical and educational professionals offering advice on the condition and so on.

There is a further complication involving definitions. The no benefit rule attached to trusteeship can be breached if, without lawful authority, a relative of the charity trustee receives a benefit. The legal position relating to trustee benefit will be discussed later but for the moment it should be noted that the law has never defined, in this context, exactly what or whom a relative is. The Charity Commissioners in CC24 consider that "relative" should be considered in the wider sense. They say:

> "Relative should be considered in the wider sense of anyone closely connected to a user who would be considered to have a clear and direct interest in how the charity is run. This might include blood relations, relatives by marriage, a partner of the same or different sex, step children or children outside marriage".

By agreeing definitions in governing instruments and in Charity Commission orders and schemes the Charity Commissioners can help to clarify these areas of legal doubt.

It should be noted that although the law relating to trustee benefits and those connected to trustees has focused on blood relatives, in the context of user trustees the person or persons connected to the user trustee will be more likely to be a friend or a neighbour. The law has nothing to say in such situations and again this is an area where the Charity Commission could help to develop model clauses for governing instruments which will clarify these areas of legal doubt.

A commonsense approach to these questions of definition might be to suggest that most people will know whether they are a "user", in receipt of a "benefit" or a "relative" but because of the lack of clear definitions, many people might be unaware that they fall within the scope of those terms or in other cases wonder whether they do or do not. In cases of doubt, the Charity Commission can provide clarification using their advisory powers under the Charities Act 1993.

5.6 Capacity to Act as a Charity Trustee

There may be some legal barriers which might prevent users from acting as trustees. This is referred to in CC24.

5.7 Age

The appointment of a minor[4] as a trustee in relation to any settlement or trust is void[5]. However, a minor can be a director of a company including a charitable company[6]. Nevertheless, the Charity Commission point out that they would have to be old enough to understand the duties of being a director[7]. Note also that the Charity Commissioners have the power to remove trustees under section 18(2) Charities Act 1993 where they have instituted a section 8 inquiry and are satisfied that there is evidence of misconduct or mismanagement and that it is necessary or desirable to protect property or secure the proper application of existing property or property coming to the charity. Therefore, if it can be shown that a director/charity trustee's lack of understanding of his or her duties has adversely affected the administration of the charity and as a result it was necessary or desirable to remove them in order to protect charitable property, then the Charity Commissioners have the power to do so.

There are many charities involving young people ranging from education to recreation. Valuable though a young person's perspective might be, charity trustees need to be satisfied that young people who are below the age of 18 have sufficient maturity to act as a director/charity trustee.

5.8 Mental Capacity

The Trustee Act 1925 provides power for the Court to appoint a new trustee or trustees in substitution for the trustee who is incapable by reason of "mental disorder" within the meaning of the Mental Health Act[8]. More particularly, charity trustees, including directors of charitable companies can be removed by the Charity Commissioners for the same reason[9].

In CC24, paragraph 48, the Charity Commissioners say that if the person lacks

---

[4] Under the age of 18 (See Family Law Reform Act 1969, s.1, s.2).

[5] Law of Property Act 1925, s.20.

[6] Unless the Articles of Association prohibits the appointment of minors as directors. Tables A and C do not.

[7] See CC24 *Users on Board: Beneficiaries who become trustees* (2000) para.48.

[8] Mental Health Act 1959, sch 7 (as amended by the Mental Health Act 1983, s.148 and sch 6).

[9] Charities Act 1993, s.18.

any capacity or comprehension to manage his or her own affairs then it will usually follow that they will not have the capacity to manage the affairs of a charity. One would therefore expect the Charity Commissioners to remove a trustee who has had a Receiver appointed under the Mental Health Act 1983 to deal with his or her affairs[10]. There may be circumstances short of a trustee's personal property being managed by a Receiver under the Mental Health Act where the Commissioners will be inclined to act but in practice it would be more difficult for them to do so without cogent evidence.

Note that the law does not prevent people from acting as trustees when they lack capacity, it just sets out the grounds for removal and the means to effect removal. But applying to the Court or the Charity Commissioners for an Order to remove a trustee is a drastic action for trustees to have to take. The solution is to provide a power for trustees to remove trustees who lack capacity in the governing instrument.

One can imagine charities which care for the elderly and the mentally disabled where capacity could become an issue. It is therefore a potential obstacle that trustees of such charities should be aware of when involving users. The solution is to make provision in the governing instrument for the trustees to be able to remove a trustee who has lost their capacity to act as a trustee on other grounds such as non-attendance at meetings which would flow from a lack of capacity. Clearly, this needs to be carefully worded! Alternatively, a procedure which would enable trustees to stand down as a trustee rather than being removed might be helpful. This would allow the trustees to make a proper assessment of a person's capacity before considering removal. It would help in cases where a trustee is suffering from a progressive condition like Alzheimer's. Persons with Alzheimer's may become legally incapacitated at some point in time but in the meantime may have physical problems or problems of concentration which hinder their ability to act as a trustee[11].

The governing instrument itself might disqualify users from becoming trustees or alternatively possess age restrictions which would disqualify them from being too old or too young. Many governing instruments disqualify trustees for acting where they are suffering from a mental disorder or where an Order has been made by the Court having jurisdiction concerning mental disorder for detention or in respect of the trustee's property or affairs under the Mental Health Act 1993.

Much will depend on the individual circumstances of each charity but the solution

---

[10] Supra, para.48.

[11] The Alzheimer's Society.

to any problems would appear to involve appropriate amendments to governing instruments, where necessary with Charity Commission consent.

5.9 Disqualification under the Charities Act 1993

Trustees can be disqualified under section 72 of the Charities Act 1993 for various reasons, including being convicted of an offence involving dishonesty or deception which has not been spent for the purposes of the Rehabilitation of Offenders Act 1974 unless the Charity Commissioners decide to waive the trustee's disqualification. The disqualification provisions under the Charities Act 1993 can prove to be an obstacle, albeit not an insurmountable one, in the case of charities involving ex-offenders. A case from practice involved a charity which was run partly by ex-offenders for the re-training and employment of ex-offenders. Part of the success of the charity depended upon ex-offenders feeling they could trust those running the charity to understand the problems of rehabilitation. Furthermore, ex-offenders who were trustees were themselves helped to be rehabilitated through their involvement in the charity. They too could be described as users. The emphasis of the charity was towards helping white-collar criminals because professionals who have been jailed and struck off their professional registers often found it more difficult to find employment than non-professionals (such as plumbers and electricians) who could simply advertise in "The Yellow Pages" and restart their self-employment on release. It was therefore ironic that the ex-offenders who were of most use to the charity as trustees were white-collar criminals with business skills but who were more likely to be disqualified for crimes of dishonesty or deception, whereas ex-offenders with no such skills to offer who had committed crimes of violence would endure no such problems of disqualification.

The solution to this problem would appear to involve a sensible use of the Charity Commissioners' power to waive disqualification in appropriate cases where the ex-offenders form a minority of the trustees on the Board.

5.10 Providing for User Trustees in the Governing Instrument

Trustees could, subject to any restriction in their governing instrument, decide to appoint user trustees on an ad hoc basis. Alternatively, the trustees could amend the governing instrument to provide for a set number of user trustees to be appointed. In CC24 the Charity Commissioners express a willingness to assist in the amendment of governing instruments to facilitate user trustees where necessary and, no doubt, where in the best interests of the charity.

On a practical note, the Commissioners point out that having some users on board might be unrealistic. They mention users who are transient such as users who seek only one-off or confidential advice and support. To add to those examples, one can readily imagine users who are too ill to act as trustees.

On a point of governance, the Charity Commissioners recommend that users should not make up more than a third of the Board so that they do not dominate matters and presumably so that they can absent themselves where there is a conflict and leave a majority of non-user trustees to decide the issues. This seems sensible and should help to avoid factionalisation or the charity becoming user led.

Most of the legal problems discussed in this paper can be resolved through agreement with the Charity Commission of express provisions in the governing instrument or through the use of the Charity Commissioner's statutory powers to assist. However, it is considered by many in the Charity Sector that there is a need for a clearer definition of what constitutes incapacity to act as a trustee. Furthermore, there is consensus of opinion that a support based approach which focuses on assisting trustees to reach their capacity is needed, as part of the wider strategy of capacity and skill development across trustee boards.

5.11 The Duty of Care

On an encouraging note some modern legal developments point towards an accommodation of user trusteeship. For example, the new duty of care contained in the Trustee Act 2000 might well assist the promotion of user trustees. Section 1 of the Trustee Act 2000 establishes "the duty of care". This is to exercise such care and skill "as is reasonable in the circumstances", depending on any special knowledge or experience the trustee has (or claims) and, in the case of a professional trustee, any special knowledge or experience that they ought to have. The new duty of care applies when the trustee:

- Exercises any power of investment;

- Buys land;

- Appoints any kind of agent, nominee or custodian;

- Exercises a power of insurance; or

- Compromises any claims under section 15(f) Trustee Act 1925.

The new duty of care is a relative duty in the sense that it is related to the individual's actual or claimed special knowledge or experience. The previous common law position in relation to asset management was that trustees' minimum duty of care to the beneficiaries was to deal with trust property as an ordinary prudent man of business would when investing for the benefit of other people for whom he felt morally bound to provide[12]. Professional trustees had a higher duty[13] and this is built into the new statutory duty of care. The new duty of care allows for a standard of care which could possibly be lower than that of an ordinary prudent man of business[14].

Potentially the new duty of care might be very good news for user trustees of charities who act on a voluntary basis out of commitment to a cause rather than necessarily because of particular business skills. If trustees consider that they lack skills then they may (unless prevented by their trust instrument) use the new powers of delegation under the Act to make sure that the powers are exercised by others who have such skills. Equally, there may be an "uplift" in the standard of care as a result of a trustee's actual or claimed special knowledge or experience. It is important to note that the new duty of care does not apply to powers conferred by a trust instrument if it appears from the trust instrument that the duty is not meant to apply.

On a point of governance, it must be sensible to retain a balance between trustees chosen for their business acumen and trustees who are chosen purely because they are users. It should be borne in mind that having user trustees on board regardless of their business skills, might actually be good business. In fundraising terms it presents a good image to the public and it shows that a charity which involves its users is actually practising what it preaches.

It might also be wise to provide training for user trustees who lack business skills so that they can partake fully as trustees rather than contributing solely to single issues. The Charity Commission has started to address the issue of trustee training in their special report: "Trustee Recruitment, Selection and Induction" (March 2002).

---

12 *Re Whitely* [1886] 33 Ch 347 per Lindley LJ at 355.

13 *Bartlett v Barclays Bank Trust Co Ltd* [1980] Ch 515.

14 Although it is argued by Reed P. and Wilson R. in *The Trustee Act 2000 A Practical Guide* Jordans (2001) that there is a basic underlying standard of care of the "reasonable trustee" which will accord to the duty of care described in *Re Whitely* ibid.

5.12 Conflicts of Interest

Undoubtedly, the main theoretical difficulty with user trusteeship is the rule against conflicts of interest. The law in relation to conflicts of interest is that a trustee must not place himself in a position where his interest and duty conflict. The law relating to conflicts of interest is inextricably linked to the law relating to trustee benefit. It was explained by Lord Herschell in *Bray v Ford*[15]:

> "It is an inflexible rule of a Court of Equity that a person in a fiduciary position is not, unless otherwise expressly provided, entitled to make a profit; he is not allowed to put himself in a position where his interests and duty conflict".

User trustees are immediately in a position of conflict of interest because they have placed themselves in that position. The key qualification made by Lord Herschell was: *"unless otherwise expressly provided"*. Indeed, he went on to comment in the same judgment that express clauses would be justified in certain cases:

> "But I am satisfied that it might be departed from in many cases, without any breach of morality, without any wrong-doing. Indeed it is obvious that it might sometimes be to the advantage of the beneficiaries that their trustee should act for them professionally rather than as a stranger, even though the trustee were paid for his services."

It has been argued that conflicts of interest are now part of life due to factors such as the commercialisation and professionalisation of the charity sector[16]. The important issue is to recognise potential conflicts of interest and to ensure that the governing instrument sets out a procedure for managing them or alternatively apply to the Charity Commission for authorisation. This seems to fit in with the approach of the Charity Commissioners generally. For example, take the case of charity trustees who are also directors of a trading company which is a wholly owned subsidiary. Theoretically, there is a potential conflict on interests between the charity trustees' duty to act in the best interests of the charity and the charity trustees' role as directors to act in the best interests of the trading company. On the other hand one could argue that the charity should be represented on the board of the trading company in order to protect its investments. In order to reconcile these two positions the Charity Commissioners advise that at least one charity trustee should not be a director of the trading company and at least one

---

[15] [1896] AC 44

[16] See Luxton P. 'Conflicts of Interest in Charity Law' in *The Voluntary Sector, The State and the Law* Hart Publishing (2000).

director should not be a charity trustee. In this way the Charity Commissioners hope that a level of objectivity is injected into both the board of charity trustees and the board of directors of the trading company. This is a good example of how potential conflicts of interest are managed by Charity Commission guidance.

5.13 Directly Affecting a Trustee

The Charity Commissioners say in CC24 that they regard a decision as directly affecting a user trustee or relative if it results in the user trustee or relative receiving something (a service, facility, funds or some other benefit) that will be personal to that trustee and not shared with other beneficiaries. The Charity Commissioners give the example of a charity that provides medical equipment for people with a particular illness, a user trustee might apply to be given a piece of equipment to ease his or her symptom. The piece of equipment would be used exclusively by that trustee. Or in the case of a charity that helps people in financial need, a trustee may apply for a grant to pay an essential bill, such as heating or water, because they cannot afford to meet the cost of that bill.

In such situations, the Charity Commissioners advise that the user trustee or relative declare an interest before discussions take place and do not take part in any such decision. In some cases, the Charity Commissioners advise that the other trustees may wish to invite the trustee involved to remain for part of the discussion to answer questions on the issue. As the Charity Commission advise, there will usually be specific provisions on dealing with conflicts of interest in the charity's governing instrument.

Specifically, in the case of user trustees the Charity Commissioners advise in CC24 that charities could establish a register of trustees' actual or potential conflicts. The Commissioners advise trustees to develop a policy where trustees withdraw from the decision-making process in respect of decisions that directly affect their own personal interests or those of their relatives.

5.14 Indirectly Affecting a Trustee

The Charity Commissioners regard a decision as indirectly affecting a user trustee or relative if:

- It results in the user trustee or relative receiving something which will also be more generally available to other users outside the trustee body; or

- It is a general policy or practice decision affecting the service in which the user trustee or relative, along with other users, participates.

The Charity Commissioners give the same example of a charity providing medical equipment for people with a particular illness, where the trustees may be making a decision on the different types of equipment that the charity will provide. Inevitably, a user trustee will have an interest in the broad categories of equipment that are provided, but the equipment will be available to all potential users. User trustees and relatives may take part in such decisions but should declare any personal interest at the outset. The issuing of this guidance indicates an acknowledgement on the part of the Charity Commissioners that conflicts do arise and the important issue is how they are managed.

5.15 The No Benefits Rule

The office of a charity trustee is gratuitous[17] and therefore unless authorised by the charity's governing instrument or the Court a trustee cannot be paid for services rendered to the charity. The Court of Appeal in *Re Duke of Norfolk*[18] decided that the Court had an inherent jurisdiction to authorise remuneration where the governing instrument failed to provide such authority. The Court of Appeal recognised that the Court would need to balance the principle that the office of trusteeship is gratuitous against the need for the trust to be well administered.

In respect of charities' the Court is more restrictive. In *Smallpiece v AG*[19] the High Court authorised past payments because the charity was in financial difficulty, its trustees had particular expertise and the amounts were reasonable. However, the Court refused to amend the governing instrument to allow the trustees to be paid in future. His Honour Judge Paul Baker QC sitting as the Deputy High Court Judge said:

> "*I would accept the formulation of the Charity Commission that in order to justify a right to charge, the trustees have to show that it is both necessary and reasonable in the interests of the charity.*" [20]

---

17 *Re Duke of Norfolk's ST* [1982] Ch 61.

18 Ibid.

19 [1990] Ch. Com. Rep.

20 [1990] Ch. Com. Rep.

Following the *Smallpiece* case the Charity Commissioners reviewed their policy in relation to remuneration and, in relation to existing charities, they have set out a series of factors which would be relevant to an application made by the charity trustees to the Charity Commissioners for authorisation for remuneration. In a nutshell, the factors relate to what would be in the best interests of the charity[21]. There is a marked reluctance to authorise the appointment of employees as trustees because of the greater risk of conflict of interest[22]. The Charity Commissioners take a more relaxed view to new charities including a provision in their governing instrument allowing trustees to receive remuneration including a procedure for avoiding conflicts of interest where a trustee has a personal interest in the matter being discussed at the meeting of the charity trustees. The procedure requires the trustee to declare an interest before discussion on the matter commences, to withdraw from the meeting whilst that item is being discussed and not to be counted in the quorum in that meeting and to withdraw during the vote[23].

CC24 does not depart from the Charity Commissioners' policy on remuneration or benefits. Their position in relation to remuneration is quite clear. Where problems might arise in practice is where a user trustee might receive a benefit which is not covered by an express provision in the governing instrument. There may be major problems deciding whether there is a "benefit" which is or is not covered by an express authorisation of the governing instrument. In such cases trustees need to seek clarification from their legal adviser and/or the Charity Commission.

One case from practice involved a major disability charity which provided its user trustees with the basic support required to attend meetings and communicate with other trustees. Such support included travel, overnight accommodation where necessary, use of a computer, a fax machine and such like. A number of issues arose which needed clarification. First, the support provided was more than able-bodied trustees would require. Did they constitute unlawful benefit? Second, would the use of such benefits outside trustee business constitute a personal benefit?

The Charity Commissioners accepted that the true analysis of the situation was that the trustees were not receiving benefits because all that was happening was that the trustees were being supported in fulfilling their role as trustees

---

[21] Ibid.

[22] Decisions of Charity Commissioners Volume 2 April 1994.

[23] Ibid.

effectively. Contrast this with the situation in the case of able-bodied trustees receiving the same level of benefits who might be in breach of the no benefits rule. Furthermore, the Charity Commissioners agreed that any personal use of equipment would be regarded as inconsequential incidental benefit which could be disregarded.

A practical solution to the problem as to what constitutes a "benefit" was devised by one major charity. Again, the charity was a disability charity and an issue arose about assessing user trustees' needs so that they could be justified. A system was devised whereby provision of facilities beyond a basic level would be subject to a two-stage process. Stage one involved trustees completing a questionnaire and listing special needs. The second stage involved an interview from a member of the College of Occupational Therapists to ascertain the trustee's needs. Alternatively, the trustee could make a self-declaration. Self-declarations would be audited by an Occupational Therapist each year on a sampling basis. The purpose of the panel was not to comment on the trustee's requirements but rather to consider the charity's ability to meet the needs. Again, the Charity Commission agreed that procedure.

These practical examples might be helpful to other charities. It will be appreciated from the examples that due weight was given to the sensitivities of user trustees.

There are other occasions where it has been generally accepted through practice and common sense (rather than by legal authority) that there is no benefit provided to the users in their capacity as trustees, for example, where members of a theatre or museum receive benefits in exchange for their subscription such as free newsletters or priority access rights to tickets that are no greater than any other member then it can be argued that they do not receive a benefit as trustees. The Charity Commissioners accept in CC24 that benefits universally available to all users, or of little discernable value will not usually cause a problem. Another example is the position of members of religious orders who are also trustees. Where the members of the order are also trustees they will be supported financially and housed by the charity. It appears to be accepted that the legal analysis is that the user trustee receives the benefits as a user rather than trustee.

It is generally thought that there could be more guidance from the Charity Commission on what constitutes a "benefit". If the Charity Commission decided to encourage more self regulation in the area of conflicts of interest then the local government grading system which distinguishes between direct, indirect, pecuniary and non-pecuniary interests might provide a possible model framework.

5.16 The Self-Dealing and the Fair Dealing Rules

Particular branches of the conflicts of interest rules are the self-dealing and the fair dealing rules.

The self-dealing and the fair dealing rules were explained by Megarry VC in *Tito v Waddell (No2)*[24]:

> *"The self-dealing rule is .... that if a trustee sells the trust property to himself, the sale is voidable by any beneficiary ex debito Justitiae, however fair the transaction. The fair-dealing rule is .... that if a trustee purchases the beneficial interest of any of his beneficiaries, the transaction is not voidable ex debito Justitiae, but can be set aside by the beneficiary unless the trustee can show that he has taken no advantage of his position and has made full disclosure to the beneficiary, and that the transaction is fair and honest."*

It is clear from the legislation governing charities and through Charity Commission practice that there is a general acceptance that conflicts of interest will inevitably exist and that rather than deprive the charity of valued trustees, conflicts of interest involving fair dealing can be overcome where it can be shown to be in the best interests of the charity. Three examples should suffice:

- *The Charities Act 1993 – Disposition of charity property to a trustee or to a person connected to a trustee*

The Charities Act 1993[25] prevents a trustee or a person connected with a trustee (as defined in the Act) from acquiring property without an order from the Charity Commission (self dealing/fair dealing).

- *Parent Governors*

In 1988[26] The Charity Commissioners advised parents serving on the governing bodies of charitable independent schools on conflicts of interest. Although not disputing that having parent governors on the Board of Governors could be beneficial, the Charity Commissioners pointed out that:

---

24 [1977] 3 All ER 29 at 241.

25 S.36.

26 Ch. Com. Rep. 1988 para.40.

"Parents with children at an independent school are, with their children, interested in and derive a benefit from the school and consequently as governors would stand in a position where their duty as trustees might conflict with their interest as parents[27]."

The Charity Commissioners therefore advised that to avoid a situation where the self-dealing rule might be breached, parent governors should not take part in decisions concerning their own children. The number of parent governors should not normally exceed one third of the total number of governors and parent governors should not be in a majority at any meeting of the governing body.

- *The Charity Law Association model of governing instruments*

The Charity Commission has accepted model governing instruments including a charitable trust, a charitable unincorporated association and the charitable memorandum and articles of association prepared by the Charity Law Association[28]. Each of the governing instruments allows a trustee to enter into a contract with a charity for the supply of goods or services in return for a payment or other material benefit subject to certain conditions, including following a procedure in order to ensure that there is fair dealing. That procedure requires that whenever a trustee has a personal interest in a matter to be discussed at a meeting of the trustees or a committee, the trustee concerned must: declare the interest at or before discussion begins on the matter; withdraw from the meeting for that item unless expressly invited to remain in order to provide information; not be counted in the quorum for that part of the meeting; and withdraw during the vote and have no vote on the matter.

These three examples show that, in practice, conflicts of interest are accepted by the Charity Commission where it can be shown to be in the best interests of the charity.

5.17 The Duty not to make a Secret Profit

Although the law relating to the "no secret profits" rule is complex and open-ended[29] it is clear that a fiduciary such as a trustee or company director (charity

---

[27] Ibid.

[28] Documents were finalised in 1997.

[29] For detailed commentary see Moffat G. *Trusts Law Text and Materials* Butterworths (1999) pp.631-656.

trustees can be both) is generally bound to account for any profit made in the course of his or her trusteeship if it flows from that trusteeship and which he or she is not authorised to retain[30]. This is a strict rule which is not dependent on the good faith of the trustee concerned[31]. There is obviously a danger that user trustees might have access to information that enables them to make a profit.

In the case of a charity "authorised" means authorised by the governing instrument or by the Court or (in practice) the Charity Commissioners. In the case of private trusts the beneficiaries can authorise the retention of profit upon receiving a full disclosure of the facts from the trustees. However, in the case of a charity the objects are charitable rather than human (although clearly humans can benefit as a result of objects). Therefore, in the case of charities the Court or the Charity Commissioners are in a position analogous to that of adult beneficiaries in private trusts. Accordingly they can give their consent to the retention profits which are not expressly authorised by the governing instrument[32].

The "no secret profits" rule is similar to the no remuneration rule. In both cases the solution is for the trustee to be expressly authorised to retain such profits by the charity's governing instrument or the Court or the Charity Commissioners.

Because it may be difficult to foresee the potential range of benefits and because clauses in governing instruments allowing either remuneration or profit by trustees are strictly construed by the courts it will be difficult expressly to provide for those benefits[33].

Even if a clause could be drafted to cover all the foreseeable circumstances where a trustee might require authorisation to make and retain a profit it is unlikely to be in the best interests of a charity to allow for such a profit. From a public relations perspective the charity might be tarnished. The better course of action would be to develop a policy on benefits and ensure that the user trustees absent themselves from the meeting and are treated by the other trustees on an equal footing to any other user.

---

[30] *Keech v Sandford* (1726) Sel Cas Ch 61; *Re Macadam* [1946] Ch 73.

[31] *Regal [Hastings] Ltd v Gulliver* [1967] 2 AC 134. Although see *Queensland Mines Ltd v Hudson* (1978) 18 ALR 2 (PC) for a more benign attitude by the court where a company rejected an opportunity which was then exploited by the managing director following his resignation and to the full knowledge of the board.

[32] *Sargent v National Westminster Bank plc* (1991) 61 P&CR 518.

[33] *Re Gee* [1948] Ch 284.

There is a pressing need for the Charity Commission to draft or approve model governing instruments which can be used generally by charities wishing to have user trustees on the Board.

5.18 Confidentiality

Following general trust law principles, trustees have no duty to inform beneficiaries of the reasons why they have reached decisions on the exercise of their discretionary powers where they have acted in good faith. This includes the agendas of their meetings and minutes of their meetings relating to the general deliberations which they engaged in before making their decisions (although the Charity Commissioners have the power to call for such documents under the Charities Act 1993).

There might be a temptation on the part of user trustees living or working with other users to disclose this information which would give them an advantage over other users or possibly cause factionalisation. This is a further reason why it is wise for user trustees to leave the room when issues arise which could potentially compromise a user's independence or affect his or her friends or relatives.

5.19 Alternatives

Charities do not need to have user trustees and, depending on circumstances, it might not always be appropriate. In such circumstances, there are alternatives to users being trustees which would allow them to remain involved.

5.20 Increasing the Level of Communication

The trustees of one charity which works with people with learning difficulties felt that having tenants on the board would be tokenism. Instead, they opened up three channels of communication with tenants, which they thought would be more meaningful:

- Tenants were encouraged to come to trustee meetings as observers.

- With more notice, they could table a paper and speak at the meeting.

The Chair would meet twice a year with the tenant group[34].

---

[34] ACEVO *Involving Users in the Running of Voluntary Organisations* (1999) p.36.

5.21 Advisory Members of the Board

Another alternative to user trustees is the involvement of non-voting advisory members of the Board. This enables users to put forward their views but avoids the obstacles associated with trusteeship such as conflicts of interest and remuneration.

5.22 Representation?

Charities need to ensure that if they wish the role of a user trustee to be that of a representative that the user trustee should be truly representative. Charities contain within them so many interested parties that there is a need to be clear about whom is being represented. Failure to resolve these issues could lead to factionalisation. It should also be appreciated that regardless of representation on the board of trustees there is often no substitute for consultation.

5.23 Conclusion

The current law does not appear to discourage the involvement of user trustees. However, this is not because it provides a useful framework or is positively encouraging. The Charity Commission therefore has a major role to play in assisting the development of user trusteeship.

There is a pressing need for the Charity Commission to draft or approve model governing instruments which can be universally used by charities wishing to have user trustees.

There is also a need for policies to be agreed between charities and the Charity Commission which would allow charities, to a certain extent, to self regulate issues such as trustee benefits without the need to be continually applying to the Charity Commission for authorisation.

Perhaps a sensible idea would be to create a permanent governance committee at the Charity Commission comprising representatives of the charity sector and other interested parties along the lines of the SORP Committee which meets from time to time to update accounting standards.

Given the general failure of the law to keep pace with modern developments in good governance such as user trusteeship, if trustees are to rely on best practice then it is important that it is universally accepted and kept up to date. It is also important to recognise, that the charity sector is diverse and that best practice for one type of charity will not necessarily be best practice in the case of another. Although CC24 is helpful guidance, individual charities might feel the need to develop their own policies on user governance which reflect their particular sectors. By agreeing such a policy with the Charity Commissioners this should leave trustees to self-regulate their affairs and only seek Charity Commission authorisation beyond what was contemplated.

Chapter 6

INVOLVEMENT OF USERS IN GOVERNANCE: SOME EXPERIENCES FROM THE NON-PROFIT HOUSING SECTOR
David Mullins[1]

6.1 Introduction

There is a long history of tenant involvement in social housing reflecting both bottom-up drivers from tenant campaigns to improve their housing conditions and, perhaps more frequently, top-down drivers from legal and regulatory expectations placed on landlords.

Locally based campaigns, rent strikes, the emergence of tenants associations and federations and of national tenant organisations and support arrangements[2] have had an enduring bottom-up influence (Cooper and Hawtin, 1998). A less widespread but nevertheless important influence has been self-help through housing co-operatives, most recently promoted as mutual ownership models for council housing transfers in England and Wales (Confederation of Co-operative Housing, 2001).

---

[1] David Mullins is Reader in Housing Studies at the Centre for Urban and Regional Studies, University of Birmingham. He has undertaken research for the Office of the Deputy Prime Minister, Housing Corporation, National Housing Federation and Audit Commission.

[2] At the national level the tenants' movement is supported by three representational bodies; Tenants and Residents Organisations England (TAROE), Housing Association Residents and Tenants of England (HARTOE) and the Association of Tenants in Control (ATIC), and a range of support bodies including an independent National Tenants Resource Centre, a Tenant Participation Advisory Service (TPAS). Mutual ownership is promoted by the Confederation of Co-operative Housing and there is a National Federation for Tenant Management Organisations.

Top-down drivers have included statutory duties on local authorities to consult tenants (Housing Act 1980) to report on their performance to tenants (Local Government and Housing Act 1989), and to deliver Best Value and Tenant Participation Compacts. Further impetus has been provided by requirements for tenant ballots before council stock can be transferred to housing associations, and by the separate regulatory expectations placed on housing associations themselves (Housing Corporation, 2002a). Funding frameworks have provided some support for capacity building to facilitate involvement (section 16, Local Government Act 1988 for local authority tenants, Housing Corporation community training and enabling grants for housing association tenants).

Programmes to improve public sector housing and to regenerate neighbourhoods have often placed an emphasis on tenant and resident involvement (notably the Priority Estates Programme, Estate Action, Tenant's Choice, stock transfer, the Estates Renewal Challenge Fund, the Single Regeneration Budget, and the National Strategy for Neighbourhood Renewal). These programmes have spawned a variety of organisational forms including Estate Management Boards, Tenant Management Organisations, community based housing associations, Local Housing Companies, community mutuals and neighbourhood management organisations with varying methods of involvement and different levels of representation of residents in governance structures.

Many attempts have been made to classify and categorise tenant involvement initiatives and the resulting levels of representation and empowerment achieved, but Arnstein's (1969) ladder of participation remains an enduring reference point. There have been differences of view as to whether this ladder represents a progression, with information provision as the lowest rung and community control as the ultimate aim, or rather a menu of possibilities from which users should choose the best fit for their needs (Riseborough, 1998). Much depends on whether involvement is seen primarily as a consumerist activity leading to improved services or as a citizenship tool to deliver higher levels of involvement (Cairncross et al, 1997). From a consumerist position an important question is whether the main aim is higher levels of involvement or better levels of service, particularly given that satisfied customers may have less motivation to get involved. From a citizenship perspective, there may be a greater emphasis on involvement per se and its links with social inclusion, community capacity building and social capital (Cooper and Hawtin, 1989).

The spectrum of involvement options presented in the Housing Corporation's (2000) *Communities in Control* document (Figure 1) continues to reflect Arnstein's ladder, with considerable emphasis given to representational rather than consumerist approaches.

Fig. 1: The spectrum of resident participation and control

	Consultation	Power Sharing	Transfer of Control	Transfer of ownership
Individual Involvement		↕		
Residents associations				
Estate agreements				
Limited delegated responsibility (power to spend money)		↕		
Estate management board			↕	
Tenant management organisation				
Local service partnership				
Housing regeneration company				
Tenants on RSL[3] board				
Stock transfer RSL with 33% tenants on board				
Resident controlled RSL (community-based RSL)				↕
Par value co-operative				
Co-ownership co-operative				

From a diagram by CDS Housing
Source: Housing Corporation (2000) Communities in Control

The remainder of this chapter focuses on the experience of involving tenants in formal governance structures. However, it is apparent that most social landlords

---

[3] RSL (Registered Social Landlord) was the name given by the Housing Act 1996 to housing associations and other non-profit landlords (such as Local Housing Companies) registered by the Housing Corporation. By the time of writing it was falling into disuse, and this chapter uses the more popular term "housing associations" to refer to all social landlords registered with and regulated by the Housing Corporation.

(with the possible exception of co-operatives and tenant managed organisations) see user representation in governance as one small part of the bigger picture of tenant involvement, and overall the housing sector is probably moving towards more consumerist approaches[4]. Thus there is a wide spectrum of involvement practices in the housing sector, the principle of tenant involvement is now well established, including representation in formal governance structures. As a result many of the dilemmas facing charities and discussed elsewhere in this volume mirror those that social landlords also face. There is clearly considerable scope for mutual learning.

6.2   Tenant Involvement in Governance

There have been substantial changes in the ownership, management and governance of the social housing sector in England over the past twenty-five years. These changes have had significant implications for tenant involvement in governance.

Local authorities remain the most significant providers, but their dominance has been substantially diminished and, within the remaining local authority stock, management and governance arrangements have been transformed. In 1979 local authorities were landlords to one in three households and owned nine out of every ten social housing dwellings. By 2000 their market share had fallen to one in seven of all households and seven out of every ten social housing dwellings. This was largely as a result of the sale of nearly 2 million homes to tenants under the Right to Buy, but also by the transfer of over 600,000 homes to housing association landlords (mainly newly established associations).

Changes in management and governance of the remaining local authority stock have sometimes included tenant co-options on to housing committees (which formerly consisted only of councillors), formal links between these committees and tenant liaison boards, the establishment of devolved management including tenant management co-operatives and estate management boards (collectively known as Tenant Management Organisations), and more recently Arms Length Management Organisations (an alternative to stock transfer to enable well performing local authorities to increase borrowing to invest in stock improvements whilst retaining ownership) with provision for tenant board members. All of these developments have increased the level of involvement of

---

[4]   Consumerist measures such as surveys, focus groups, tenants' juries and panels, newsletters and customer and neighbourhood forums are seen by many social landlords as the main focus for tenant involvement activity. Best Value has also placed an emphasis on involving residents in service reviews.

tenants in the governance of local authority housing from a previously low base. Tenant Management Organisations have been growing in importance since the 1970s and can be depicted as progress to a fairly high rung on Arnstein's ladder of participation (Hawtin, 1998). It is therefore instructive to review how these organisations are managing the governance tensions explored in this volume (see Case Study 2 below).

Housing associations are non-profit organisations governed by voluntary boards. Their role has grown substantially as a result of public funding (from 1974), transfer of local authority new build funding (from 1979), private finance (from 1988) and stock transfer (from 1988, but accelerating after 1997). Two thousand associations now manage over 1.4 million homes in England but exhibit a wide variety of institutional and governance forms reflecting their diverse origins. For the sake of brevity three main types of association are discussed: philanthropic bodies, stock transfers and co-operatives.

The oldest philanthropic associations (nineteenth century trusts) were generally governed in a paternalistic style and issues of user involvement came quite late to their agendas. The social action associations of the "Cathy Come Home"[5] era of the 1960s and early 1970s placed a greater emphasis on tenant involvement from the start, but generally not as members of formal governance structures. Black and Minority Ethnic (BME) housing associations formed from the 1970s onwards are distinguished by 80% of the boards being drawn from BME communities and were often rooted in local communities. All of these types of associations have been transforming their governance arrangements over recent years as a result of the top-down influences described at the start of the paper. The National Housing Federation's Code of Governance highlights the impact of these changes:

"the involvement of residents must be the main form of accountability"

(National Housing Federation (NHF), 2000, p.21).

Stock transfer has boosted tenant involvement through requirements for a ballot of all tenants before transfer can proceed and the associated consultation processes. It has also introduced new governance models into the sector and strengthened the representation of tenants on the boards (Mullins, 1998). Since 1996 the standard "local housing company" model adopted by most transfers has been for a third of board members to be tenants. However, the Housing

---

[5] "Cathy Come Home" was an influential TV documentary about the plight of homeless people in the 1960s. Shelter, the national campaign for the homeless, was formed in 1966 and a new generation of housing associations was formed by local groups, with involvement of the major churches to provide alternative housing.

Corporation's registration arrangements provide greater flexibility than this and following discussions with the Corporation and, where relevant, with the Charity Commission (see below) some partial transfers (of individual estates or neighbourhoods) have adopted resident majority and resident controlled models. These stock transfer models have also had a wider impact on thinking about governance in the housing association sector (NHF, 1997), encouraging associations to explore accountability to a range of stakeholders and not just to shareholders. The position of tenant board members in stock transfer associations has been receiving increasing attention, particularly the relationship between tenant participation structures and governance structures and the expectations sometimes placed on such board members to play a representational role[6].

Co-operatives and community-based associations have a different tradition, with tenant majorities or tenant controlled boards, but have played a relatively minor role within the sector as a whole[7]. However, recent proposals for stock transfers in England, Scotland and Wales have placed an increasing emphasis on options for tenant controlled housing. The Confederation of Co-operative Housing has developed proposals for a "community gateway model" whereby management after transfer could be devolved to tenant controlled bodies and has proposed that:

> "*stock transfers should only take place if they provide opportunities for community control*"

(CCH, 2001, p.1).

In Walsall existing tenant management organisations have grouped together to form an umbrella body (WATMOS) to receive part of a proposed whole stock transfer. Devolution to tenant controlled bodies has also formed part of Glasgow's whole stock transfer, building on an earlier tradition of community based housing associations there, and similar approaches have been supported by the National Assembly in Wales (NAW). These developments reflect a growing interest in the potential of mutual and community ownership models for managing public services (such as hospitals, schools and housing estates) in preference to traditional state, market and philanthropic forms (Hargreaves, Mills and Michie, 2001).

---

[6] The Joseph Rowntree Foundation is funding research led by Barbara Reid and Cathy Davis at South Bank University on tenants, governance and social housing; lessons from large-scale transfer associations to explore these issues.

[7] In Scotland there has been a greater tradition of community-based associations, with over 50 such bodies established as community ownership transfers (Clapham and Kintrea, 1994, 2000).

A countervailing force to the general increase in pressure for tenant involvement in governance has been the growing organisational scale in the housing association sector and the emphasis of the role of boards in organisational leadership rather than community representation. 90% of housing association stock is now controlled by just 200 associations. Stock transfer has been a major contributor to increasing scale and over 50% of associations with more than 5,000 homes are now stock transfer landlords. Many larger associations have been reviewing their governance arrangements in recent years in the light of their growing asset base and risk exposure and the expectations of the Housing Corporation that:

> *"Housing associations should be headed by an effective board with a sufficient range of expertise supported by appropriate governance and executive arrangements that will give capable leadership and control."*
> (Housing Regulatory Code 2002a, paragraph 2.2).

Furthermore, since the mid-1990s there has been a rapid increase in the numbers of associations joining Group Structures consisting of two or more housing associations and often including other types of social business to serve housing association tenants or the wider community (Mullins, 2000). These organisations are developing complex governance structures and it is instructive to observe how these groups are balancing tenant involvement and accountability with sound organisational management and business efficiency (see Case Study 1 below).

6.2.1 Regulatory and Constitutional Issues and Interaction with Charity Law

Housing associations are non-profit organisations and are currently prescribed from distributing surpluses (although earlier in the century the most common form of organisation involved the payment of dividends to shareholding members and the issuing of loan stock) [8]. The Housing Associations Act 1985 section 15 places strict limits on the financial benefits that can be provided to committee members. This includes the award of contracts and provision of employment opportunities to committee members or their relatives. There are some exemptions for co-operatives and community-based housing associations, and associations are able to pay reasonable expenses (e.g. to cover travel to meetings, and child care provision). The Housing Corporation is currently (Housing Corporation, 2002b) consulting on the possibility of allowing associations to relax these provisions and to introduce payments for board members.

---

[8] See for example Gulliver (2000) for an account of how one organisation, Focus Housing, formerly COPEC, operated from its formation in 1926 until 1939 on the basis of share issues with the possibility of a dividend and loan stock issues with a 4% rate of return. The association's committee decided to drop distribution and became a charity in 1939.

Further regulatory pressures on housing association governance depend on whether the associations are registered as Industrial and Provident (I&P) Societies, Companies limited by guarantee or as charities (including I&P exempt charities).

A majority of housing associations are I&P Societies and issue £1 shares to members who formally elect committee members (usually for a three years term, with results announced at an annual general meeting). However, often memberships are low, AGMs are poorly attended and elections un-contested. Tenant membership is variable but some associations have actively promoted tenant membership. Practice in the election of tenant board members also varies, but some I&P societies (particularly stock transfer landlords) have established constituencies whereby tenant board members are elected by tenant members and other voluntary board members by the remainder of the membership. However, this practice is not common in traditional (non-transfer) I&P associations, who may elect tenant board members through the general shareholding route, but make no special provisions to ensure tenant involvement in their formal governance procedures.

From the mid-1990s there was increasing adoption of the Company model, particularly by new stock transfer landlords wishing to involve tenants and councillors in constituency models of governance (since 1996 the most common board structure for stock transfer landlords has been a third tenants, a third council representative and a third independent members). This approach was promoted by the Chartered Institute of Housing (Zitron, 1995) and recognised by the Housing Corporation as a good way of incorporating tenants in governance:

> *"tenant representation on an area or estate by estate constituency basis may be easier to achieve as a company"*

(Housing Corporation, 1998, p.10).

Three quarters of registered housing associations are either registered charities or exempt charity I&P societies. Charitable housing associations are subject to the same governance requirements as other registered charities. During the 1990s there was some debate about the limitations that charitable status might place on the representation of 'beneficiaries' in governance; and there were doubts about whether it was acceptable for tenants to comprise more than a third of the board of charitable housing associations (Housing Corporation, 1998). However, the position was clarified by joint Housing Corporation/Charity Commission guidance in 2002 which applied more general guidance on user trustees (CC24, Charity Commission, 2000) to housing associations.

In an article introducing this guidance, Chapman (2001) pointed out that user involvement is welcomed by the Charity Commission and that there is no legal bar on the number or proportion of tenant board members; therefore

> *"in principle a social landlord with a resident majority on its board can achieve charitable status".*

However, it is necessary to demonstrate to the Charity Commission that all trustees are acting in the best interests of the charity and not their own, or their particular group's private interest or gain. In practice this means that there must be transparent arrangements for dealing with potential conflicts of interest.

One way of ensuring that users are not seen (rightly or wrongly) to be taking control of a charity for their own interests has been to place limits on the proportion of trustees that are made up of beneficiaries (stock transfers with a third tenant board members is seen as providing such a safeguard).

Neighbourhood regeneration projects are seen as one example where higher proportions of resident board members may be desirable. In such cases the Charity Commission expects to see robust arrangements for avoiding conflicts of interest. The Joint Guidance (Housing Corporation/Charity Commission, 2002) includes model clauses with three main provisions:

- Meeting agendas should identify any items where board members are known to have a relevant personal or financial interests (direct or indirect).

- Board members must declare any relevant interests (direct or indirect) arising from any items to be discussed or decided by the Board (whether or not it has been identified in the agenda).

- Tenant board members must exclude themselves from any discussion or decision involving a direct benefit to their family or individual dwelling.

Thus the regulatory framework has provided considerable support to facilitate tenant involvement in formal governance of housing organisations, including provision for user majorities subject to appropriate safeguards. This is consistent with the position in the charity sector generally where a recent Charity Law Unit seminar concluded that:

"the current law does not appear to discourage the involvement of user trustees"[9],

But in many ways goes beyond it to actively encourage tenant board members. But how have such provisions been used in practice and what organisational and legal and constitutional issues have arisen? We now explore these questions with reference to two contrasting types of housing organisations.

6.3 Housing Sector Case Studies

6.3.1 Case Study 1: Housing Association Group Structures

The development of group structures is now a dominant trend in the restructuring of the housing association sector. Group structures consist of a number of separate organisations with formal connections controlled by a 'parent organisation'. A majority of the housing stock managed by larger housing associations is now part of a group consisting of two or more associations. Research undertaken by the author for the Audit Commission (Audit Commission, 2001)[10] has highlighted the extent of this trend and charted some of the main reasons for the establishment of group structures by housing associations.

While groups have been around for a long time they have recently increased in importance and changed in nature. 'Traditional' groups usually comprised a landlord organisation with a number of special purpose subsidiaries set up to undertake specific functions (e.g. to provide low cost home ownership at a time when it was not clear that such activities would be consistent with charitable status). These groups did not pose particular issues for accountability to tenants since there were no changes in the landlord part of the organisation.

Since the mid 1990s "modern" groups have been developed with a different "umbrella" structure. These groups comprise a non-landlord parent providing central services and strategic direction to a number of special purpose subsidiaries which include at least one landlord body, but may also encompass a wide range of other social businesses. For example the East Thames Housing Group comprises a parent with no housing stock, two landlord subsidiaries, a care subsidiary and a foyer (providing homes and training for young people). Groups have been established for a variety of purposes, but the prospect of economies

---

9   See *'Involvement of Users in Governance'*.

10   Comments and interpretation included in this chapter are those of the author alone.

through avoiding corporation tax[11], value added tax and scale economies (including cheaper borrowing rates) have been particularly important drivers.

Diversification by associations into new activities (such as social care and regeneration) has continued to be an important driver, while stock transfer from local authorities has recently boosted groups in two main ways. Firstly established housing associations have set up local subsidiaries to receive housing stock (usually individual estates, but sometimes the whole of a local authority's stock)[12]. Secondly, Government limits on the amount of stock that can be transferred to a single landlord (normally 12,000 homes) has led to transfers of a local authority's stock to a new group comprising a parent and two or more "independent" subsidiaries (five in the case of Sunderland and Bradford). In both of these types of stock transfer groups locally based subsidiaries usually have tenant involvement and are seen to provide a basis for local accountability while the parent board handles the wider strategic issues. Local accountability becomes more important in groups where the parent is geographically distant from the subsidiary landlords.

"Modern" groups raise greater issues for accountability to tenants than "traditional" groups did and one of the questions explored in the case studies undertaken by the author as part of the Audit Commission project was the impact of group structures on accountability to tenants and communities and implications for the role of tenant board members. The research found that (with the exception of stock transfer groups) tenants were rarely fully consulted on decisions by their landlord to form or join a group structure. This contrasts with decisions by local authorities to transfer stock which require evidence of majority tenant support (usually through a ballot) before transfer can proceed.

Group structures are usually more difficult to understand than free-standing associations and governance arrangements (for example the powers of different subsidiary boards vis-à-vis the parent board) are often less transparent. Yet few groups have published clear "plain English" descriptions of how they operate and what they are expected to achieve (Reading, 2000). Some groups took the view that tenants would only be concerned with the "front end" services provided to them by their landlord subsidiary and therefore as one board member put it that:

---

[11]   The removal of Corporation tax relief for non-charitable housing associations after 1996 led to a boom in group structures through which surpluses could be gifted to charitable subsidiaries. Over a three year period associations reduced tax liability by £40 million by this means.

[12]   As in the case of the transfer by Carlisle council in December 2002 of its 7,200 dwellings to Carlisle Housing Association, a newly created subsidiary of Riverside Housing (the parent body of which is located in Liverpool).

> *"tenants know little and care less about the group parent"*.

There appears to be a trend towards the exclusion of tenants from the small business boards and executive committees that are being set up by some parent organisations to set the strategy for groups. Meanwhile, tenant involvement is focused on the landlord subsidiaries and increasingly through other mechanisms (outside of formal governance structures) such as customer panels. In some respects this trend would appear to run counter to regulatory requirements for associations to conduct their business so that they are:

> *"accountable and transparent to residents and other stakeholders"* (2.3.3)

and

> *"to enable residents to play their part in decision making"* (2.5.3)

(Housing Corporation Regulatory Code 2002a).

However, it may be that housing associations are seeking to meet these demands for tenant and community accountability and the competing demands of organisational leadership and strategy (*"capable leadership and control"* (2.2), *"viable businesses"* (1.1), *"effective identification and management of risk"* (1.2)) through different elements of their governance structures. This may be resulting in an increasing separation of tenants, even those involved in the formal governance structures, from the forums in which the major strategic directions (e.g. business expansion and diversification, risk management and funding) are determined.

The role played by tenant board members in group structures was explored in a limited way in case studies involving stock transfer, where tenants made up a third of all board members[13]. A central issue was the role conflict experienced by some tenant board members arising from perceptions that they are "representatives", when the constitutional arrangements require that they must always pursue the best interests of the company. In many ways the election of tenant board members (e.g. for geographical constituencies as in the New Charter Group) tended to heighten these perceptions that they were "representatives". This case study noted:

> *"it is not always clear how far tenant directors are representatives of the tenants who elected them. How far should they put their views as*

---

13   More detailed research on the role of tenant board members in stock transfer associations is currently underway by Barbara Reid and Cathy Davis.

> *representatives and how far should they provide feedback to other tenants on board deliberations? Whatever the legal position this can be a dilemma."*

(Audit Commission, 2001, p.74).

As a recent Charity Law Unit seminar concluded there is a need for careful thought on what users are representing and what they should be representing.[14]

Other issues emerging for tenant board members from these case studies were:

- Expectations of tenant board members by their neighbours place greater pressures on them than are faced by other voluntary board members who are not tenants and do not live in the immediate community. It is less easy to "clock off" from the job.

- The need for capacity-building and training to enable tenants to play a full role in governance.

- The impact of elections for tenant board members on the build up of experience within this constituency (tenant board members appear to be more subject to electoral defeats than other voluntary board members whose places are less likely to be contested). This can build in inequalities and instabilities.

- The need to clarify the relationship between tenant board members and consultation structures established by the landlord to report back to and gauge the views of tenants. The main conclusion was that the former should not be confused with the latter and that tenant representation in governance is no substitute for effective consultation mechanisms.

- Some potential constraints experienced by tenant board members as a result of the conflict of interest provisions set out by the Housing Corporation and Charity Commission (2002). Because housing associations are often significant employers and may be involved in training schemes, it may be necessary for tenants to make choices between involvement as board members or as employees. This issue also arose in the TMO case study below.

---

14   See *'Involvement of Users in Governance'*.

6.3.2 Case Study 2: Tenant Management Organisations

At the other end of the organisational spectrum to housing association group structures are Tenant Management Organisations (TMOs). TMOs have recently been described as *"one of the most important developments in tenant empowerment in recent years"* (Cairncross et al 2002, p.15). The "Right to Manage" (Leasehold Reform, Housing and Urban Development Act 1993) gave local authority tenants' groups covering areas with more than 25 properties the right to set up organisations to provide a range of management and maintenance functions on behalf of their local authorities. This encompassed two earlier forms of organisation; tenant management co-operatives whose boards usually consisting entirely of tenants (and leaseholders) and who usually employed their own staff had been in operation since 1975; estate management boards had been established from around 1988 on a number of larger less popular council estates with resident majority boards working with staff seconded from the local authority (Hawtin, 1998). In both types of TMO the local authority remains the owner and contracts specified management and maintenance services to the TMO using a management agreement. TMO boards take decisions about the devolved budgets for contracted services and undertake day-to-day management and maintenance functions in conjunction with either directly employed or seconded staff.

A recent comprehensive evaluation for the Office of the Deputy Prime Minister (ODPM) (Cairncross et al, 2002) has charted the growth, objectives, success and problems encountered by more than 200 TMOs that by 2002 were responsible for the management of 84,000 council dwellings. TMOs are concentrated in larger urban authorities (notably in inner London, the North West and West Midlands), particularly where there is support from local authorities and promotional agencies (which draw on grants under section 16 of the Local Government Act 1988 to provide training and capacity building for tenants wishing to set up TMOs). The mean size of TMOs is 400 properties, with tenant management co-operatives generally covering less stock than estate management boards. The largest TMO (in Kensington and Chelsea) has over 12,000 properties, the smallest has twelve. The most important reasons for setting up TMOs were for tenants to have more say, and to improve the repairs and maintenance service. There was also an interest in improving housing management and the physical appearance of estates and improving security and safety. 97% of TMOs had local offices, a feature which was highly valued by tenants, a similar proportion were responsible for day to day repairs, over 80% had other housing management functions but only a quarter were responsible for capital works. As in an earlier evaluation (Price Waterhouse, 1996) in most cases TMOs were seen to be doing better than their host local authorities. TMOs were generally seen as very successful in improving services and creating a better physical environment as well as strengthening community spirit. Successful TMOs were seeking to expand their role, for example by taking on wider neighbourhood management functions or becoming involved as stock transfer landlords where their local authorities were proposing to transfer (Cairncross et al, 2002).

The ODPM evaluation also considered a number of issues arising from tenant involvement in governance. These findings are reviewed before introducing a mini-case study by the author of some governance issues in one of the larger TMOs. The size and composition of boards was found to vary considerably by type of TMO. Size of board ranged from 8 to 22 members; in the case of co-operatives all members were residents but others were sometime co-opted onto the board; in the case of estate management boards there were usually local authority representatives and sometimes other board members. Some boards had some reserved seats for leaseholders or owners (who had bought their properties), but in most cases tenants were in the majority. Meetings were frequent (generally monthly) and there were sometimes sub-committees. Practice varied as to whether meetings were closed or held in public. Successful committees tended to have experienced Chairs and a good skills mix; there was evidence that boards were involved in policy decisions and some board officers spent a lot of time at the TMO offices and were sometimes involved in day to day management decisions. Larger TMOs with substantial staffing tended to delegate more issues to paid staff and to seek external help and advice on personnel; management issues such as appraising their Chief Executive. Despite these successes 70% of TMOs reported difficulties in attracting new board members, elections were often not contested, AGMs had low turnouts and there were often vacant seats. However, there was still optimism about future survival and when tenants were re-balloted (usually after a five year term) they did not vote to return to the council (Cairncross et al, 2002, Chapter 4).

Some further insight into governance issues in a large TMO was provided by a case study by the author[15]. This TMO was well established and had recently had its mandate extended for a further five years following a positive tenant vote. The TMO had taken on a very wide role, employing over 50 staff (including local authority secondments) to provide housing, community support and leisure facilities to an estate of 1000 dwellings. There had been substantial improvements to the external environment, a major emphasis on community safety (including the establishment of a base on the estate for local police services for the wider area), high standard leisure facilities and a plethora of community advice and support groups were housed in former retail premises on the estate. Despite these improvements the long-term future of the estate was still in doubt as a result of

---

15 This was kindly facilitated by the Chief Executive of the TMO who was a participant on the MBA programme at the University of Birmingham directed by the author.

low demand and some underlying physical problems. Occupancy had been increased through representation of asylum seekers on NASS licences and there was also a strong demand for tenancies from refugees with leave to remain who valued the diverse and balanced community on the estate.

The senior officers of the board were extremely dedicated and spent many hours in the TMO offices, but there had been difficulties in filling the 16 resident places on the Board. Board meetings were often poorly attended and a recent AGM had been inquorate. Over and above the factors which might be expected to militate against participation relating to social deprivation, high property turnover and the "disorganised lives" of some residents, there were also concerns about the style and nature of board business, which had been increasingly concerned with major strategic issues including the future of the wider geographical area in which the TMO was located. Some board members were more interested in day-to-day management issues and staff found that informal interaction outside of board meetings provided better opportunities for engagement and involvement. There had also been some difficulties involving a council co-optee to the board who had some differences of view with other board members and staff about TMO policy and relationship to the local authority.

There were important barriers to participation in governance by residents on the estate. First, in order to prevent conflicts of interest, the constitution does not allow staff to be members of the board. While this might appear quite a reasonable provision, in practice it is quite constraining for those residents who wish to make a contribution to the TMO. As noted the TMO is a significant employer, providing 50 direct jobs and supporting training schemes and community organisations, providing pre-school facilities, leisure facilities etc on the estate. Residents who wish to "get involved" are more likely to be attracted by the opportunities for paid employment than by involvement in a voluntary board. Without provision for payment of board members or the possibility of staff co-options this is an unequal contest which is likely to adversely affect the quality of board recruitment as well as shifting the focus of resident involvement away from the boardroom. A second barrier affected the significant number of asylum seekers living on the estate, some of whom were very interested in becoming more involved in the TMO. Because membership of the TMO is open only to tenants, and asylum seekers placed by NASS occupy on licences, they are excluded from voting or standing as board members. This new "democratic deficit" might be seen as a barrier to social inclusion and cohesion, but there were opportunities for asylum seekers to become involved in some of the community organisations operating on the estate.

Interestingly, some of the solutions being considered to the governance dilemmas of this TMO at the time of this case study[16] have some parallels to the developments described earlier in relation to the housing association group structures. There were proposals to "modernise" the strategic board by slimming down the numbers involved and by co-opting other stakeholders including staff and non-resident "experts". This would enable a better fit with the broad strategic focus of this board and expectations being placed on it in relation to the wider regeneration of the area. At the same time there were proposals to develop new arrangements to maximise the input of service users through customer panel type arrangements and to delegate more operational matters to the paid staff.

In summary TMOs provide for high levels of resident involvement in governance, and unusually, in the housing sector, they provide the possibility for governance bodies that are made up entirely of service users. While there may be problems of recruitment of board members and participation levels in elections, AGMs and board meetings may be quite low; a comprehensive evaluation found that this was little risk to the long term sustainability of TMOs. The strategy/operations divide is a real one and many tenants are most interested in the day-to-day management issues that they can "feel" and "touch" and may prefer to engage with the TMO outside of formal meetings. This can lead to a mismatch between the governance structures needed to meet external expectations (e.g. in relation to regeneration strategy) and the structures required to harness residents' wish to engage in service delivery issues. Furthermore there can be perverse disincentives for tenants who want to get involved in TMOs; paid employment opportunities are likely to be more attractive but conflict of interest rules may disqualify employees from becoming involved in governance. The occupancy status of asylum seekers as licensees can prevent their involvement in membership of TMOs and therefore from participation in elections or board membership.

6.4 Conclusion: Some Emerging Issues

The case studies in this chapter have highlighted some aspects of the experience of tenant involvement in two very different governance forms in the housing sector. Each of these forms is becoming increasingly important as the social housing sector restructures. This means that issues emerging from the case

---

[16] These discussions were at an early stage of development but do provide a good indication of some of the underlying governance dilemmas that were concerning the CEO and Chair of this well-established TMO.

studies are important for the future of the sector. There may also be some resonance for developments elsewhere in the non-profit and charity sectors. Essentially the two forms derive from the twin pressures of efficiency and accountability that have underscored the agenda for the delivery of public services by the non-profit sector.

Group structures are emerging as an organisational solution to a variety of different problems but place a particular emphasis on achieving efficiencies through scale and separation of functions between a strategic parent body and a number of special purpose subsidiaries. TMOs place a premium on accountability to service users and have much in common with new models of public service provision embodying the concepts of mutuality and public interest rather than simply business efficiency. Perhaps surprisingly some of the underlying governance issues emerging from these two case studies are similar as our concluding review demonstrates. We look first at the organisational issues and finally at the legal and constitutional issues emerging.

6.4.1   Organisational Issues

Three main organisational issues have emerged from the case studies; convergence of governance models, transparency and accountability and incentives for users to participate.

6.4.1.1 Convergence of Governance Models?

A core issue of corporate governance is the boundary between strategic and operational activities and determining appropriate levels of delegation. This issue is writ large in voluntary controlled organisations that have responsibility for major strategic decisions (e.g. in relation to investment and risk management) but where some voluntary board members may have greater interest in operational matters. In some cases this results in a "reverse delegation" in which boards ponder over operational detail while the paid Chief Executive and Directors are left to get on with the "big picture" strategy. This is most likely to happen where greater importance is placed on the community involvement function of boards than on their organisational leadership role, where the organisation is required to take major strategic decisions and where staff with strategic management skills are employed (perhaps the larger TMOs are particularly subject to these conditions). However, such a solution fails to provide effective organisational accountability.

The housing association sector has also been influenced by private sector models of corporate governance which place a premium on effective organisational accountability. Many larger associations are moving towards governance structures with small strategic boards recruited on the basis of strategic management competences. Meanwhile operational and user involvement issues are delegated to other structures. Group structures sometimes accentuate this division with parent boards being the focus for strategic decisions and subsidiary boards having an operational focus. The impact on tenant involvement in governance is compounded when (unlike most of the stock transfer models) there are lower levels of tenant representation on the parent board than on the subsidiaries.

The case studies suggest that there may be a degree of convergence in governance models emerging between the two forms of organisation. This may be the result of a growing emphasis on the organisational leadership function of boards and the use of alternative structures to achieve community involvement. Even in tenant controlled organisations there may be tendencies towards streamlined boards and co-options of staff and external "experts" to assist in strategic decision-making. In such circumstances user involvement may develop through alternative structures such as customer panels and informal consultation methods which may have a wider "reach" to tenants as a whole than representational models of involvement.

6.4.1.2 Transparency and Accountability

One of the major advantages enjoyed by the TMOs is their transparency and closeness to tenants. A local office and daily face-to-face contact with senior staff and board members was a key feature of the case study TMO. However, it is important to recognise that small locally accountable organisations may still be subject to unaccountable influences and control from Government, funders and regulators (Clapham and Kintrea, 2000) as well as the potential for delegation of strategy to paid staff described above. The contrast with Group Structures is apparently quite stark given the failure of many groups to place an emphasis on making their overall structure transparent, preferring to focus user attention on 'front end' subsidiaries providing their housing service.

However, an alternative view would see Group Structures as a device to *"act locally while thinking globally"* enabling large and well resourced organisations to deliver services that are also locally accountable by involving local people in the governance structures of subsidiaries.

6.4.1.3 Incentives for Users to Participate

A final organisational dimension emerging from both of the case studies was the common issue faced by voluntary organisations in a changing society –why participate? Levels of participation in voluntary activity are declining and barriers to involvement are many (including some of the legal and constitutional issues discussed below). Incentives for service users to become involved in governance structures are often particularly weak unless there are either specific problems or opportunities (e.g. to influence major housing refurbishment programmes). Housing stock transfer provides a good example of the creation of new opportunities for involvement at the same time as spending programmes for housing improvements. Yet even in these examples there is evidence that participation levels can reduce once the ballot for transfer has been won and other priorities take over (setting up the new organisation and arranging the finance), and once the refurbishment programme has been completed. The preference for operational over strategic issues may also be a disincentive to become involved in formal governance structures, providing further support for landlords to develop informal involvement mechanisms.

6.4.2 Legal and Constitutional Issues

The Charity Law Unit has identified a number of legal and constitutional issues arising from involvement of users in charity governance[17]. The housing case studies have provided an opportunity to explore these issues in a specific sector context.

Overall the case studies confirm the Charity Law Unit finding that there are no general legal obstacles preventing the involvement of users in formal governance structures. In the housing sector it has proved quite possible for users to form a majority or even the entirety of boards. Model clauses have been developed (Housing Corporation/Charity Commission, 2002) to enable housing organisations to manage the issues such as the definition of direct and indirect benefits and potential conflicts of interest arising from having "users on board" and self-assessment frameworks for board performance have been developed (Housing Corporation, 2001).

Issues of capacity building to enable users to take part in governance have been addressed in the housing sector through grants available to tenant groups (section 16 grants for local authority tenants and community training and enabling grants for housing association tenants) and there is a fairly well developed "industry" facilitating tenant and board member training, including a National Tenants Resource Centre. However, as the case studies have demonstrated there may be mismatches between the issues that tenants wish to be involved in and the strategic decision making functions required of boards.

---

[17] See *'Involvement of Users in Governance'*.

Both case studies reveal some problems arising from the way in which organisations have sought to guard against conflicts of interest in compliance with good practice guidance and regulatory requirements. The most significant issues arise from prohibitions on committee members (and sometimes family members) being employed by their organisations. In communities with high levels of exclusion from the labour market the employment opportunities provided by landlords, especially when these extend into community activities and training schemes are particularly important for local residents. Where residents want to get involved, it is natural that they will first explore the paid employment opportunities offered by their landlord. Attempts to prevent conflicts of interest may create perverse disincentives to involvement and deprive committees of some of the most committed potential members.

Some specific problems also arise in relation to restriction of opportunities for involvement to tenants (and in some cases leaseholders). The exclusion of licensees such as asylum seekers can result in fairly high levels of resident disenfranchisement on some estates.

The housing sector has provided some interesting experience in relation to Charity Law Unit discussions about the "representative role" of user board members. Despite the constitutional requirement for all board members to pursue the best interests of the organisation and not to pursue sectional interests, frequently different expectations are placed on tenants than on other board members. Tenant board members may sometimes be subject to different methods of appointment to Boards with resulting differences in security. There are unresolved conflicts in parts of the housing sector arising from the simultaneous operation of principles of representative governance on the one hand and of unified governance on the other. The tensions arising from these conflicts are being managed on a day-to-day basis by unpaid tenant board members.

Constituency based models of governance in stock transfer associations (commonly a third tenants, a third local authority and a third independent board members) and the increasingly common practice of electing tenant board members (either from the entire tenant population or from among tenant shareholding members) tends to increase these expectations. In some cases where tenant board members have been elected from the whole tenant body, turnout has been higher than in local government elections, strengthening the notion of "mandate". Similarly where tenant board members are elected from area based tenants' forums or federations there can be expectations of direct accountability.

In stock transfer organisations there are usually separate constituencies for tenant and "independent" board members and this can result in differences of treatment. Tenant elections are more likely to be contested and this can result in a greater frequency of tenant board members having to stand down at the end of their term. This can prevent expertise building up, and may be contrasted with the position in TMOs where tenants form a single constituency and where the national evaluation found a strong relationship between the level of experience of Chairs and organisational success.

Finally the housing case studies provide strong support for the proposition that inclusion of users on a trustee board is not a substitute for consultation with users in general. The housing sector places greater emphasis on consumerist models of user consultation. However, it is usually the case that such consultation is focused on operational matters with very limited user involvement in the major strategic decisions. Ironically even where there are high levels of user representation in governance, the major strategic decisions may get less user attention than day-to-day operational matters. This may occur in a number of ways including the "delegation" of strategy to parent boards, executive committees or employees.

Bibliography

Arnstein S (1969) A ladder of citizen participation. *Journal of American Institute of Planners* 35(4) 214-224.

Audit Commission (2001) *Group Dynamics. Group structures and registered social landlords*. London, Audit Commission and Housing Corporation.

Cairncross L, Clapham D, Goodlad R (1997) *Housing Management, Consumers and Citizens*. London, Routledge

Cairncross L, Morrell C, Darke J and Brownhill S (2002) *Tenants Managing. An Evaluation of Tenant Management Organisations in England.* London, ODPM

Chapman R (2001) Charities, housing associations and resident controlled boards. *Housing Today*

Charity Commission (2000) *Users on Board. Beneficiaries who become trustees*. (CC24). London, Charity Commission

Clapham D and Kintrea K (1994) Community ownership and the break up of council housing in Britain. *Journal of Social Policy 23(2) 210-245.*

Clapham D and Kintrea K (2000) Community-based Housing Organisations and the Local Governance Debate. *Housing Studies 15 (4) 533-559.*

Confederation of Co-operative Housing (2001) *Stock Transfer-creating community controlled housing*.

Cooper C and Hawtin M (1998) *Resident Involvement and Community Action. Theory to Practice*. Coventry, Chartered Institute of Housing.

Gulliver K (2000) *Social Concern and Social Enterprise. The origins and history of Focus Housing*. Warwick, Brewin Books.

Hargreaves I, Mills C and Michie J (2001) *Ownership Matters. New mutual business models*. London, Mutuo.

Hawtin M (1998) Estate Management Boards; their development and significance in Cooper C and Hawtin M (eds) *Resident Involvement and Community Action. Theory to Practice*. Coventry, Chartered Institute of Housing

Housing Corporation (1998) *No time to lose! Key issues for board members of start up 'transfer' organisations*. London, Housing Corporation

Housing Corporation (2000) *Communities in Control*. London, Housing Corporation.

Housing Corporation (2001) *Treading the Boards. A self-assessment framework for board performance*. London, Housing Corporation.

Housing Corporation (2002a) *The way forward. Our approach to regulation*. London, Housing Corporation

Housing Corporation (2002b) *Board member remuneration*. Consultation Paper. London, Housing Corporation

Housing Corporation and Charity Commission (2002) *Guidance for Charitable Registered Social Landlords (including the acquisition of tenanted housing and tenants as members of Governing Bodies*. London, Housing Corporation and Charity Commission

Mullins D (1998) More choice in social rented housing? in Marsh, A and Mullins, D (eds) Housing and Public Policy. Citizenship, Choice and Control. Buckingham, Open University Press.

Mullins D (2000) *Constitutional and Structural partnerships: Who benefits?* Housing Research at CURS no 8. University of Birmingham.

National Housing Federation (1997) *Action for Accountability. A Guide for independent social landlords.* London, National Housing Federation

National Housing Federation (2000) *Competence and Accountability. Code of Governance* London, National Housing Federation

Price Waterhouse (1996) *Tenants in Control. An evaluation of tenant led housing management organisations.*

Reading J (2000) *How Groups Work, Management and Accountability in Housing Groups.* London, National Housing Federation.

Riseborough M (1998) More choice and control for users? Involving tenants in social housing management. in Marsh, A and Mullins, D (eds) Housing and Public Policy. Citizenship, Choice and Control. Buckingham, Open University Press.

Zitron J (1995) *Local Housing Companies. A Good Practice Guide.* Coventry, Chartered Institute of Housing.

Summary 2

INVOLVEMENT OF USERS IN GOVERNANCE

Capacity of Users to be Involved in Governance

- A clearer definition of what constitutes incapacity to act as a trustee is needed.

- Provision for trustees to stand down for a period in order to address problems affecting capacity is needed as an alternative to removing incapable trustees.

- A support-based approach that focuses on assisting trustees to reach capacity is needed, as part of a wider strategy of capacity and skill development across trustee boards.

Benefits and Conflicts of Interest

- Clearer definitions and guidance are needed in this area. Clarification of what constitutes a benefit is particularly important.

- A policy of grading interests would provide trustee boards with a structured framework, enabling them to develop clear procedures regarding declarations of interest and potential conflicts. These procedures can in turn assist individual trustees to focus on and define their interests before problems arise.
  The local government grading system, which distinguishes between direct, indirect, pecuniary and non-pecuniary interests provides a possible model for such a scheme.

- The creation of universal governing document clauses to deal with potential conflicts of interest would enable greater self-regulation in the area. These need to be drawn up on a sector by sector basis.

- User trustees can be discouraged by the attention currently focussed on the legal problems surrounding conflicts of interest. Many potential problems in this area can be negated by openness and careful policy implementation.

Users on Trustee Boards

- Whilst the promotion of users on trustee boards is generally advantageous, it is not automatically so.

    - A small group of users may not be truly representative of users in general.

    - If a group of user trustees becomes a dominant element, they may compromise the independence of the board.

    - Conversely, a perception of the user trustees by themselves or the other trustees as 'representative' can translate into tokenism and render them ineffectual.

    - Prescriptive board forms, which specify quotas of users and other members may be too rigid in practice, and may compromise the presence of a diverse and effective skill base.

- Users as Representative

    - There is a need for careful thought on what users are representing and what they *should be* representing.

    - The law may need to recognise that user trustees *are* representative and may need to consider creating two types of trustee.

    - Users who are elected are *perceived* as representative. Greater attention should therefore be given to election procedures.

    - The tensions faced by user board members need to be recognised.

- Users as trustees need not be seen as representative but as a way of diversifying Board membership and acquiring new, necessary skills.

- Importance of Consultation

  - Inclusion of users on a trustee board is not a valid substitute for consultation with users in general.

  - Trustees need to be alerted to the importance of user consultation, and encouraged to adopt it as part of good practice. However, this imposes a greater burden on trustees and exacerbates the existing problems in trustee recruitment.

  - Key strategic decisions often need to be made without consultation, and knowing which issues to consult on is an area in which trustees need increased guidance.

- Effectiveness of Law

  - The current law does not appear to discourage the involvement of user trustees. However, this does not appear to be because it provides a useful framework or is actively encouraging, but because it is largely ignored. The development of model clauses and the promotion of self-regulation are therefore greatly needed.

Chapter 7

STRATEGY OR MANAGEMENT BY TRUSTEES?
Michael Carpenter[1]

7.1 Introduction

Charities do not exist in a vacuum. They exist to carry out particular charitable purposes. But unless established in corporate form[2], a charity has no distinct legal personality. It can only live and breathe through the leadership and direction of its trustees.

The trustees are ultimately responsible for the charity – its policies and its execution of them. This can lead to liabilities falling on the trustees in a number of ways:

1. Financial liability. Unless liability can be limited to the assets of the charity from time to time (for example by contractual agreement with a bank in relation to a loan facility) the rights of a third party are not constrained by the value of charity property.

2. Vicarious liability. Trustees can be liable not only for their own conduct, but also for the conduct of others which they have authorised or ratified. They may also be liable for the conduct of others – although neither authorised nor ratified by the trustees – which takes place in the course of a business which the trustees conduct and where there is a close

---

[1] Michael Carpenter retired at the end of September 2002 after nearly five years as the executive Legal Commissioner at the Charity Commission. Before joining the Commission he spent over 30 years in private practice as a solicitor, specialising in charity, private client and taxation work. At the time of preparing this paper Michael Carpenter was the executive Legal Commissioner at the Charity Commission. He retired at the end of September 2002. The views expressed in this paper are his own.

[2] This paper focuses on trusteeship of charitable trusts. It does not seek to identify the circumstances where the responsibilities and liabilities of charity trustees of charities in corporate form might be different.

connection between the conduct and what the wrongdoer was employed to do. This principle can extend to the conduct of volunteers.

3   Liability for loss as a result of breach of trust. If a trustee commits a breach of trust then the trustee concerned should expect to be called upon to restore the charity to the state it should have been in, if the breach of trust had not occurred.

4   Reputational liability. With ever-greater public interest and scrutiny of the actions of charities, poor leadership can be exposed, and reputations of the individuals responsible can be blighted.

5   Regulatory sanctions. Whenever the Commission finds *any* misconduct or mismanagement in the administration of a charity then the door is open to a number of remedial sanctions. These stretch to the possible removal of a trustee where the trustee has personally been responsible or privy to the misconduct or mismanagement - or has by his conduct contributed to it or facilitated it.

Under most constitutional arrangements the powers, duties and responsibilities attached to the promotion of the charitable purposes are vested in the trustees and nobody else. Trustees "carry the can". This stark reality helps to set the framework within which charities operate.

7.2   The Governing Instrument

Although charitable purposes and activities through which these purposes are to be promoted are often set out with some precision in the governing instrument, nowadays trustees have considerable flexibility as to the administrative arrangements which they can adopt. If insufficient (or out of date) powers are set out in the governing instrument then the Commission (within limits, primarily around private benefit) will readily grant extra powers or bestow on trustees a power to add administrative powers themselves should the trustees identify a "missing" power which would be useful. The Commission takes the view that it is unlikely to serve the best interests of charities and their charitable beneficiaries if the trustees find themselves unnecessarily constrained by administrative limitations in their governing documents. What matters is the quality of judgments rather than the narrowness of supporting powers.

The governing instrument (supplemented by legislation) represents the starting point. A well-drawn modern governing instrument will help the trustees not only to focus on key strategic issues but also provide coherent leadership and direction without requiring the trustees personally to stick on all the stamps.

The traditional position used to be that trustees did everything associated with the trust. This was based on the proposition that those who assume the burden of looking after the property of someone else cannot "pass the buck" to a third party. This reflected the personal nature of trusteeship - "I trust X so I ask him to manage my affairs – but I do not know Y so why should he be let loose on my affairs without my specific approval?"

However this purist approach could not stand the test of time. How could a trustee buy and sell shares if he was not a stockbroker or convey land if he was not a solicitor? Can trustees realistically be expected to have personally all the expertise necessary to achieve the best results for their beneficiaries?

The Trustee Act 1925 represented statutory recognition that trustees had their limits. But its distinction between a narrowly drawn list of "ministerial" acts which could be handled by a narrowly drawn list of third parties —and other more "fiduciary" powers (e.g. which investments to buy) which could not, has proved to be inflexible and potentially damaging. It has become almost universally recognised that the role of a trustee should be that of "conductor" rather than the player of all the instruments.

Many relatively modern governing instruments will have recognised the statutory limitations and will be constructed so as to maximise the prospects of the trust achieving its objectives. In principle a well-constructed governing instrument should ensure that if a particular course of action or internal management arrangement proposed by the trustees satisfies a "common sense" test then the trustees will not be inhibited from proceeding.

The Trustee Act 2000 has now brought the statutory framework into line with best drafting practice. The position in relation to charitable trusts is that trustees may now:

- Delegate any function *consisting of carrying out a decision the trustees have taken*.

- Delegate any function relating to the investment of assets (subject to the standard investment criteria and other requirements in relation to the performance of investment functions).

- Delegate any function relating to the raising of funds otherwise than by means of profits of an "integral" trade.

- Delegate any other function prescribed by an order of the Secretary of State (none yet).

This highlights the point that delegation as such is not wrong – indeed it may be highly desirable or even essential – but there must be some authority which permits it – whether this in the governing instrument or under the Trustee Act 2000.

In practice it has long been the position (from well before the Trustee Act) that charities employ staff if there is a need to do so, relying either on specific authority in the governing instrument or - because it is obviously necessary to enable the charity to function properly (or at all) - on an "unexpressed" but clearly ancillary power which marches hand in hand with the charitable purposes. It is inconceivable that the Courts or the Commission would take the view that where the employment of staff is clearly necessary nevertheless the trustees should be personally accountable for staff costs on breach of trust grounds. For example, many charities are service providers and in the context of employing staff to deliver the service the natural comparators are service providers in the public (and in some cases the private) sector rather than the completely different world of private family trusts around which many of the statutory and judicial developments of trust law have taken place.

Under the Trustee Act 2000 the key principle for trustees is the observance of the "duty of care". In relation to the functions to which it applies, trustees must exercise "such care and skill as is reasonable in the circumstances". In judging this it is necessary to take into account any special knowledge or experience that he has or holds himself out as having. You cannot leave your brains behind when acting as a trustee. And if you are a trustee in the course of a business or profession (i.e. as part of the day job for which you are remunerated) then the standard requires the trustee to exhibit any special knowledge or experience that it is reasonable to expect of a person acting in the course of that kind of business or profession - not what you in fact know but what a competent professional should know.

This provides a framework from which to draw out the primary functions of trustees. These include:

- The exercise of discretions.

- The determination of strategy and strategic objectives.

- The control of resources.

- Accountability for the charity.

- The entitlement (but not the obligation) to delegate the *execution* of decisions taken by trustees (but not the decisions themselves) and when this occurs to hold the delegate to account.

- In relation to all delegations (including investment and fund raising) the obligation to keep the delegations under review, to consider whether to exercise their power of intervention and where there is a need to do so then to intervene. This power of intervention includes a power to give directions and to revoke any authorisation given to the agent.

Although the Trustee Act 2000 continues to use the term "agent" (better than "master and servant"!) it is not defined. It is a word of wide meaning and embraces internal delegations to staff and external delegations to "sub contractors" for the trustees.

The Trustee Act 2000 is welcome for the introduction of "default" powers as well as for the clarification it has brought to this issue. This approach has been followed, for example, in the guidance from the Commission on Electronic Banking[3] which illustrates the shift in the debate from whether trustees can bank electronically to the key issue of the management of risk.

Section 97 of the Charities Act 1993 defines "charity trustees" as the persons having *"the general control and management of the administration of a charity"*. The provisions in the Trustee Act 2000 are consistent with this. There will always be "charity trustees" of every charity – and often there will be others with key contributions to make to the effective delivery of charitable services but who do not carry directly the risks and responsibilities of trusteeship (and do not qualify as charity trustees).

Effective charities will have management structures designed to provide the best leadership and management through which to promote the charitable purposes. Depending on the circumstances these structures can be quite complex.– They may well be hierarchical. It would be absurd, in practice, to expect trustees to take every decision, however small, which involves any element of discretion and equally absurd to disenfranchise staff from taking substantive decisions in pursuance of the strategy laid down by the trustees.– In my view the Courts would not be impressed by any challenge to a decision of a charity solely on the grounds that an employee took the particular decision within the framework of

---

[3] This is on the Commission website (www.charity-commission.gov.uk) and can be found under "Useful Guidelines – Supporting Charities" within the "Publications" section.

the policy laid down by the trustees. For example a decision on whether to open a new care home (or close an existing one) would fall naturally to the trustees but a decision whether to admit a particular person (consistent with charity policies) would not, even though a clear element of discretion will be involved. Another simple example might relate to a school offering scholarships. Once the scholarship policy has been determined it would be "reasonable" for any discretion within the framework of the policy to be exercised by persons other than the trustees.

In my view it must be implicit that any charity which carries out activities in furtherance of its purposes must be able to employ appropriate staff with the right mix of skills to carry out those activities properly and exercise the necessary judgments that go with this.

In common governance models, trustees take the key strategic decisions (the super decisions). Following on from this a whole raft of further specific decisions will need to be taken to implement the "top level" decision. In practice the employer (the trustees) and key staff have a contractual relationship, underpinned by employment law. Within the contractual arrangements employees are directly acting for the trustees and the charity.

In theory a governance model of unpaid trustees devoting part of their time to leading a charity supplemented by paid staff to implement their policies sounds fine. But this requires trustees who have the skill and judgment to make wise strategic decisions and who are able to recognise that real expertise on key issues will often lie outside the trustee body (amongst the staff or with external consultants and advisers).

A key message for trustees is to ensure there is clarity in all arrangements involving delegation, whether to staff or external parties. The less clarity, the more likelihood there is that difficulties will arise as to the scope of the delegated authority. Where tensions occur at the top of a charity as between the trustees and key senior staff they can often be traced back to this lack of clarity.

If trustees comply with the procedures in the Trustee Act 2000 (or in their governing document) including the review duty they can insulate themselves from some personal liability. This will not, however, provide protection against claims under financial contracts which cannot be met by the charity (unless these arrangements include contractual terms which cap the liability of trustees). But the duty of care is all-important both initially at the point of delegation and subsequently through monitoring and review. If this is breached the protection under the Trustee Act disappears.

As a result the Trustee Act is not a green light to delegate inappropriately. But it is part of the framework within which effective and appropriate delegation can take place.

In the context of investment where the Trustee Act includes specific powers, it recognises the practical reality which is that most trustees do not have detailed investment expertise. Markets are technical, global, sophisticated and fast moving. The execution of the investment strategy laid down by the trustees requires constant vigilance. I accept that it may be an open question as to whether the delegation of investment powers to investment "experts" has produced better or worse results for charity than investments made by decision of the trustees (having regard to professional advice which has been received!).

Where the trustee body includes "experts" in particular fields the temptation exists to let the experts get on with it (they are after all trustee colleagues). But even in areas involving technical issues the views of the trustees who do not claim particular expertise are important. They too need to be satisfied about the appropriateness of a proposed course of action in the best interests of the charity. It is easy to state that the "challenge" responsibility in relation to any advice given to trustees - —whether by one of their number, a member of staff or an external adviser - falls on the trustees individually but it is not always easy to carry through in practice. This illustrates the importance of clarifying the ground rules at the beginning by open policies so that there can be no surprise if the non expert trustees test vigorously any advice wherever it comes from before making up their minds. This point also applies where particular functions are delegated to particular trustees on behalf of the whole body. The trustees collectively must review what has occurred and be prepared, if necessary or appropriate in the interests of the charity, to withdraw or change the delegation arrangements.

7.3 Liability of Trustees

Inevitably trustees will be concerned about personal financial exposure. They will, rightly, feel they are contributing their time and their talents for no reward. If in return their own financial well-being is put additionally at jeopardy merely because the charity operates in trust rather than corporate form this may well act as a disincentive to serving as a trustee. It is in this context that the concept of a new form of charitable vehicle - the Charitable Incorporated Organisation (the "CIO") - has attracted widespread interest and support. In its Report "Private Action, Public Benefit" published in September 2002 the Strategy Unit has responded by specifically recommending that the CIO should be introduced as a new constitutional form exclusively for charities. When the CIO becomes available it will widen the choice for promoters whilst existing charities will be able to convert easily. Amongst other features the CIO would have the flexibility of a trust but would offer the limited personal liability of a company.

The issue of personal liability will not disappear at a stroke with the advent of the CIO. Many charities will continue in unincorporated form (and company law – on which the provisions about personal liability are likely to be linked – does not protect the directors/trustees in all circumstances).

In thinking about personal liability trustees will no doubt consider:

- Does the trust deed provide any protection to trustees, in the form of an exculpatory clause?

- If not should the charity incorporate even if this might not otherwise be the preferred model?

- Or should the trustees take out trustee indemnity insurance? Whilst few (if any) claims have been made on these policies they do provide some peace of mind.

Only incorporation will help trustees who enter into financial commitments which they find they are unable to honour from charity resources. It is simplistic to suggest that if trustees enter into "uncovered" financial obligations then on their own head be it. (In this area corporate primary purpose trading charities will need to be aware of the consequences of "insolvent trading" and other requirements of company law.)

Urgent charitable need waits upon nobody and trustees may consider that they must take immediate steps in the interests of the charitable beneficiaries in the confident (and risk assessed) expectation that resources will "catch up". But their expectations may not then be met. Charities do not harbour reserves for the sake of it. They are expected to be lean and mean.

Personal liability for a breach of trust is unlikely to occur where accepted good practice has been adopted. But it does not automatically follow that actions of trustees which do not comply with good practice represent misconduct or mismanagement or will lead to restitution claims if loss ensues.

This is emerging as a key topic. The statutory environment (e.g. Trustee Act 2000) and the regulatory environment (for example the Commission's new policy on Orders[4]) is moving from a "thou shalt not" approach to one where trustees can

---

[4] See Operational Guidance OG1 in the "Supporting Charities" section of the Commission website.

(broadly) acquire ALL the powers they consider they need to carry out their tasks properly. Instead of regulation being a process of checking whether the trustees have been acting within their powers (if yes, then all is well but if no, some regulatory intervention may follow), the focus has shifted to whether trustees are exercising their powers prudently in the interests of the charity. There are no absolutes here which determine whether or not the actions of trustees satisfy the requisite fiduciary standard. The Trustee Act 2000 describes a standard of care that must be complied with in relation to the exercise of specific functions set out in the Act but it did not invent fiduciary standards. In practice trustees were, prior to the Trustee Act, subject to a common law duty of care (that of an ordinary prudent man of business) in relation to investment issues and were under a statutory duty of care in exercising their limited powers of collective delegation[5]. Nevertheless it is extremely helpful to have a clear statutory articulation of the standard of care. Where the Commission bestows additional administrative powers on charities (or gives them a power to amend or add to their administrative provisions – effectively a DIY power) it will impose the same standard of care on trustees as appears in the statute which will apply whenever the trustees exercise their new powers (and if trustees exercise the power of amendment or addition to take new or varied administrative powers then the standard of care will also apply whenever the new or varied powers are themselves used)[6]. Following due process may represent a first line of defence for trustees particularly if their decision is one that reasonable trustees could have reached.

Trusteeship is complex. Trustees are not required to have any formal training. Without published guidance from the Commission and others, in a number of key areas trustees would be left to make the best of the job from their own knowledge and experience. What the Commission is able to do is to draw on long corporate knowledge and experience in order to identify ways in which good outcomes are more likely to be achieved and bad outcomes more likely to be avoided. Guidance and advice is provided in a number of ways by the Commission:

- The CC range of guidance publications.

- Operational Guidance (now being released on the website) which is prepared for the assistance of Commission staff.

---

[5] See the Law Commission and the Scottish Law Commission report on Trustees' Powers and Duties (Law Cm 260) p.33 et seq.

[6] OG1 – see above.

- Regulatory Studies[7].

- Specific guidance in response to specific issues (whether given in response to issues raised by charities with the Commission or where the Commission identifies an apparent need for guidance in the course of case handling which it then offers proactively).

- The Annual Report of the Commissioners.

- The Education and Outreach programme.

- The Review Visits programme.

- In conjunction with the process of registration (what has become known as the "gateway" approach).

7.4 Do Trustees Need to Take Notice of Commission Guidance?

The Commission (without prejudice to its specific powers and duties under other enactments) has the general function[8] of promoting the effective use of charitable resources by:

- Encouraging the development of better methods of administration.

- Giving charity trustees information or advice on any matter affecting the charity.

- Investigating and checking abuses.

In addition the Commission has the general object[9] so to act in the case of any charity (other than altering its purposes) as best to promote and make effective the work of the charity in meeting the needs designated by its trusts (but the Commission does not itself have power to act in the administration of a charity).

This function and this object give the Commission legitimacy to address good practice issues (and it would be failing in its statutory responsibilities if it did not address them vigorously).

---

[7] See, for example, Regulatory Study 1 on Trustee Recruitment Selection and Induction.

[8] See Charities Act 1993, s.1(3).

[9] See Charities Act 1993, s.1(4).

But does any of this advisory/promotional work (other than investigating and checking abuse) have any teeth? The Commission cannot itself become involved in the administration of a charity so it cannot compel trustees to take particular decisions. At one level, therefore, the advice would seem to be influential but not obligatory. But this may be somewhat simplistic. It may all depend upon the circumstances in which the advice is given.

Helpful comments are contained in the judgment of Mr Justice Neuberger in the case of *Arthur Scargill v Charity Commissioners and Attorney General* [10]:

> "*The public interest in the affairs of charities being properly conducted is, I would have thought, self-evident. The public should be entitled to have confidence that the relevant authorities, namely the Commissioners and the court, will take appropriate steps to ensure that the affairs of charitable trusts are properly conducted*".

The Attorney General plays a role in proceedings relating to charities precisely because of the public interest in seeing charities properly administered. See the judgment of Lord Macnaughten in the Privy Council in *Wallis v Solicitor General for New Zealand*[11] in which he stated:

> "*It is the function of the Crown as parens patriae to enforce the execution of charitable trusts, and it has always been recognised as the duty of the law officers of the Crown to intervene for the purpose of protecting charities and affording advice and assistance to the Court in the administration of charitable trusts*".

However, these comments need to be balanced by further comments from Mr Justice Neuberger in the *Scargill* case:

1   "*I think it is legitimate for the court to bear in mind that making or upholding an order removing a person as charitable trustee could, at least in some circumstances, discourage people who might otherwise be prepared to do that which is self-evident in the public interest, namely to act as charitable trustees. The court should, in principle, not be anxious to find fault with charitable trustees who, while doing their best, make honest, even stupid, mistakes.*"

2   "*I would have thought that any self respecting charitable trustee would,*

---

[10]   Heard in 1998 but unreported.

[11]   [1983] AC 173

in the absence of a very good reason to the contrary, cooperate with the reasonable requirements and requests of the Commissioners, even in the absence of any statutory obligation to do so."

These comments need to be seen in context. The following tentative conclusions can be drawn:

- Charitable trusteeship is an important public service.

- The public is interested in seeing charities run properly.

- The Commission has its statutory general function and its general object. It is entitled to give advice on anything affecting a charity.

- Advice from the Commission does not mean that trustees MUST follow it.

- Nevertheless, advice from the Commission is of a different dimension from advice from a professional or other adviser obtained by trustees. The Commission has a statutory function which includes providing advice. Specific advice may be given under s.29 of the Charities Act 1993. And in some cases (e.g. guidance the Commission is required to give under the Trustee Act 2000 about nominees) it is mandatory.

- Trustees should consider the advice carefully. Both the trustees and the Commission should, after all, have the same objective of seeing the charity flourish in pursuit of its charitable purposes. If trustees do not even consider the advice then they may have made themselves particularly vulnerable to claims of breach of trust if the problems continue and loss ensues. If trustees consider the advice carefully (and this can be demonstrated) but then conclude that it would not be in the interests of the charity to follow it then so be it – but again if problems continue or are made worse then the trustees may be called to account for their judgment.

- If trustees rely on advice given by the Commission then whether or not this is formal advice under s.29 of the Charities Act 1993 the trustees will be insulated from criticism of the consequences which flow from following the advice.

- Making honest mistakes will not normally bring down the wrath of the Courts or the Commission if the trustees are prepared to take steps to face up to issues or are prepared to mend their ways for the future.

- At the end of the day the interests of the charitable beneficiaries are paramount.

In some circumstances advice from the Commission may represent a last chance to avoid an investigation and the possibility of the imposition of a remedial sanction. In such circumstances refusal to consider and follow advice may represent the straw that breaks the camel's back.

General statements of good practice (i.e. not specifically directed to a specific charity) are primarily designed to give trustees a framework for their own decision-making and an awareness of what others in similar circumstances are doing. The very diversity of the sector (in charitable purposes, activities and organisational form) means that general advice will not fit all charities the same. But once a charity has been challenged about the effectiveness of its arrangements and has been given good practice guidance the pressure is on trustees to respond.

Good practice guidance sets aspirational standards. If trustees comply with the governance arrangements in their constitution then it would be difficult to blame trustees for continuing as they are – although at some point these arrangements may be so defective that by continuing to rely on them the trustees could be seriously hindering the fulfilment of the charitable purposes. There may come a point where failure to approach the Commission for improved constitutional arrangements may itself amount to mismanagement.

One precondition for formal intervention under s.18 of the Charities Act 1993 is the identification at any time of misconduct or mismanagement in the administration of the charity. It does not matter by whom or when the misconduct or mismanagement took place. Alternatively the Commission can intervene if it is necessary or desirable to act for the purpose of protecting the property of the charity or securing its proper application for the purposes of the charity. It may not be too fanciful to suppose that ignoring Commission advice could fall foul of either or both of these preconditions. However to move on to the possibility of removing a trustee (or making a remedial scheme) the individual concerned has to be associated with the misconduct or mismanagement AND the property has to be at risk.

At the very least failure to take note of Commission advice may be a factor in considering whether an inquiry might be opened and if opened whether a remedial sanction is appropriate.

Misconduct or mismanagement will usually mean that a breach of trust (or a failure to meet minimum fiduciary standards) has occurred. It is possible that an exculpatory clause may have set the standard for breach of trust lower than its normal setting - although in common forms they do not adjust the height of the bar in judging what is a breach of trust but rather provide protection from the consequences[12]. But an exculpatory clause does not convert misconduct or mismanagement into acceptable conduct or management. In cases where trustees are protected from the financial consequences of their failures the Commission can, of course, still intervene.

A breach of trust may be a prelude to seeking restitution from the trustees. In this context:

- There will need to be some demonstrable loss which would not have arisen if there had been no breach of trust.

- Poor trusteeship but no loss would not enable a restitution claim to be made notwithstanding that this amounts to a breach of trust.

- The trustees may have the benefit of a "protective" clause in the governing instrument – although this would not cover "gross negligence".

- If there is no protective clause but there is trustee indemnity insurance, restitution would be sought from the trustee who would then in turn seek to be indemnified out of his insurance.

7.5 Can Poor Decisions Be Set Aside?

Trustees are always taking decisions. Nobody would expect to get every decision right. But what makes a decision vulnerable to challenge?

There are a number of factors:

7.5.1 Was the decision within the powers of the trustees?

This is simply judged against the governing documents and any relevant statutory provisions. See *Re Hastings-Bass*[13] where the Court of Appeal indicated (*inter*

---

[12] See *Armitage v Nurse* [1998] 1 Ch 241; *Bogg v Raper* [1998] The Times 22 April; the appeal to the House of Lords in *Walker v Stones* is eagerly awaited. The Law Commission is currently reviewing Trustees' Exemption Clauses.

[13] [1975] Ch 25

alia) that it would not interfere with the *bona fide* exercise of a discretion by trustees unless what the trustees did was unauthorised by the relevant power which the trustees purported to use. It is not, of course, enough to show that a particular act is within the powers of the trustees – it could still be challenged under one of the following categories.

7.5.2 Was the decision made by the trustees one which a reasonable body of trustees could have made (or was the decision perverse or irrational)?

Charity trustees must act in the interests of the charity and its beneficiaries, both present and, where appropriate, future, in carrying out the charity's purposes. It is not enough to demonstrate that another body of trustees might have reached a different decision. The question is whether on the evidence and in the circumstances "was this a decision which no reasonable body of trustees could have taken?". In *Wight v Olswang*[14] Mr Justice Neuberger reiterated the principle that:

> *"Beneficiaries of a trust did not have a claim against a trustee who made an investment decision unless they could establish that the decision was one that no reasonable trustee could have made".*

In the absence of fraud or bad faith what is important is the ultimate decision – it is not appropriate to look at every aspect of the decision making process to identify whether at any stage there has been something which can be characterised as a breach of trust and stop there. There is the question of whether any breach of proper process caused the trustees to make a decision they would not otherwise have made. But no matter how a particular decision is reached – in compliance with process or not – if the ultimate decision was one a reasonable trustee could have reached an adverse claim could not succeed. Following good process may well in most situations increase the likelihood of a good decision being taken but it is not by itself a guarantee that the decision will be good.

7.5.3 Did the trustees act in good faith?

A lack of good faith may be demonstrated, by way of examples, where trustees ignore a relevant conflict of interest, prefer their own or other irrelevant interests to the interests of the charitable beneficiaries, ignore clear warnings in reports from experts, or disregard inconvenient financial information. This is an essential ingredient for a valid trustee decision. In *Armitage v Nurse*[15] Millett LJ stated:

---

14 [2001] WTLR 291; see also *Nestle v National Westminster Bank plc* [1994] 1 All ER 118.

15 [1997] 2 All ER 705

> *"It is the duty of a trustee to manage the trust property and deal with it in the interests of the beneficiaries. If he acts in a way which he does not honestly believe is in their interests then he is acting dishonestly. It does not matter whether he stands or thinks he stands to gain personally from his actions. A trustee who acts with the intention of benefiting persons who are not the objects of the trust is not the less dishonest because he does not intend to benefit himself".*

7.5.4   Did the trustees take into account any factors which it was not proper for them to take into account?

In *Dundee General Hospitals Board of Management v Walker and Another*[16] Lord Reid stated:

> *"If it can be shown that the trustees considered the wrong question, or that, although they purported to consider the right question they did not really apply their minds to it or perversely shut their eyes to the facts or that they did not act honestly or in good faith, then there was no true decision and the court will intervene".*

However, the fact that trustees had taken into account matters that were not relevant did not in the particular case invalidate the decision because it was justified by other matters which had properly been considered.

In *Stannard v Fisons Pension Trust*[17] the Court of Appeal struck down the exercise of a discretion. In this case the trustees had relied on an outdated valuation and as a result were not able to give properly informed consideration as to whether the amount of assets to be transferred from one pension fund to another should be calculated on the total service reserve method or the past service reserve method.

7.5.5   Did the trustees fail to take into account any factors which they should have taken into account?

In *Mettoy Pension Trustees Limited v Evans*[18] Warner J considered that the reasons for the trustees failing to take into account considerations they ought to have taken into account were immaterial:

---

16   [1952] 1 ALL ER 896

17   [1992] 1 RLR 27

18   [1991] 2 All ER 513

> "Where a trustee acts under a discretion given to him by the terms of the trust, the Court will interfere with his action if it is clear that he would not have acted as he did had he not failed to take into account considerations which he ought to have taken into account".

It is not enough for the principle to apply that it should be shown that the trustees did not have a proper understanding of the effect of their act. It must also be clear that, had they had a proper understanding of it, they would not have acted as they did.

Edge v Pensions Ombudsman[19] neatly covers points 7.5.4 and 7.5.5 in the context of the ordinary duty which the law imposes on those with responsibility for exercising discretionary powers - has the trustee exercised *"the power for the purpose for which it is given, giving proper consideration to the matters which are relevant and excluding from consideration matters which are irrelevant"*? This case is interesting for the way in which the court makes clear how the test for challenging the exercise of a trustee's discretion is very closely aligned to the test for administrative law. Would trustees have acted the same way if they had considered all relevant factors and not considered irrelevant factors?

7.5.6   Did the trustees adequately inform themselves in order to make the decision in question?

In *Scott v National Trust*[20] Robert Walker J stated:

> *"Trustees must act in good faith, responsibly and reasonably. They must inform themselves before making a decision of matters which are relevant to that decision. These matters may not be limited to simple matters of fact but will on occasion (indeed quite often) include taking advice from appropriate experts. It is however for advisers to advise and for trustees to decide."*

In the cases referred to the issue was whether the decisions of the trustees could stand (rather than whether the trustees were vulnerable to a breach of trust claim). Clearly trustees will want to take valid decisions which cannot be overturned by the courts. It is in this area of effective valid decision making that advice to trustees (and development of good practice) assumes particular significance.

There is some tension here in relation to remedies. The Commission cannot by

---

19   [1999] 4 All ER 546

20   [1998] 2 All ER

itself unravel a poor decision taken by trustees – this is a matter for the courts in relation to proceedings instituted under s.32 of the Charities Act 1993. But this is not always the most attractive way of addressing these issues – litigation is not good for the reputation of charities, it rarely serves the beneficiaries well, it can be costly, the procedures can take time and there are few "guaranteed" winning cases.

Some further helpful guidance is contained in the case of *The Public Trustee v Cooper*[21] (known as the *Mansfield Brewery* case).

A few conclusions:

- In the first instance it is for trustees to take their own decisions. If the courts are asked to review a decision that trustees have already taken they will only interfere, in effect, if the *Wednesbury* principles have been breached.

- The law is not entirely clear! In *Scott v National Trust*, Walker J appears to have applied a *Wednesbury* type approach but it remains unclear whether the test is whether the trustees if properly advised would have acted differently or merely might have acted differently. In *Mettoy*, Warner J had applied a "would" test whereas in *Stannard* the Court of Appeal had applied a "might" test without analysing the important difference between the two. This is of considerable importance in the context of pensions law because the "might" test runs the risk of undermining certainty and the finality of trustees' decisions. It is probably not such a crucial issue for charities if only because challenges to the exercise of trustees' discretions are fairly rare (no doubt because of the cost and the filtering effect of needing to obtain prior approval from the Commission).

- Where the courts are asked to sanction a proposed action (which would normally only be considered if a particularly momentous decision fell to be taken) the approach is likely to be one of testing the soundness of the process by which the trustees had reached their conclusion, weighing up the contrary arguments, assessing the full weight and thoroughness of the professional opinions and for the judge to be satisfied that the trustees have been conscientious and careful and have considered the matters they were entitled to consider in sufficient detail to enable them to reach a proper and reasonable judgment. The courts would not take over the discretion of the trustees and would not substitute their views for the

---

[21] (2001) 2 WTLR 901

views of the trustees. The courts would leave the primary responsibility for decision making to the trustees but would "check it out".

7.6 What Does all this Amount to?

It is interesting that all these key decisions have centred around the actions of trustees. They do not relate to issues decided by a Chief Executive or other employee.

Whilst trustees set strategy they cannot just wash their hands of management. What they can do is build in sound reporting systems so that they can be satisfied that their policies have been effectively implemented as intended. But reporting systems work both ways. Skilled professional staff will not be willing to show the requisite commitment if their contribution is undervalued, or considered second class or they are not properly engaged in the process of developing or refining strategy.

A division between strategy and management with never the twain do meet will not in practice work. What is essential is the development of a vision of shared partnership and shared leadership. Trustees and staff may have specific responsibilities but neither set of responsibilities can be carried out in isolation.

Charity and trust law has developed on the back of the concept of trusteeship with its particular brand of personal accountability. But in the modern environment this can sound artificial and outmoded.

Nevertheless it is important for trustees and the staff of a charity to be aware where responsibilities begin and end. There is at present considerable support for the concept of altruistic trusteeship whilst recognising that the organisation needs to attract the right mix of skills in its paid workforce. This creates the divide between "gratuitous" trusteeship and "paid" staff. Unkindly this can be described as amateurs leading professionals. This misses the point as all contribute to the totality, albeit in different ways. Leadership is not the sole preserve of the trustees.

A few further legal points:

- Charities do not have shareholders. Issues of accountability would be confused if trustees could be self-perpetuating and paid. Who sacks those who under-perform? A paid trustee might be particularly reluctant to stand down if his/her livelihood and eventual pension was dependent on continuing to work. And in the context of a trust can you really employ yourself?

- Trustees provide the mechanism for employing and remunerating staff, for setting objectives and managing appraisals, and where necessary for dispensing with the services of those who under-perform. Whilst employment law provides safeguards for employees, at the end of the day somebody needs to assert the interests of the beneficiaries in priority to the interests of any other party.

- Chief Executives and other staff do not normally qualify as being "charity trustees". Even without being charity trustees the Commission can suspend employees and agents. If they have been associated directly with misconduct or mismanagement the Commission can remove employees or agents of a charity. It is also interesting to note that the definition of misconduct or mismanagement specifically extends to the-

    "employment for the remuneration or reward of persons acting in the affairs of the charity, or for other administrative purposes, of sums which are excessive in relation to the property held by the charity"

    - this point applies notwithstanding anything in the governing instrument.

7.7 Conclusion

Focussing on legal issues can sometimes blur the bigger picture. An effective charity will have clear objectives (refreshed from time to time) led by committed trustees and staff with a common purpose and clear recognition of the separate responsibilities.

The function and object of the Commission supports this approach. Each charity will be focussing primarily on what it does within its own context but a full appreciation of wider developments of interest or concern is also essential.

The Commission opens around 315 investigations a year. The number of trustees who are removed is tiny. The number of cases going to court where an attempt is made to overturn decisions of trustees is also tiny. The vast majority of charities have no truck with abuse or bad practice. The trustees, the volunteers and the work force want to make a real difference in areas which matter greatly to them.

In looking at some of the relevant legal issues, inevitably the focus shifts to areas of poor practice and abuse. Identifying where the law allows interventions to occur is interesting because it sets the bottom line – but few charities are interested in performing with poor governance and management arrangements even if these scrape above the bar. Concentrating on good practice issues and bringing these to the attention of trustees produces significant dividends in improved performance and over time is likely to raise the level at which the bar is set for judging mismanagement and breach of trust issues. To the extent that the law does not specifically colour in all the squares, judgments about "reasonableness" will continue to be necessary – and what is reasonable will be influenced through the dissemination of good practice.

Chapter 8

STRATEGY OR MANAGEMENT BY TRUSTEES: CORPORATE GOVERNANCE
Roger Singleton CBE[1]

I have been asked to address the issue "Strategy or Management by Trustees" by utilising a case study approach. I will endeavour to respond to that remit but first some preliminaries.

I guess that lawyers are well represented at this seminar and you have already had a comprehensive paper from Michael Carpenter. I make no pretence to legal expertise in charity law and my contribution will focus on the practical and day-to-day applications of the law as they relate to the relationship between trustees and senior management. It is obvious, therefore, that I will draw from the experience of those charities who actually employ staff and where issues of "Who does what?" frequently arise[2].

I should, perhaps, present my credentials for being vain enough to believe that I have something worthwhile to contribute to the seminar.

Firstly, a personal interest in the whole issue of governance within not-for-profit organisations. My trustees kindly provided me with the opportunity to study governance formally at the Institute of Management at Cambridge and I was also able to spend time looking at governance practice in the United States, Australia and New Zealand. In this country I have been involved with a number of organisations as they have contemplated changes to their governance structures

---

[1] Roger Singleton CBE is the Chief Executive of Barnardo's – the UK's largest children's charity. He has a background in education, children's services, policy and management, is trustee of several charities and is accredited to mediate disputes within the private, public and voluntary sectors.

[2] Extracts from ACEVO *Leading the Organisation: The Relationship between Chair and Chief Executive* (2002) have been used to describe relevant governance issues on the topics covered in this presentation.

and led conferences and courses designed to promote good practice. Secondly, I have gained some experience as the Chief Executive of Barnardo's.

The principal aspects of the relationship between governance and management on which I wish to focus are:

- Determining the vision and purpose.

- The strategic plan.

- The major policies.

- Resource deployment.

- Risk Management.

- Public image.

- Delegation, reporting and reviewing.

I propose to make a few comments about each of these aspects and then invite you to consider how changes to the law, to Charity Commission guidance, to conventional wisdom on good practice, and how resort to consultancy and mediation might assist in addressing some of the issues to which it gives rise.

Finally, I want to identify the general approach I bring by reminding you of what Michael Carpenter said:

> "*A division between strategy and management where never the twain do meet will not in practice work. What is essential is the development of a vision of shared partnership and shared leadership. Trustees and staff may have specific responsibilities but neither set of responsibilities can be carried out in isolation*" [3].

By partnership I do not imply a lack of clarity about who is responsible for what. On the contrary I would advocate absolute clarity about what are the distinctive functions of trustees and management. But any delineation will leave substantial grey areas. It is those which will require the greatest attention. As an American governance guru John Carver says:

> "*The board and its chief executive constitute a leadership team. Their*

---

[3] See para 7.6

contributions are formally separable, and once clearly differentiated, the two roles can be supportive and respectful of each other. As in sports, the team functions only so long as the positions are clearly defined at the outset. Teamwork is not the blurring of responsibilities into an undifferentiated mass. The foremost expectation of mutual support is that each function remains true to its peculiar responsibility. The chief executive must be able to rely on the board to confront and resolve issues of governance, while respectfully staying out of management. The board must be able to rely on the chief executive to confront and resolve issues of management while respectfully staying out of governance."

I have never found myself able to recognise that Carverian world which appears to have no place for such human characteristic as personal power, ambition, motivation or political game playing but I accept the generality of what he aspires to delineate.

8.1 Determining the Vision and Purpose

By law, trustees must ensure the charity operates within its permitted objects as laid down in its governing instrument. Typically trustees do this by determining which objects to focus on at any particular time and within the framework of objects they may agree a vision for what they wish to achieve and a mission and/or purpose. They may also determine some values which guide how things should be done.

Barnardo's objects are outlined in its Memorandum & Articles, which state that the Association is established for:

- The relief and assistance of children and young people in need.

- The promotion of the education of children and young people.

- The promotion among children and young people of the knowledge of the Christian faith or the faith in which they were brought up.

- The relief of the poor, sick, handicapped and aged.

Barnardo's values are: respecting the unique worth of every person; encouraging people to fulfil their potential; and working with hope to achieve these aims.

Barnardo's vision & purpose is periodically reviewed by Council, and has recently been revised for the 2001-06 corporate plan. Barnardo's vision is that the lives of *all* children and young people should be free from poverty, abuse and discrimination. The contribution which Barnardo's as an organisation can make towards the achievement of this vision is expressed as our purpose, namely to help the most vulnerable children and young people transform their lives and fulfil their potential.

Barnardo's 2001-06 strategic objectives are to:

- Meet the needs and requirements of children and young people with excellent service.

- Improve the circumstances in which children and young people grow up by influencing decision-makers.

- Embed the perspectives and participation of children and young people at the heart of everything we do.

- Gain greater public recognition and support by promoting Barnardo's brand name.

- Enable employees and volunteers to achieve exemplary performance.

- Generate the income and support we need.

- Balance the revenue budget and meet the reserves policy.

Trustees develop and apply the objects, vision, purpose and strategic objectives in the following ways:

- They charge the CEO and Directors with preparing a 5-year Corporate Plan which recommends the vision & purpose, after consultation with all stakeholders, and an environmental scan. These are debated and agreed at Council.

- Any major changes in direction or new developments are brought to Council for approval.

- Through visits to the organisation, trustees gain an understanding of Barnardo's current operations and aspirations of staff, volunteers, service users, supporters and other stakeholders.

- Through six Council meetings per year they gain an understanding of key developments and issues.

- A Basis & Values Committee oversees the application of the value statements.

The role of management is as follows:

- The CEO gives direction to the formulation of the organisation's philosophy, objectives and strategies and annual targets, and develops the 5-year Corporate Plan.

- The CEO and Directors identify key developments that may impact upon the overall vision & purpose and bring these to Council for consideration.

- They are also responsible for ensuring that Basis & Values are applied throughout the organisation.

Problems do occasionally arise in making these roles work in practice.

- Trustees will have different motivations and may have differing positions on the extent to which the various objects and values should be prioritised. Their perspectives may also differ from those of staff and volunteers.

- There are sometimes differences in culture and language between trustees, managers and staff - e.g. on the meaning of "poverty" in the UK.

8.2 The Strategic Plan

By convention trustees are expected to set the overall strategic direction of the organisation and the framework within which the organisation has to work. They should ensure that within this framework, the chief executive prepares a more detailed strategic plan with annual targets.

Consideration needs to be given as to how and when ideas from all those with an interest in the work of the organisation (trustees, staff, volunteers, members, service users, beneficiaries, funders) can inform the process for making strategic and major policy decisions. It should be remembered, however, that the final decisions can only be made by the trustees.

Trustees should be able to contribute ideas about strategic and policy direction at any time. In a large charity, trustees often make decisions following staff presentations.

At Barnardo's the CEO is charged with preparing the Corporate Plan every 5 years, with annual updates, assisted by the Head of Organisational Planning and Change and the UK Directors. The draft plan is shared with trustees at all stages of the process, so they can feed in their views on priorities as well as providing feedback to the Directors about their proposals. The CEO has to operate with the framework determined by trustees - e.g. preparing environmental scans and financial information, and consulting at particular times with trustees and other stakeholders.

Trustees check the plans are robust through discussion and debate with the CEO and Directors at Council. Further details or evidence may be requested on a particular point (e.g. benchmarking information against other providers of children's services, or market research on the profitability and risks of certain fundraising initiatives). Visiting also enables trustees to gauge whether the top-level strategic plan fits with the predominant issues expressed in the field.

The final plan is approved by Council and performance against the plan is monitored at subsequent meetings. Each year an annual review of the plan is prepared for Council, detailing how the organisation is meeting its purpose and objectives and proposing any course corrections that need to be agreed in light of emerging circumstances.

In practice, there is only limited time available for involving trustees as they are volunteers with other full time jobs. This can lead to the feeling that the plan is a fait accompli by managers, with little opportunity for anything more than minor amendments by trustees. This is why it is essential to engage with Council at every stage of planning, not just when it is nearing completion. Sometimes trustees' appetite for involvement can exceed their capacity. The chair and CEO must carefully steer the Board on this aspect.

8.3 The Major Policies

Trustees are expected to ensure that they are up to date with the work of the charity and the field within which it is operating. The CEO brings to their attention the need for any new policies and proposals. Trustees also have a need for wider information about how the internal and external environment is changing, to base their decisions on e.g. unions, positions on adoption/fostering, regional boundaries etc. The CEO is responsible for the management and administration of the organisation in the execution of the Council's policies.

Problem areas can arise if the need for policy development or change is not recognised or agreed.

8.4 Resource Deployment

Trustees must ensure the charity's property is protected and that all funds not immediately required are invested properly in accordance with its investment powers. The charity must also comply with the requirements of the Charities Acts re. filing of returns and accounts, sale of property, disclosure of charitable status etc. If the charity is also a company, it must comply with the requirements of the Companies Acts as well.

By convention trustees are expected to monitor the overall financial performance of the organisation against agreed budgets and agreed internal financial controls. Trustees are under a duty to keep proper accounting records for their charity which are sufficient to show and explain all the charity's transactions. The charity must comply with the relevant Charity Commission Statement of Recommended Practice (SORP) when preparing its annual reports and accounts. This would include carrying out regular risk analyses, reviewing reserve policies and imposing strict financial controls.

This is applied by trustees by receiving and scrutinising financial reports. The Treasurer has particular responsibilities for checking financial performance, and ensuring that areas of concern are brought to the attention of Council. Furthermore, Barnardo's has a committee of Council for monitoring its investments. On the management side, the Company Secretary and UK Director of Finance and Corporate Services are responsible for bringing management information, plans and reviews to Council. An internal audit department also monitors resource deployment.

Problems encountered include selecting appropriate levels of reserves and managing financial risk, to ensure that services received by users have secure financial backing, whilst satisfying donors that funds are being fully utilised.

8.5 Risk Management

Trustees should take professional advice where appropriate, which may include exploring matters which they believe to pose serious risks to an organisation. Furthermore, trustees are expected, by convention, to set a code of conduct for themselves, and also to ensure the charity's management style reflects up-to-date employment conventions.

Barnardo's trustees discharge their risk management responsibilities through an Audit Committee, and by receiving audit reports. It is the conjoint duty of trustees and senior staff to identify the major risks to which the charity is exposed. It is the staff's responsibility to develop a programme of work which minimises and manages risk, as well as reporting on risk management annually. This process is supported by Barnardo's internal audit team. External audits provide an additional level of comfort to trustees.

It is not always easy to get the right balance between risk aversion and prudent risk-taking to achieve the organisation's objectives, in work such as child protection.

8.6 Public Image

Trustees must act at all times in the charity's best interest, and not obtain any personal benefit from being trustees. A failure to do so brings significant risks to the charity, including long-term damage to the organisation's reputation amongst users, staff, funders, donors and other stakeholders. Trustees must also ensure the charity does not engage in improper political activities.

Furthermore, trustees should set the framework for the potential campaigning role of the charity, and which types of fundraising and types of donor are acceptable to the organisation. Initiatives and spend for changing or protecting Barnardo's public image are brought to Council for consideration. This has included an approach for educating the public that we no longer run orphanages. Trustees sign off campaigning issues and any contentious policies. Managers prepare the rationale and plans for such approaches.

It can be difficult to find accord between perceptions of trustees, staff, service users and donors about an acceptable public image for such a large and diverse organisation. The content and spend on advertising can also raise significant debates.

8.7 Delegation and Reporting

Trustees must ensure the charity complies with relevant legislation regarding, for example, health and safety, employment, equal opportunities and disability discrimination. They should monitor the ways the staff plan to achieve organisational aims and objectives and whether the organisation is making sufficient progress towards its goals. They are also expected to evaluate the work of the charity - in terms of the impact the organisation is having in its field and on its users, or its clients, and, where possible, the impact current activities might have on future generations of users or clients. Furthermore, they should appraise themselves, as individuals and collectively.

Council and its sub-committees receive a wide range of reports to meet these requirements. External demands have increased in recent years for trustees to be more closely involved in scrutinising activities at all organisational levels. Consequently Barnardo's recently established Committees in Scotland, Wales and Northern Ireland, and Trustee Groups in the English regions have taken on enhanced reporting duties on behalf of Council. However, trustees still depend on management's integrity in reporting honestly on reviews and information gathering exercises that have been conducted. The increased levels of reporting do increase the potential for confusion about the distinction between governance and management.

Chapter 9

CORPORATE GOVERNANCE AND PERFORMANCE IN LARGE UK NONPROFITS
Gregory Jobome[1]

9.1   Introduction

This paper examines the pattern of the adoption of key corporate governance mechanisms by large UK nonprofits and assesses the performance implications of this. It is motivated by the fact that while many nonprofits have begun adopting business-type corporate governance practices, there is hardly any empirical evidence that provides pointers about the potential impact of this adoption. This is especially important because of the growth that has taken place in the sector in recent years. Total UK voluntary sector income grew by 7% in real terms between 1996 and 2000, reaching about £15 billion. Of this, about £7 billion is accounted for by charitable donations, which grew by 26% over the same period[2]. For this growth to be sustained, governance practices in the sector need to be based on probity, accountability and transparency to maintain the support of contributors. It is for this reason that many large nonprofits are looking to the business sector which has had a head-start in designing and implementing mechanisms to achieve same.

There are obviously parallels which suggest that the governance problems of the nonprofit sector are similar to those of businesses and so the same corporate governance prescriptions should work. For example, all professionally managed organisations (whether profit or nonprofit) are characterised by the separation of management from shareholders (or donors/recipients) and so are potentially exposed to similar issues of ensuring that both groups of stakeholders are working towards the same objective with the same motivations. In this context,

---

[1]   Gregory Jobome is Lecturer in the Department of Economics and Accounting at the University of Liverpool where he teaches Corporate Governance, Finance and Transitional Economies.

[2]   Mintel (2001)

any mechanisms designed to ensure congruence should be equally applicable. Reflecting this similarity of intention, the pace of work on corporate governance committees such as Cadbury (1992), Greenbury (1995), Hampel (1998) and Turnbull (1999) was only just ahead of charitable, "quango"[3] and public sector counterparts such as Nolan Committee (1994 and 1997), Statement of Recommended Practice (SORP) (1995 and 2000), Cabinet Office (1997) and HM Treasury (2001). However, this parallel with business needs to be balanced against the fact that nonprofits *are* different from businesses. Nonprofits have different goals, different structures and are run by people motivated differently from the business sector, and so the specific mechanisms that are likely to be effective could also be different. This raises the question whether nonprofits have similar governance problems to the business sector which the adoption of typical corporate governance mechanisms would help overcome. This paper estimates the effect of the adoption of some typical corporate governance recommendations on the performance of a set of the largest UK charities, with performance defined in two ways - the ability of the nonprofit to raise funds from private (voluntary) donors, and its effectiveness in channeling such funds to the donor-intended charitable objects.

The remainder of this paper is organised as follows. Section 2 briefly describes the theoretical framework, especially issues about agency costs, and stresses how the framework may be usefully extended to the analysis of charities. Section 3 describes the sources of funds for charities, emphasising issues of donor motivation, voluntary contributions, government grants and fundraising activities. Section 4 summarises the framework typically employed in assessing the performance of nonprofits, highlighting the empirical approaches and the evidence, and how these may usefully be extended in the context of the present study. In Section 5, the empirical models and estimation procedures are presented while Section 6 describes the nature of the data employed in estimation, drawing out some stylised facts. Finally, Section 7 presents the results of empirical estimation.

9.2 Nonprofits and Agency Problems

Agency theory has become well established as a major theoretical construct in explaining firm governance issues[4]. With its roots in work such as Berle and

---

[3] Some of the nonprofits studied in this paper are Non-Departmental Public Bodies (NDPBs), also called Quasi-NGOs.

[4] Other firm theories have been employed in the context of governance. For discussions on a *transactions costs* perspective see Coase (1937), Williamson (1988) and Hart (1995 and 1996), and for a *property rights* approach see for example Alchian and Demsetz (1972) and Frech (1976).

Means (1932), the agency perspective notes that while shareholders provide the funds for a firm, control is delegated to professional managers, with the shareholders being limited in their ability to constrain the behaviour of management. The separation of ownership and control generates agency problems as epitomised by misalignments in risk preference, incentives, effort level and timing (Rediker and Seth, 1995). To illustrate, Hart (1995) posits that the typical agency problem involves the owner hiring a manager to run his firm, with the firm's performance (represented by gross profit, π) being dependent on the manager's effort level e, and chance ε. Thus, $\pi = g(e, \varepsilon)$ with effort encouraged via a governance mechanism such as compensation (or other incentives, and disincentives), as a means of aligning manager vis-à-vis owner preferences. However, because of information asymmetry regarding the manager's effort choice, contracts which make the manager's compensation (I) a direct function of e cannot be enforced. Thus, to mitigate this moral hazard problem, the compensation incentive must be tied to actual performance (gross profit), such that:

$$I = I(\pi).^5$$

In sum, in the absence of effective control mechanisms, managers are more likely to make decisions that do not coincide with shareholders' interests. This "managerial" behaviour could be reflected in shirking, wasteful expenditure, perquisites, inefficiencies, fraud and ultimately, failure. In this construct, corporate governance arises as a means of generating the structures and mechanisms that would engender goal and preference congruency between shareholders and senior managers and thereby lead to the maximisation of value for shareholders. This conventional corporate governance perspective is clearly plausible in the case of large companies, but can this analytical framework be usefully extended to the governance of large nonprofit organisations? Two reasons may justify an extension. First, it is generally supposed that agency issues characterise all professionally managed firms, whether profit-making or not. Second, many large nonprofits also own commercial subsidiaries that make up a significant part of their income generation activities, thereby again being subject to the same agency and governance issues. In fact, it may be argued that agency problems are worse in nonprofits because of the absence of some incentive-aligning tools available to profit-making firms. For example, the nondistribution constraint implies no stockholding and concomitantly that there is no stock

---

5   Formalised treatment and further details about agency costs and implications may be obtained from work such as Jensen and Meckling (1976), Fama (1980), Fama and Jensen (1983), Hart (1995 and 1996) and Shleifer and Vishny (1997).

market-based managerial incentive alignment mechanism (Preyra and Pink, 2001)[6].

However, nonprofits are different in ways which suggest that the typical agency perspective needs to be reinterpreted in their case. For example, there are no "owners" in the usual sense, who invest in the hope of reaping a financial reward, who closely monitor their investment and can potentially vote out a weak board. Also, Rose-Ackerman (1987) raises the possibility that managers in the nonprofit sector are relatively less motivated by financial gain than their for-profit counterparts. She hypothesises that *"nonprofit managers are much more directly interested in the character of the services they provide than are for-profit managers"* (p.811, 812). She alludes to a selection mechanism whereby *"people attracted to managerial positions in the nonprofit sector are those who care relatively little about financial gain and relatively highly about putting their own ideals into practice"* (p.812). Thus, nonprofit "managerial" behaviour in this thinking is not so much in the excessive consumption of perquisites, shirking, and so on, but more that *"their choice of service quality may not perfectly match the preferences of either donors or clients"* (p.812).

In other words, the agency issue here is about nonprofit managers pleasing themselves via their service mix choice, possibly at the expense of satisfying donors' goals, rather than a concern about outright shirking. It raises the possibility that typical corporate governance mechanisms may not work in the same way as for business[7]. For example, a package of financial incentives may not add much in motivating a manager who is already fully committed to a charitable cause; on the other hand, measures which restrict his or her discretion over funds may be more effective. These and other testable implications which arise from the foregoing theoretical discussion are empirically tested subsequently.

9.3 Donor Motivation and Nonprofit Fundraising

The performance of a nonprofit may be gauged in at least two ways - how much income it is able to generate through fundraising, and, how much of its income it is able to distribute to donor-preferred beneficiaries and purposes. This section highlights the former, with the latter discussed in Section 4. Charities and other nonprofits raise funds from two broad sources - private (voluntary) donations and

---

6 See, for example, their discussion on p.510.

7 Note that even for business, empirical studies of the performance implications of many governance mechanisms have found ambiguous results. See, for example, Bruce and Buck (1997) on weak pay-performance linkage.

government grants, in varying proportions, depending on their objectives, nature and legal status (nonprofit characteristics). Arguably, the nonprofit has a more active role to play in determining how much voluntary donations it is able to raise, and perhaps less so for government receipts. The nature and implications of these fund sources are discussed in turn, starting with the former.

The amount of private donations raised by nonprofits depends *ceteris paribus* on the willingness of donors to give. The literature identifies several reasons why individuals donate to charitable purposes. These include "pure altruism" [8], or deriving utility from donations providing a public good (Olson, 1965; Becker, 1974), "impure altruism" or "warm glow" effect (Andreoni, 1989) and "prestige", "signaling" or "snob appeal" (Glazer and Konrad, 1996; Harbaugh, 1998; Romano and Yildirim, 2001). Once one recognises more than an altruistic or warm glow motive in giving (which are outside the nonprofit's control), and moves towards the prestige and signaling type hypotheses, then it is possible to characterise the dynamic interaction between the charity and the donor. For example, Harbaugh (1998) models a process whereby charities supply prestige to donors by publicly reporting the amounts donated, with the charity in turn exploiting this prestige effect in increasing contributions. Further, Harbaugh shows that in such a prestige model, category plans are more effective than reporting the exact amount of donations, in stimulating contribution by donors. Harbaugh then uses the prestige model in explaining the behaviour of different types of charities. First are charities such as educational and local cultural organisations; these are characterised by a limited group of donors with long-term ties to the charity. These charities would usually solicit large contributions and report individual donations in detail. In their reporting, they mostly use contribution categories, and these tend to be far apart. Second, there are the broad-based national charities such as environmental and social welfare groups. These tend to have donors with comparatively fewer long-term ties (and or lower demand for prestige), solicit smaller donations and in most cases do not report individual contributions. Third, cartel type charities which raise funds on behalf of member charities. Harbaugh argues that this latter type is ideally placed to exploit the prestige effect. This is because these charities are able to work locally (thus able to report on the charities with the highest ability to provide prestige) and since they are cartelised they are also able to increase donations via using categories. Several testable implications arise from the foregoing. For example, while donor motivation may not be directly observable, it is possible to test whether particular kinds of nonprofit organisations are better able to raise funds, perhaps because they espouse causes donors feel more motivated to contribute to

---

[8] See Andreoni (1988) which shows that many of the predictions of the altruistic model are not consistent with the empirical evidence. For example, the prediction of near complete crowding out of voluntary contributions by public expenditures, or that only the wealthiest will contribute, and that average contributions should approach zero.

or because they use fundraising methods (prestige supplying, etc.) that coincide with their motivations.

On the role of the government, the theoretical rationale for intervention is often premised on the argument that as a result of free-rider problems, relying on private donations would lead to under-provision of charitable activities (Sugden, 1982)[9]. However, the involvement of the government in the nonprofit sector is generally viewed as a two-edged sword. Financial contributions by the government have been hypothesised to affect the amount of private donations generated by nonprofits. There are two theoretical perspectives on this. In the first, where a public good is funded via private contributions (as in charitable giving), government spending on the public good would be neutral, tending to crowd-out private donations. Thus, there is a substitution effect between government spending and private donations, as demonstrated theoretically by for example Warr (1982), Roberts (1984), Bergstrom et al (1986) and Cornes and Sandler (1996). On the other hand, the second view (for example, Khanna and Sandler, 2000) raises the possibility that private and government spending are in fact complementary, such that government grants stimulate charitable contributions by individuals and we have instead a *crowding-in* effect. This view is related to the notion (for example, Andreoni, 1998) that government grants could play the role of seed money which "guarantees" a certain minimum size and quality before private contributors are induced to donate, or, the argument in Rose-Ackerman (1987) that government grants could enhance the reputation of nonprofits in the view of voluntary contributors.

In addition to the above quantitative effects, the government represents an external source of monitoring and control that serves to reinforce the internal corporate governance mechanisms adopted by nonprofits. This may be viewed as the sum total of the laws and procedures aimed at safeguarding the interests of donors and the public at large from shirking or own-agenda managers. In the UK, for example, this role is reflected in the various reporting and compliance relationships between nonprofits and the relevant regulatory body. Depending on the legal status and size of the nonprofit, this may be one or more of the Charity Commission, Companies House, the supervising government department or the Treasury. Again, several testable implications emerge from the above discussion. These include testing: the crowding-in *versus* crowding-out hypotheses, the fundraising implications of government monitoring or supervision and whether exogenous and unrestricted government grants encourage own-agenda behaviour by nonprofit managers.

---

9   See specifically the discussion on page 342; and the rest of the paper for an alternative theory.

9.4 Assessing the Performance of Nonprofits

The main function of nonprofits is to raise funds *and* then to effect a redistribution of funds from donors to recipients[10]. However, there are agency type problems implicit in the nonprofit manager-donor relationship, which provide an incentive for nonprofit donors to establish information and governance mechanisms that would ensure that the intended amount is distributed and target recipients are reached. That is, there is both a quantity (right amount) and a quality (right recipient) dimension to the problem. The amount actually raised in donations provides an indication of the former, while the "passthrough rate" (the fraction of funds distributed to recipients) of nonprofits could provide an approximation of the divergence between donors' preferences and managers' behaviour. Clearly, the governance and other monitoring mechanisms put in place to induce incentive-compatible behaviour by nonprofit managers would influence the passthrough rate of individual nonprofits. The weaker the monitoring and scrutiny provided by corporate governance mechanisms and external regulatory arrangements, the larger the discretionary margin potentially available for managers to exploit in the form of own-agenda activities and the lower the passthrough rate will be.

Empirical assessments of the performance of nonprofits have typically estimated models which seek to explain either the amount of private donations (so-called *donations function*, for example, Khanna et al, 1995; Khanna and Sandler, 2000; Okten and Weisbrod, 2000) or the passthrough rate (*passthrough function*, for example, Feigenbaum, 1987), in terms of a range of variables which reflect some or all of: the implicit price of giving, alternative funding sources, fundraising expenditure, market structure and organisational characteristics.

9.4.1 Donations functions

The donations functions essentially estimate the demand for the output of the nonprofit, under the assumption that donors view their marginal contribution to output to be proportional to their money donations. In Okten and Weisbrod (2000), for example, the donations function expresses the willingness of potential contributors to donate as a function of price and quality as well as the information about price and quality available to the donor. They posit that the fundraising expenditures of a nonprofit are analogous to advertising in for-profit firms, and thus provide information on the quality of its output. However, they hypothesise two opposing effects of fundraising expenditures on donations. First, they reduce information costs for donors, thereby directly increasing contributions. Second, they increase the price of giving (via devoting an increased share of income to

---

[10] The discussion here draws on insights offered in Feigenbaum (1987).

fundraising activities rather than to output) thereby reducing contributions. The sign and size of the total elasticity of donations with respect to fundraising expenditures is the net effect of these two opposing influences. They also control for other factors, including the crowding-out (or -in) potential of other sources of income such as government grants and autonomous (self-generated) income. The empirical model they estimate (using US panel data) states donations as a function of fundraising expenditures, price, age of nonprofit, government grants received, self-generated income and the interaction of age and fundraising expenditure. Their findings broadly support their hypotheses; for example, fundraising expenditures both directly increase and indirectly reduce contributions, and in total show a positive net effect. They also find evidence for crowding-in, both from government grants and from self-generated income. Broadly similar results (though with some variation) are also reported in Posnett and Sandler (1989), Khanna et al (1995) and Khanna and Sandler (2000), using UK data and varying methodologies.

In these models, price, p, is typically derived as the implicit cost to the donor of raising the output of the nonprofit by £1. Thus,

$$p = (1-t)/[1-(f+a)]$$

where t is the marginal tax rate and f and a are respectively the proportion of total expenditure spent by the nonprofit on fundraising and administration.

Clearly the donations function is useful in explaining the performance of charities in terms of their ability to generate funds. However, given the objective of this present study, there are two extensions that appear warranted. First, it is important to recognise and estimate the potential importance of corporate governance and other monitoring mechanisms in stimulating donor contribution. While nonprofit characteristics such as age have been employed as proxies to test the impact of reputation, this is no substitute for the explicit testing of the effect of adopting specific governance mechanisms. Second, the donations function focuses relatively more on explaining the *quantity* aspect of nonprofit performance. Thus, there is a need for alternative specifications which explain the extent to which nonprofits are able to redistribute the donations received to the donor-intended beneficiaries. The passthrough functions, which focus relatively more on explaining these qualitative aspects are briefly considered next.

9.4.2 Passthrough functions

While not as commonly estimated as donations functions, passthrough functions provide an alternative way of explaining the performance of nonprofits. They are adapted from structure-conduct-performance (S-C-P)[11] type models. In estimating S-C-P models, some measure of firm performance or innovation is typically expressed as a function of market structure, as proxied by a measure of concentration in the market in which each firm competes. Feigenbaum (1987) utilises this framework in estimating nonprofit performance (passthrough rate) as a function of four-firm concentration ratios, controlling for other firm characteristics, such as age and size. She derives four-firm concentration ratios by focusing on US charities involved in the medical research funding 'industry' and which compete in one of seven metropolitan markets. Her results indicate a negative and significant impact of market concentration on passthrough rate, suggesting that higher competition for donations constrains nonprofit managers to spend less of the discretionary margin on expense-preference behaviour and more on reputation-enhancing behaviour. Size was hypothesised (and found) to be positively and significantly related to passthrough rate, which she attributes to the possibility that larger organisations attract more monitoring, both from donors and from the relevant government agencies. Finally, age was hypothesised (and found) to exert a negative and significant effect on the passthrough rate, which finding was attributed to likelihood that older organisations, having cultivated a reputation over time, appear more trustworthy and so might attract less monitoring by donors and the authorities.

The passthrough function is clearly useful in explaining the qualitative success of the nonprofit. However, despite efforts to reflect monitoring intensity via proxies such as age and size, the empirical model needs to be extended to explicitly incorporate the incentive-aligning and monitoring-engendering effects of corporate governance mechanisms. This is especially important for passthrough functions because, as highlighted in Section 4, the effectiveness of governance mechanisms can influence the discretionary margin available for managers to exploit via shirking or own-agenda activities and ultimately, the passthrough rate.

9.5 Empirical models and Estimation Procedure

This paper estimates corporate governance-augmented versions of both donations and passthrough functions with a view to explaining both the quantitative and qualitative aspects of nonprofits' performance.

The donations function estimated is of the form:

$$PIN_i = \alpha + \beta P_i + \gamma FEX_i + \lambda GIN_i + \vartheta AIN_i + \psi_i COG_i + \mu AGE_i + \phi SIZE_i + \varepsilon_i$$

---

[11] These go back to early work by Bain (1951), among others.

where the subscript i denotes charity i, and the explanatory variables are respectively, price, fundraising expenditure, government grants, autonomous income from investments, corporate governance, age, size and error term. *COG* is a vector of corporate governance variables that proxy for various aspects of monitoring, control and accountability. These include variables typically employed in the empirical corporate governance literature to depict the mechanisms put in place to align manager-owner/donor/board incentives, reduce agency costs and engender accountability. These include: board size (*TRUSTNO*), use of the recommended board committees for nominations, audit and remuneration (respectively the dummy variables: *NOMCO*, *AUDCO* and *REMCO*), chief executive remuneration (*CEOPAY*), audit quality (the dummy variable *AUDQUAL*) and "tied" funds ratio (that is, restricted-to-total funds ratio) (*REST*). In this equation, all the *COG* variables serve as signals to potential donors about the likelihood of the nonprofit to judiciously apply resources, and so an incentive to contribute. With the exception of *TRUSTNO*, all the corporate governance variables are hypothesised to exert a positive influence on private (or voluntary) income, *PIN*. *TRUSTNO* is expected to have a negative influence based on the premise that larger boards are more unwieldy, more likely to have "free-riding" trustees and more likely to shirk with respect to commitment to effective monitoring and control of senior management. The anticipated signs on the other variables are as suggested by demand theory and the crowding-out hypothesis, as highlighted in the studies reviewed in Section 5. Precise definitions of all variables and anticipated signs are provided in Table 1.

The passthrough function estimated is of the form:

$$PR = a + bFEX_i + cMEX_i + dAGE + eSIZE_i + fGOV_i + gFINV_i + gCOG + \mu_i$$

where the dependent variable *PR* is the passthrough rate and the explanatory variables are respectively fundraising expenditures, management expenditures, age, size, government grants, financial investments and corporate governance; μ_i is the error term[12]. Again, *COG* is a vector of corporate governance terms, as per earlier discussion. The fraction of donations successfully redistributed to recipients is hypothesised to depend on the level of fundraising and management expenditures as well as the strength of the monitoring and governance mechanisms in place to reduce incentives for managers to engage in expense-preference and or own-agenda behaviour. As in the donations function, all *COG* variables except *TRUSTNO* are expected to have a positive influence. *AGE* is expected to have a negative effect, following the argument in Feigenbaum (1987)

---

12   Note that this specification is not strictly S-C-P since it does not include market structure terms; rather it is more 'C-P', just as Feigenbaum's (1987) specification was more 'S-P'. The sample of nonprofits studied did not permit detailed market definitions.

cited above. *GIN* is intended to proxy for the intensity of external monitoring by government agencies and hypothesised to exert a positive effect on passthrough rate. However, it should be recognised that in some cases, especially true for NDPBs, government involvement usually means "outside" appointments and "meddling" by the government, a practice that could affect the dynamics of the existing board with possible negative effects on monitoring and control. *FINV* could also have a mixed effect depending on whether its effect is shown up as subtracting from the funds available for charitable purposes (negative) or as providing exposure to the governance practices of commercial enterprises (positive). *SIZE* controls for size effects and could also pick up any residual external monitoring effects, in line with the argument in Feigenbaum (1987) that larger nonprofits are likely to attract more monitoring. See Table 1 for a summary of variable definitions.

Table 1: Variable Definitions and Expected Signs

Variable	Definition	Expected Sign	
		Donations	Passthrough
PRICE	Implicit price of generating £1 of donations, calculated as $p = 1/[1-(f+a)]$	Negative	Na
FEX	Publicity and fundraising expenditures (£m)	Positive	Negative
MEX	Management and administration expenditures (£m)	Na	Negative
GIN	Public grants received; the sum of local and central government grants as well as lottery grants (£m)	Positive/negative	Positive/Negative
AIN	Autonomous income received from investments in financial assets, real estate, fees and charges and net income from non-charitable trading (£m)	Positive/negative	Na
FINV	Financial assets held (£m)	Na	Positive/Negative
AGE	Number of years since founding	Positive	Negative
SIZE	Total funds (£m)	Positive	Positive
REST	Total funds restricted (£m)	Positive	Positive
TRUSTNO	Number of trustees in post during financial year	Negative	Negative
NOMCO	1 = existence of a nominations committee	Positive	Positive
REMCO	1 = existence of a remuneration committee	Positive	Positive
AUDCO	1 = existence of an audit committee	Positive	Positive
CEOPAY	Annual remuneration of highest paid officer (£'000)	Positive	Positive
AUDQUAL	1 = audited by a Big Five auditor, as defined	Positive	Positive
MEMB	1 = existence of a membership-based structure	Positive	Positive

9.6 The Dataset and some Stylised Facts

9.6.1 Sources and nature of data

Estimation is based on two broad kinds of data, financial and governance. The financial data were obtained from the Top 100 UK charities ranked by income, extracted from *Dresdner RCM Global Investors Top 3000 Charities: The Guide to UK Charities* 2002. Based on these Top 100 charities, a matching governance dataset was then constructed, from a detailed manual inspection of the qualitative information provided in each individual charity's published annual report. Some features of these two broad sources are briefly described in turn.

The *Dresdner RCM Top 3000 Charities* financial data are compiled by CaritasData mainly from the annual reports of charities, in addition to supplementary information obtained directly by them from charities themselves and from the Charity Commissioners. The Top 100 charities comprise a very diverse group of nonprofits. They all have charitable status; however, they are not all charities in the conventional sense. Several are Non-Governmental Public Organisations (NGPBs) which tend to be "exempt" charities, and a few are "excepted" charities (both these groups do not have to register with or report to the Charity Commission)[13]. They operate in a wide range of "markets", covering: overseas aid, poverty, education, medical research, religion, disability, care of the elderly, arts and culture, children and disaster relief, among others. This data source has the advantage that the data have been adjusted and restated on a more comparable basis and also made more consistent with the reporting format implied by the Charities SORP. The focus on the Top 100 charities is because these charities are also more likely to have the variety and complexity that agency issues and governance mechanisms are more likely to be relevant for. Regarding the matching governance data, it is assumed that nonprofits that have established the key corporate governance mechanisms suggested by the various Reports and Standards, would disclose this fact in their annual reports. This is considered to be a plausible assumption because in recent years corporate governance has come to be viewed as a driving force for performance and accountability, and so charities that have adopted some or all of these mechanisms would take pride in reporting them to potential donors, recipients and their members.

---

[13] Exempt charities need not register with or report to the Charity Commission, but must still maintain proper accounts and make these available for public inspection, e.g. many NGPBs. Excepted charities also need not register with or report to the Charity Commission, being excepted by Order or Regulation; they must however also maintain proper accounts, e.g. many religious bodies. For further details see Charity Commission, at www.charity-commission.gov.uk.

Most of the financial data is as of March 31, 2001 and so the governance information is matched as closely as possible to prevailing arrangements as of that date. The governance dataset is particularly interesting because it captures the charity sector at a threshold of change in governance arrangements. Since the last few years, several of the larger and more complex charities have begun adopting business sector type governance mechanisms. This dataset therefore provides a unique opportunity to test the potential effect of this change, since it contains a good mix of charities which have adopted some or all of these mechanisms, and those which have not, as of March 31, 2000.

9.6.2 Stylised facts

Figures 1 to 12 present some stylised facts for the financial aspects of the nonprofits in the sample. Figures 1 to 5 depict the sources of income, while 6 to 9 provide highlights of the expenditure patterns. Figure 1 indicates that about 45% of the nonprofits obtain 10%, or less, of their income from private contributions. Many of these would tend to be NGPBs, typically museums, arts councils and organisations, examination bodies and academies; they generally receive more state support and or have scope to charge fees for their services. The "average" nonprofit obtains 26% from this source. Figure 2 indicates that autonomous income from investments (mainly securities and real estate) is not a significant source of income for most of the nonprofits, with nearly 80% of them obtaining 10% or less of income from this source.

Fig.1: Private (Voluntary) Income as % Total Income
Total Number of Charities: 100 Average: 26%

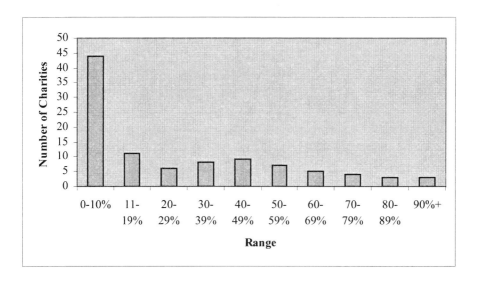

Fig.2: Autonomous (Investment) Income as % Total Income
Total Number of Charities: 100 Average: 10%

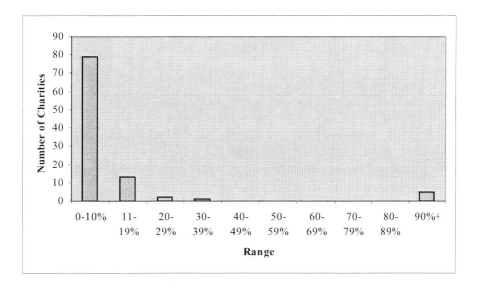

Note that autonomous income, in this narrow definition, excludes income from fees and charges, which are often implicitly state-influenced and protected. For example, charges by examination and assessment bodies and entrance fees for a museum. It also excludes income from commercial trading (charity shops, etc.). However, were these sources to be included, then in this broader definition of autonomous income, Figure 3 shows more income being generated autonomously, averaging 39% across the sample.

Fig.3: Autonomous (Investment+Fees+Trade) Income as % Total Income
Total Number of Charities: 100 Average: 39%

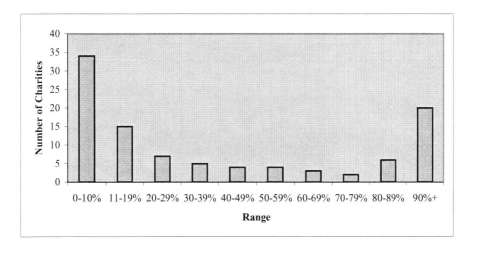

Fig.4: Public Grants Received as % Total Income
Total Number of Charities: 100 Average: 28%

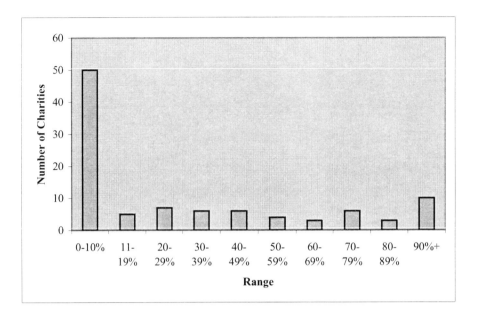

Figure 4 provides an indication of how much the nonprofits received in public grants. It shows that about half of them received 10% or less of their income from the government. These are typically the more "traditional" charities - poverty relief, hospitals, medical research, disability and religious organisations. As noted earlier, NGPBs receive a higher level of government funding, with about 10 of them receiving 90% or more of their income from the state. The "average" nonprofit in the sample obtained 28% of its funding from the government. The possible monitoring implications of the level of government support were considered briefly in Section 6. Subsequently, among other things, the study tests the hypothesis that the higher the *fraction* of income provided by the government, the higher the intensity of monitoring provided by government agencies is likely to be and that this will have a salutary effect on the passthrough rate.

Figure 5 shows the proportion of their income that the nonprofits obtain from legacies. It indicates that this is not a significant source for most of them, with close to 80% deriving 10% or less. The average share of legacies in revenue generation is 7% across the sample.

Fig.5: Legacy Income as % Total Income
Total Number of Charities: 100 Average: 7%

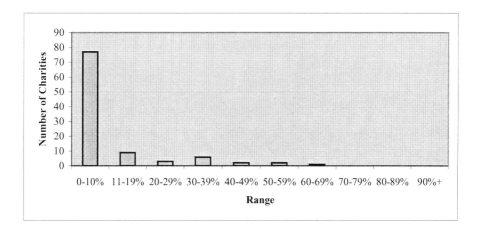

In the next set of figures, the study highlights how the nonprofits allocated their expenditures across charitable and non-charitable purposes. A key test of the effectiveness of a charity is how much it spends on its primary objects. In Figure 6, it is shown that 43% of the nonprofits spent 90% or more of their total expenditure on charitable purposes. These highest spenders tend to cut across different types (and purposes), indicating that the proportion spent on the primary charitable purpose is down to individual management and governance practices, rather than the "market" they operate in or where they get their income from. It averages 82% across the sample.

Fig.6: Charitable Expenditure as % Total Expenditure
Total Number of Charities: 100 Average: 82%

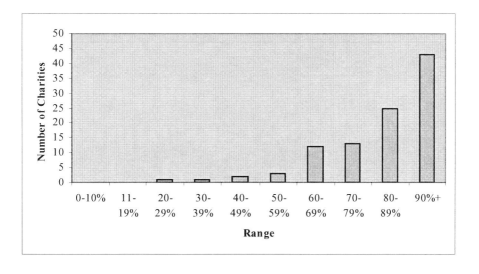

Fig.7: Passthrough Rate - Charitable Expenditure as % Total Income
Total Number of Charities: 100 Average: 78%

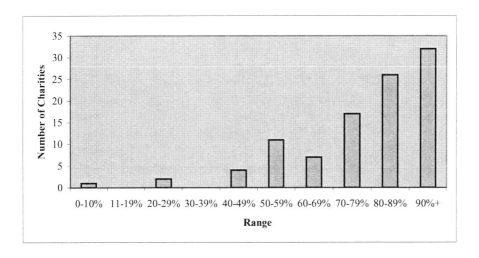

In keeping with earlier discussions in Sections 5 and 6, it is perhaps more instructive to look at what fraction of *income* generated is ultimately redistributed to the recipients in whose name it was collected. In other words, the passthrough rate. Figure 7 provides the passthrough rate for the sample. In comparison with Figure 6, the charities do not perform quite as well, with the highest spending category now comprised of 32, compared to 43 observed previously, using expenditure shares. Also, the average passthrough rate is 78%, lower than the 82% charitable expenditure share average. The passthrough rate is lower because it is a fraction of income, which is usually higher than expenditure. That is, most nonprofits in the sample have a positive net revenue (total income minus total expenditure) which, in principle, goes to boost reserves. Plausibly, when nonprofits accumulate reserves, they are thus strengthened and better positioned to deliver on their charitable objects in the future. However, from a governance and accountability point of view, this has got to be balanced against the possibility that reserves are aimed at managerial empire building rather than for the benefit of intended recipients and the concern that donors' immediate intention to reach the beneficiary is thus truncated. It is at least partly these concerns that motivated the SORP to stipulate that charities clearly enunciate their unrestricted reserves policy and justify their level of reserves in their published annual accounts[14].

---

14 See Hind (1995), Chapter 9, for a discussion on charity reserves policy; and in fact the rest of the book for details on the operations of UK charities.

Fig.8: Fundraising Expenditure as % Total Expenditure
Total Number of Charities: 100 Average: 5%

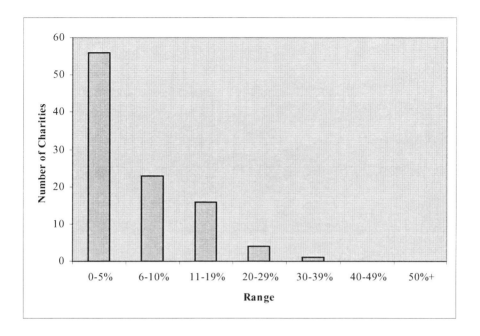

Related to the foregoing is the issue of how much charities spend on publicity and fundraising expenditures. In general, the more that is spent on fundraising, the less that will be available to meet charitable objects. But just like the above issue with reserves, there is a balance to be struck between ensuring that adequate resources are deployed to facilitate on-going revenue generation and at the same time achieving a "reasonable" passthrough to beneficiaries. For the nonprofits in the sample, well over half of them spend 5% or less on fundraising, averaging 5% across all 100, as depicted in Figure 8.

Fig 9: Total Expenditure
Total Number of Charities: 100 Average: 4%

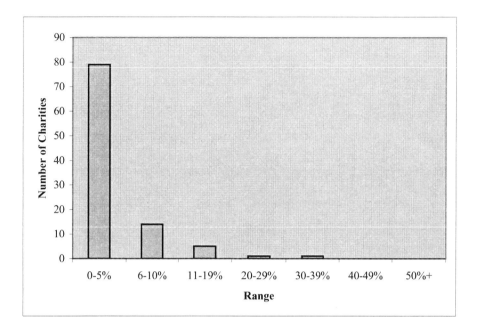

Figure 9 provides comparable information for management and administration expenses; it indicates that about 80% of the nonprofits spend 5% or less on management expenses, averaging 4%. Again, it is stressed that there is no one acceptable share of management costs, with each charity needing to balance management capacity building with achieving a reasonable passthrough to beneficiaries. Taken together, these stylised facts show that on average the charities in the sample devoted less than 10% of expenditures to fundraising *and* management costs. It is often suggested that this ratio should ideally not exceed between 20 and 30%[15]. On this index, it seems that the charities in the sample have on average performed well. This may be attributed to the fact that the charities in the sample tend to be relatively large, with the possibility for economies of scale in fundraising and management costs. Further, many of them are NGPBs with the implication that they need to spend less on fundraising activities since they do not depend mainly on voluntary contributions. On the other hand, smaller charities rely more on voluntary contributions and so may need to spend proportionately more on publicity and fundraising activities.

---

15 See for example, Hind (1995).

Figures 10 and 11 provide a summary of how the "average" charity in the sample raised its income, and how its spending priorities were ordered, respectively.

Fig.10: Sources of Income for "Average" Charity in Sample

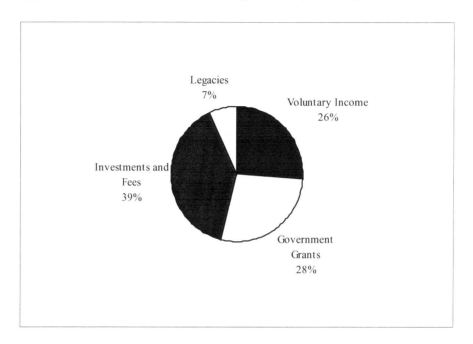

Fig.11: Spending Behaviour of 'Average' Charity in Sample

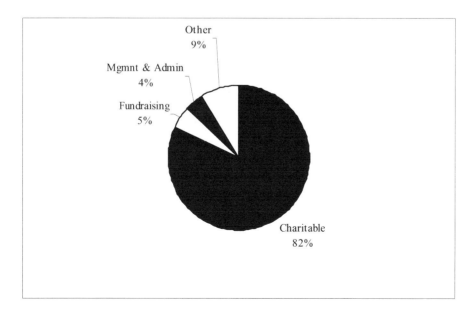

Taking a close look at Figures 10 and 11, one might contend that government grants, investment income and legacies tend to be relatively more stable or predictable sources of funding than voluntary income. It is arguable therefore that publicity and fundraising expenditures (and in fact, reserves coverage) are really mainly needed for the more volatile voluntary donations. Figure 12 therefore recasts the information in the context of how much voluntary income is raised per pound spent on fundraising[16]. It indicates that about three quarters of the sample received £10 or less per £ spent on fundraising, averaging £12 across the sample, less glowing than the 5% fundraising expenditure share suggested.

Fig.12: Voluntary Income Raised Per £ of Fundraising Expenditure
Total Number of Charities: 76   Average: £12

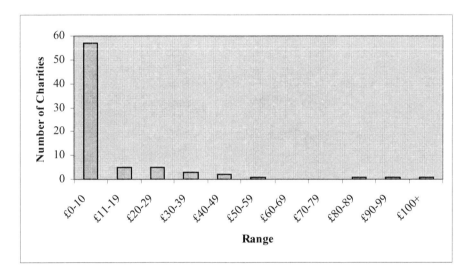

Next the study presents some stylised facts on the corporate governance characteristics of the nonprofits in the sample. Clearly, it is a difficult task to adequately reflect the rich variety of governance structures and processes that characterise the nonprofit sector. In spite of this constraint, the annual reports of the sampled charities yield information that is useful in characterising governance practices. Figures 13 to 16 highlight some of these. The size of the board of directors, as represented by the number of trustees, is depicted in Figure 13. It shows that about half the sample have between 10 and 19 trustees on their boards, with an overall average of 21. This is larger than the average of 11 members reported in the survey-based FitzGerald (2001) and larger than the 12 - 15 commonly recommended for charities. This is likely to be due to the relatively larger size and possibly the complexity of the nonprofits sampled. Generally,

---

16   Note that the sample in this case reduces to 76 because there are a number of (mainly NGPBs) charities that have zero fundraising expenditure and zero voluntary contributions.

larger boards are seen as unwieldy and less governance- (and performance) friendly.

Fig.13: Board Size - Number of Trustees
Total Number of Charities: 87   Average: 21

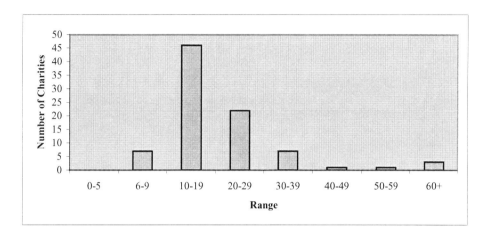

Fig.14: Chief Executive Remuneration
Total Number of Charities: 76   Average: £105,000

	% Legacies		%Exp Charitable
0-10%	77	0-10%	0 0-10%
11-19%	9	11-19%	0 11-19%
20-29%	3	20-29%	1 20-29%
30-39%	6	30-39%	1 30-39%
40-49%	2	40-49%	2 40-49%
50-59%	2	50-59%	3 50-59%
60-69%	1	60-69%	12 60-69%
70-79%	0	70-79%	13 70-79%
80-89%	0	80-89%	25 80-89%

Table 14 shows the estimated pay of chief executives of nonprofits. The annual reports indicate how many employees are in wage bands starting from £40,000 and above. It is assumed that the chief executive is the highest paid employee (and so in the highest wage band), and that he or she earns the upper end of that band. The amount (and the structure) of CEO pay is seen as a key incentive-aligning mechanism and so an important governance indicator. Figure 14 indicates that about half the charities pay their CEOs between £80,000 and

£110,000, with an overall average of £105,000. Whether pay level acts as an incentive to stimulate CEO (and overall managerial) performance, reduce shirking and feed through to enhanced fundraising and or passthrough rate is ultimately to be decided from subsequent empirical estimation.

Fig.15: Discretion Over Funds: Restricted Funds as % Total Funds
Total Number of Charities: 76   Average: 37%

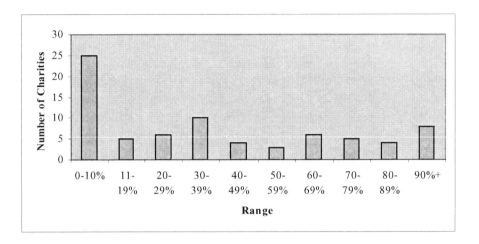

Clearly, where donors specify what use contributed funds are to be put to, agency issues between donors and trustees/managers are thereby curtailed and this would ultimately be reflected in a higher passthrough rate. Figure 15 provides an estimate of the discretion enjoyed by trustees and senior management in terms of the deployment of the funds of the charity, as shown by the fraction of total funds represented by tied or restricted funds. For about a third of the sample, restricted funds represent 10% or less, with an overall average of 37%, of total funds. This suggests that, for this sample, trustees and managers have a wide discretion over funds and so the *potential* for misuse and shirking is present.

Figure 16 summarises a set of mechanisms and structures that are viewed as governance- (and performance) enhancing, if adopted by the nonprofit. The first three "stacks" are the three board/management committees recommended by the Cadbury Committee and since widely adopted by private sector firms[17]. Briefly, they relate to the recruitment of the 'right' trustees, ensuring financial probity and transparency and managing the pay and incentives of senior management, respectively. The constitution of these committees is clearly important as well.

---

[17] Note that some of the governance mechanisms prescribed by business-based committees such as Cadbury were also recommended by public sector-based ones. For example, the Cabinet Office's (1997), *Guidance on Codes of Practice for Board Members of Public Bodies* recommended the establishment of Audit Committees.

One broad principle is that the CEO should not be too involved in them, and certainly should not be on the remuneration committee. This is buttressed by the fact that the committees should provide a useful forum for trustees to meet and interact with other employees, without being "teleguided" by the CEO. They are therefore an important check on the CEO. Consistent and detailed information on the composition of these committees is not available for the sample. However, the study is able to identify which organisations have reported the use of any of these committees.

Fig.16: Governance Committees Adopted and Other Governance Features

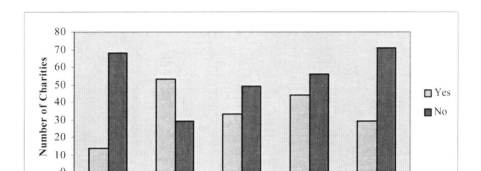

Of the 82 nonprofits that gave committee-related information in their annual report and accounts, only 17% indicated having a nominations committee, while 65% and 40% reported having an audit and a remuneration committee, respectively. Clearly there is some way to go still in terms of the adoption of the nominations and remuneration committee. It is more than likely that some of the roles expected of the committees are being at least partly provided by some other mechanism. For example, some charities have committees called "executive" or "general" that fuse some of these roles. Thus, the argument is not that these roles are not being performed at all; rather it is that setting up a 'dedicated' committee to handle the respective issues sends a signal of commitment to monitoring, control and accountability that the board, managers and donors are likely to respond to. Interestingly, the rather slow pattern of adoption of the nominations committee mirrors the experience in the business sector. For example, Conyon and Mallin (1997) found that while 98% of the sampled 298 large British quoted companies by market value had implemented audit and remuneration committee proposals by 1995, only 51% had complied with the nomination committee recommendation. One explanation for this experience might be that a nominations committee effectively takes away board recruitment from the CEO. While trustee recruitment is usually a board-level decision, in practice many CEOs are also actively involved in the process. Thus, established CEOs, whether in the nonprofit or for-profit sector, could see the committee as a threat to their power base, and so would be slower in urging the adoption of that aspect of governance reforms.

The last two "stacks" in Figure 16 indicate two governance characteristics that could potentially enhance monitoring, accountability and transparency. For example, organisations that are membership-based have certain advantages. First, such membership would tend to include present or potential recipients, donors and other interested stakeholders. Thus, their involvement provides an opportunity for trustees and managers to gauge the requirements of their stakeholders and so enrich their fundraising practices and passthrough rate to ultimate beneficiaries. Second, in many cases, members have the opportunity to vote for trustee re-(appointment) at annual general meetings, thus providing an extra level of scrutiny and accountability. On audit quality, better quality audits should provide more accurate and reliable information to donors and recipients, and in fact to all stakeholders, thereby enhancing accountability. It is assumed that auditors with the most experience are likely to provide better quality audit. Dresdner RCM Top 3000 Charities provides a ranking of the Top 100 charity auditors. Thus, if a charity is audited by any of the "Big Five" [18], it is considered as having a better quality audit. The experience from the nonprofits sampled is that about 30% of them have a membership of one form or another while 44% may be considered as having relatively better audit quality, as defined.

Overall, the stylised facts discussed in the foregoing facilitate a characterisation of the financial and governance aspects of the large nonprofits studied, in the context of the theories and governance standards highlighted in the earlier sections. With a relatively large board size, large discretionary "margin" over funds and the slow adoption of the recommended board committees, the "average" charity in the sample seems to have only modestly adopted the typical governance prescriptions. However, with an average passthrough rate that is close to 80%, many would contend that the nonprofits sampled perform well on the financial side. This raises the question of what role corporate governance mechanisms played in this process, ultimately answered by recourse to the empirical evidence.

---

[18] "Big Five" in this case refers to the Top 5 auditors by number of charity clients. These include PricewaterhouseCoopers, Baker Tilly, KPMG, Horwath Clark Whitehill and Delloite & Touche.

9.7 Empirical Results

Prior to estimation, Table 2 depicts the estimated correlation among the corporate governance variables. Generally, there is relatively low correlation among the variables, most with an absolute value of around 0.10. The only noticeable exception is *REMCO* which has a correlation of 0.48 with *AUDCO* and 0.33 with *CEOPAY*; *REMCO* is therefore excluded in the econometric estimation, to avoid potential difficulties with disentangling its separate effect.

Table 2: Estimated Correlation Matrix of Corporate Governance Variables

	TRUSTNO	MEMB	REMCO	NOMCO	AUDCO	AUDQUAL	CEOPAY
TRUSTNO	1.000						
MEMB	0.289	1.000					
REMCO	-0.088	-0.126	1.000				
NOMCO	0.087	0.000	0.172	1.000			
AUDCO	-0.130	-0.073	0.482	0.094	1.000		
AUDQUAL	0.118	0.157	0.258	0.085	-0.002	1.000	
CEOPAY	-0.003	-0.096	0.333	0.104	0.245	0.165	1.000

The results from the estimation of the donations function are presented in Table 3. Model 1 gives the results for the "base" model[19], i.e. the typical donations function, in the spirit of Khanna and Sandler (2000), Okten and Weisbrod (2000) and others, controlling for age and size. Model 2 then investigates the potential impact of the adoption of some recommended corporate governance mechanisms, for example by signaling that the nonprofit is more likely to make judicious use of funds raised. The model also estimates the impact of other governance and accountability structures such as *REST*, *AUDQUAL* and *MEMB* which are other means by which the nonprofit may signal good governance. Model 3 re-estimates Model 2 in a more parsimonious form, by dropping from the latter any variables with t-ratio of 0.5 or less[20].

The final estimates in Model 3 indicate that *PRICE* has a negative and significant effect, in line with the theory of demand. Also, *FEX* is positive and significant, indicating that fundraising expenditures stimulate voluntary contributions, a result that mirrors the role of advertising for commercial enterprises. There is some evidence for crowding-out, both for government grants and for autonomous income, albeit not significant for the former. The significant crowding out effect

---

19 Note that *PRICE* is computed as $p = 1/[1-(f+a)]$, following Posnett and Sandler (1989), Khanna et al (1995) and Khanna and Sandler (2000).

20 There was no indication of heteroscedasticity or other econometric problems.

of income from investments, fees and charges suggests that the availability of such autonomous income implies less effort by the nonprofit to generate voluntary income and also signals to potential donors that control over resources could be less strict, especially where such funds are unrestricted. *AGE* is positively and significantly related to the level of voluntary income generated, confirming the intuition that older nonprofits have accumulated experience in fund raising which they bring to bear in stimulating voluntary contributions.

Table 3: Parameter Estimates: Donations Function

	Model 1		Model 2		Model 3	
	Coefficient	*t-ratio*	*Coefficient*	*t-ratio*	*Coefficient*	*t-ratio*
CONST	41.60	0.82	112.55	2.16*	110.51	2.19*
PRICE	-32.08	-0.68	-97.97	-2.05*	-97.28	-2.08*
FEX	2.60	3.21*	2.66	3.31*	2.63	3.33*
GIN	-0.04	-0.35	-0.08	-0.74	-0.09	-0.82
AIN	1.39	1.39	-0.21	-1.76	-0.23	-2.32*
AGE	0.08	2.39*	0.07	2.18*	0.07	2.22*
SIZE	-0.04	-1.40	0.04	1.08	0.04	1.13
REST	-	-	-0.04	-0.97	-0.04	-1.02
TRUSTNO	-	-	-0.18	-0.68	-0.15	-0.62
NOMCO	-	-	20.08	1.94*	20.32	2.01*
AUDCO	-	-	6.83	0.91	6.21	0.87
CEOPAY	-	-	-29.49	-0.32	-	-
AUDQUAL	-	-	10.28	1.48	10.24	1.52
MEMB	-	-	2.75	0.37	-	-
N	81		81		81	
$\bar{R}^2$	0.20		0.24		0.26	

*Significant at 10% or better

SIZE also exerts a positive influence, suggesting the presence of economies of scale in fund generation, although it is not significant. *REST* (restricted funds) exhibits a counterintuitive negative sign. Being an indication of the funds that are restricted as to purpose (and so their disbursement are in line with donors' wishes), one would expect *REST* to be a positive signal to potential donors. One possible explanation for this is that while *REST* may signal the disposition of funds already generated (being a cumulative balance), it does not say much about how funds generated today will be disbursed, unless similarly restricted by the donors.

In terms of the corporate governance mechanisms adopted, they mostly exhibit the expected signs. *TRUSTNO* has a negative, though not significant, effect, while *NOMCO*, *AUDCO* and *AUDQUAL* are all positive[21]. Thus, the adoption of some of the recommended key corporate governance mechanisms would be salutary for the generation of voluntary income. The greatest (statistically significant) impact would come from the setting up of a nominations committee (*NOMCO*). Again, this is plausible because the nominations committee influences who gets appointed to the board in the first place and so potentially sets the tone for all other board mechanisms and practices. It visibly takes the role of trustee appointment away from the CEO, who in practice wields considerable influence in the process. In the words of ACENVO (1998):

> *"The operational reality, especially for large national charities, is often that of effective control being to all intents and purposes in the hands of the chief executive, leaving the chair and trustees exposed to the management practices and perspectives of the chief executive"* (p.30).

How do these results compare to prior findings? There is no directly comparable evidence because the existing UK donations functions do not consider the effect of corporate governance and they also use different specifications, methods and data coverage. However, the "base" (non-governance) part of the model accords largely with the near-unanimous full-sample evidence in UK studies such as Sandler (1989), Khanna et al (1995) and Khanna and Sandler (2000), with price and fundraising expenditures having similar signs and significance. There is more variation (across all studies) in terms of crowding-in (-out), both from government grants and from autonomous income, due possibly to the differences highlighted above[22].

Table 4 presents the estimates of the passthrough function. Here, the emphasis is on monitoring and control. Specifically, given the amount of income raised (from all sources), what mechanisms and structures influence how much of that income is ultimately passed through to intended beneficiaries. As in the donations functions above, the approach is to first present the "base" model estimates in Model 1 and then in Model 2 to add the influences from corporate governance mechanisms, and in Model 3 to present more parsimonious estimates having dropped variables with t-ratios of 0.5 or less. Expectedly, fundraising and management expenses negatively affect the passthrough rate, significantly so in the case of fundraising expenditures. Age exerts a negative and significant effect. This lends support to the view that older charities have built up a reputation over the years which leads donors and regulators to believe they require less

---

[21] Note from Model 2 that *CEOPAY* has a negative but insignificant effect; perhaps suggesting that donors view higher executive pay in the same light as perquisites and so are discouraged from contributing.

[22] No problems are suggested regarding heteroscedasticity or other econometric issues.

monitoring. As a result, the discretionary margin is likely to increase with age, ultimately leading to a lower passthrough rate.

Table 4: Parameter Estimates: Passthrough Function

	Model 1		Model 2		Model 3	
	Coefficient	*t-ratio*	*Coefficient*	*t-ratio*	*Coefficient*	*t-ratio*
CONST	0.86	28.17*	0.85	13.32*	0.84	15.92*
FEX	-0.01	-3.19*	-0.01	-2.43*	-0.01	-2.46*
MEX	-0.003	-0.61	-0.002	-0.39	-	-
AGE	-0.0005	-2.72*	-0.0005	-2.67*	-0.0005	-2.89*
SIZE	0.00006	3.05*	-0.0001	-0.40	-	-
GIN	-	-	0.0004	0.62	0.0003	0.49
FINV	-	-	-0.0002	-1.21	-0.0002	-1.57
REST	-	-	0.0003	1.46	0.0003	1.95*
TRUSTNO	-	-	-0.0002	-0.12	-	-
NOMCO	-	-	-0.07	-1.27	-0.09	-1.63
AUDCO	-	-	-0.03	-0.78	-0.03	-0.80
CEOPAY	-	-	0.46	1.02	0.47	1.10
AUDQUAL	-	-	0.01	0.28	-	-
MEMB	-	-	-0.01	-0.21	-	-
N	81		81		81	
$\bar{R}^2$	0.27		0.26		0.30	

*Significant at 10% or better

Size was hypothesised to exert a positive influence because larger charities are expected to attract greater scrutiny by donors and regulators. This was corroborated in Model 1, but once corporate governance effects are directly reflected in (Models 2 and 3), size becomes insignificant. *GIN* and *FINV* are incorporated to reflect the potential effect of external supervision and exposure. The more grants supplied by the government to a charity, the more likely that government will be involved in monitoring, either through the usual bodies (for example, Charity Commission) or more directly via appointments to the board, etc. *GIN* shows a positive but weak effect on the passthrough rate. The effect of *FINV* is negative but insignificant. The negative sign on it suggests that the acquisition of financial assets substitutes for charitable spending and that the potential positive governance effects are not enough to reverse this. *REST* was expected to, and in Model 3 shows, a positive and significant effect on the passthrough rate. It is clearly plausible that the more funds are purpose-restricted by donors, the less the discretionary margin available to charity managers and the higher the passthrough rate will be. In terms of the adoption of governance mechanisms, the results are somewhat mixed. For example, *TRUSTNO*, *CEOPAY* and *AUDQUAL* show the expected signs while *AUDCO* and *NOMCO* display counterintuitive signs. In any case, they tend to be statistically insignificant, suggesting that once the basic spending pattern is recognised, and some basic governance structure (e.g. restricting the use to which funds may be put) is in place, there is little additional explanatory power from the adoption of governance committees in this (passthrough) regard.

Overall, the econometric estimates indicate that corporate governance mechanisms could have an important role to play in the *generation* of funds by nonprofits. This operates via the fact that the adoption of these mechanisms signals to potential donors that the organisation is positioned to undertake the successful distribution of their contributions to the intended recipients. In terms of explaining the actual *redistribution* done, governance committees provide weak (and conflicting) additional effects. However, governance structures that encourage donors and regulators (and perhaps charities themselves) to purpose-restrict contributions would reduce nonprofit managers' discretionary margins and improve the redistribution rate.

9.8 Summary and Conclusion

Nonprofits, like all professionally managed organisations, face agency type governance and accountability problems, along with the asymmetric information and moral hazard issues that under lie these problems. However, the nature of most nonprofits is such that these problems may be tempered, or at least different, from those encountered by businesses. For example, it is a view often expressed that nonprofit managers are more committed to the causes espoused by the charities they manage and that they are less motivated by financial incentives. Given this background, this study examines the performance implications of the adoption of conventional corporate governance mechanisms, using a sample comprised of the 100 highest earning nonprofits in the UK where governance concerns are likely to be very relevant. The performance indicators employed are "bottom line" ones which ask how much the nonprofit generates in income and how much of that income is redistributed to intended beneficiaries. The corporate governance indicators are a mixture of "traditional" mechanisms such as the purpose-restriction of donations, and the rate of adoption of recently recommended governance committees. After controlling for other phenomena such as age, size, crowding-out effects and so on, the empirical evidence suggests that the adoption of the recommended governance committees could be important factors driving how much large nonprofits are able to raise in donations. This is especially significant where the nominations committee is adopted. On the issue of how much of the income raised is redistributed to ultimate beneficiaries, traditional governance structures such as the purpose-restriction of fund uses by donors are highlighted.

The broad implication of these findings is that even though nonprofits face agency and governance issues that may be different from those encountered by business, they would do well to accelerate the pace at which the recommended mechanisms are implemented, especially the nominations committee. These seem to signal to donors that the nonprofit is positioned to ensure that their contributions would be judiciously employed. At the same time, in ensuring that donors' preferences are attained, purpose-restriction and the other more traditional characteristics of the sector (for example, trustee/manager commitment, non-remunerated trusteeship) would continue to play an important role. These are some of the un-modeled factors that no doubt contributed to the delivery of an average 80% passthrough rate for the sample. This pilot paper is probably the first to empirically assess the implications of corporate governance for performance, at least for UK nonprofits and there is clearly scope for further research in this area. Several possible extensions are indicated. First, the extension of the sample to include more large and medium sized nonprofits. Second, the creation and application of a matching comprehensive database of governance practices, to bring out more details on board-CEO relations, chairman-CEO relations, and individual trustee and CEO characteristics. Third, the application of alternative econometric methods and specifications.

References

ACENVO (1998), *Partners in Leadership*, Harrow, Middlesex: ACENVO (Association of Chief Executives of National Voluntary Organisations).

Alchian, A. A. and H. Demsetz (1972), Production, information costs and economic organisation, *American Economic Review*, vol. 62, pp. 777-795.

Andreoni, James (1988), Privately provided public goods in a large economy: The limits of altruism, *Journal of Public Economics*, vol. 35, pp. 57-73.

Andreoni, James (1989), Giving with impure altruism: Applications to charity and Ricardian equivalence, *Journal of Political Economy*, vol. 97, no. 6, pp. 1447-1458.

Andreoni, James (1998), Towards a theory of charitable giving, *Journal of Political Economy*, vol. 106, no. 6, pp. 1186-1213.

Bain, Joe S. (1951), Relation of profit-rate to industry concentration: American manufacturing, 1936-1940, *Quarterly Journal of Economics*, vol. 65, pp. 293-324.

Becker, G. (1974), A theory of social interactions, *Journal of Political Economy*, vol. 82, pp. 1063 - 1094.

Bergstrom, T., L. Blume and H. Varian (1986), On the private provision of public goods, *Journal of Public Economics*, vol. 29, pp. 25-49.

Berle, A. and G. Means (1932), *The Modern Corporation and Private Property*. New York: Macmillan.

Bruce, Alistair and Trevor Buck (1997), Executive reward and corporate governance, in eds. Kevin Keasey, Steve Thompson and Mike Wright, *Corporate Governance: Economic, Management and Financial Issues*, Oxford: Oxford University Press.

Cabinet Office (1997), *Guidance on Codes of Practice for Board Members of Public Bodies*, Cabinet Office, available at: www.archive.official-documents.co.uk/caboff

Cadbury, A. (1992), *Report of the Committee on the Financial Aspects of Corporate Governance,* London: Gee Publishing.

Coase, R. (1937), *The Nature of the Firm*, Economica, vol. 4, pp. 386-405.

Committee on Corporate Governance (1998), *The Combined Code, London Stock Exchange Limited*. London: Gee Publishing.

Conyon, Martin and C. Mallin (1997), A review of compliance with Cadbury, *Journal of General Management*, vol. 2, no. 3, pp. 24-37.

Cornes, R. and T. Sandler (1996), *The Theory of Externalities, Public Goods and Club Goods*, second edition, Cambridge: Cambridge University Press.

Dresdner RCM Global Investors (2002), *Top 3000 Charities: The Guide to UK Charities*, London: CaritasData Limited.

Fama, E. F. (1980), Agency problems and the theory of the firm, *Journal of Political Economy*, vol. 88, no. 2, pp. 288-307.

Fama, E. F. and M. C. Jensen (1983), Separation of ownership and control, *Journal of Law and Economics*, vol. XXVI, pp. 301-325.

Feigenbaum, Susan (1987), Competition and performance in the nonprofit sector: The case of US medical research charities, *Journal of Industrial Economics*, vol. 35, no. 3, pp. 241-253.

FitzGerald, Paddy (2001), *Corporate Governance in the Public and Voluntary Sectors*, Bristol: Royal Society of Arts, available at www.rsa.org.

Frech, H. E., III (1976), The property rights theory of the firm: Empirical results from a natural experiment, *Journal of Political Economy*, vol. 84, no. 1, pp. 143-152.

Glazer, Amihai and Kai A. Konrad (1996), A signaling explanation for charity, *American Economic Review*, vol. 86, no. 4, pp. 1019-1028.

Greenbury, R. (1995), *Directors' Remuneration: Report of a Study Group Chaired by Sir Richard Greenbury*. London: Gee Publishing.

Hampel, R. (1998), *Committee on Corporate Governance: Final report*. London: Gee Publishing.

Harbaugh, William T. (1998), What do donations buy? A model of philanthropy based on prestige and warm glow, *Journal of Public Economics*, vol. 67, pp. 269-284.

Hart, O. (1995), Corporate governance: Some theory and implications, *Economic Journal*, vol. 105, pp. 678-689.

Hart, O. (1996), *Firms, Contracts and Financial Structure*. Oxford: Oxford University Press.

Hind, Andrew (1995), *The Governance and Management of Charities*, High Barnet, Herts.: The Voluntary Sector Press Ltd.

HM Treasury (2001), *Executive NDPBs Annual Reports and Accounts Guidance*, London: HM Treasury, Central Accountancy Team, available at: www.hm-treasury.gov.uk.

Jensen, M. C. and W. H. Meckling (1976), Theory of the firm: managerial behaviour, agency costs and ownership structure, *Journal of Financial Economics*, vol. 3, pp. 305-360.

Khanna, Jyoti, John Posnett and Todd Sandler (1995), Charity donations in the UK: New evidence based on panel data, *Journal of Public Economics*, vol. 56, pp. 257-272.

Khanna, Jyoti and Todd Sandler (2000), Partners in giving: The crowding-in effects of UK government grants, *European Economic Review*, vol. 44, pp. 1543-1556.

Nolan Committee (1994), *Committee on Standards in Public Life, First Report*, London: HMSO.

Nolan Committee (1997), *Review of Standards of Conduct in Executive NDPBs, NHS Trusts and Local Public Spending Bodies, Fourth report*, London: HMSO.

Okten, Cagla and Burton A. Weisbrod (2000), Determinants of donations in private nonprofit markets, *Journal of Public Economics*, vol. 75, pp. 255-272.

Olson, M. (1965), *The Logic of Collective Action*, Cambridge, MA: Harvard University Press,

Posnett, John and Todd Sandler (1989), Demand for charity donations in private non-profit markets: The case of the UK, *Journal of Public Economics*, vol. 40, pp. 187-200.

Preyra, Colin and George Pink (2001), Balancing incentives in the compensation contracts of nonprofit hospital CEOs, *Journal of Health Economics*, vol. 20, pp. 509-525.

Rediker, K. J. and A. Seth (1995), Boards of directors and substitution effects of alternative governance mechanisms, *Strategic Management Journal*, vol. 16, pp. 85-99.

Roberts, A. (1984), A positive model of private charity and public transfers, *Journal of Political Economy*, vol. 92, pp. 136-148.

Romano, Richard and Huseyin Yildirim (2001), Why charities announce donations: A positive perspective, *Journal of Public Economics*, vol. 81, pp. 423-447.

Rose-Ackerman, Susan (1987), Ideals versus dollars: Donors, charity managers and government grants, *Journal of Political Economy*, vol. 95, no. 2, pp. 810-823.

Shleifer, A. and R. W. Vishny (1997), A survey of corporate governance, *Journal of Finance*, vol. LII, no. 2, pp. 737-783.

SORP (1995 and 2000), *Statement of Recommended Practice on Accounting and Reporting by Charities*, Charity Commission, available at: www.charity-commission.gov.uk.

Sugden, Robert (1982), On the economics of philanthropy, *Economic Journal*, vol. 92, no. 366, pp. 341-350.

Turnbull Committee (1999), *Internal Control: Guidance for Directors on the Combined Code*, London: Institute of Chartered Accountants in England and Wales.

Warr, P. (1982), Pareto optimal redistribution and private charity, *Journal of Public Economics*, vol. 19, pp. 131-138.

Weisbrod, Burton A. and Nestor D. Dominguez (1986), Demand for collective goods in private nonprofit markets: Can fundraising expenditures help overcome free-rider behaviour? *Journal of Public Economics*, vol. 30, pp. 83-95.

Williamson, O. E., (1988), Corporate finance and corporate governance, *Journal of Finance*, XLIII, 3, 567-591.

Summary 3

STRATEGY OR MANAGEMENT BY TRUSTEES

Trustee Liability: Clarity

- Greater clarity is needed on how the law affects trustees and the directors of charitable companies differently. Particular clarification is needed regarding the delegation of functions.

- Greater awareness must be generated within charities of the need to incorporate clear delegation policies and procedures into governing documents.

Trustee Liability: Effect

- Personal liability and the SORP guidelines are both sources of concern for trustees, probably exacerbated by trustee indemnity insurance marketing. This concern can affect how trustees exercise their powers of delegation.

- In some circumstances it may cause trustees to delegate functions such as investment more readily to experts.

- In others it may have the opposite effect of causing trustees to be more hesitant to delegate functions generally.

Board Dynamics and Influence

- Current advice on dealing with board conflicts is aimed at the board as a whole, yet conflict by its very nature breaks down the collective body and isolates members. More advice aimed at individual trustees is needed.

- Guidance is needed on constructive handling of experts who are board members, particularly on how to incorporate appropriate challenge mechanisms.

- Where charities become involved in seeking funding from external bodies there is a danger that they may become 'funding-led'. Boards need to be aware of this and ensure that their strategy does not become distorted and divert from the charity's purposes.

Board Conflicts: Mediation

- There were different opinions on the best course of action where there was conflict between the Board and Chief Executive Officer. There was some support for the idea of mediation, for a number of reasons. As well as introducing a neutral third party to the equation, it may avoid the expense of litigation and preserve the reputation of the charity and the trustees by resolving the conflict before too much public awareness is generated.

- However, mediation needs to be used to facilitate the creation of a new strategy, rather than just to solve current problems. In this way it can solve the root issues and prevent similar problems from occurring in the future.

Time Limited Posts

- The possibility of limiting the length of tenure for trustees, chairs and Chief Executives may be a method of preventing stagnation and conflicts, but there are a number of complicating factors.

- If changes are made too often, the kudos and 'historic pull' of the organisation may be affected. Whilst this can be a negative consequence in some circumstances, in others it is a positive and necessary step forward. Some felt that whilst limiting the Chair's length of tenure would be useful, the same would not apply to the post of Chief Executive.

- Methods of preventing stagnation, such as tenure limitations and skills audits assume that there is a free choice of trustees. It is important when considering such strategies to note the current trustee (and particularly chair) recruitment problem.

- The tendency of trustees boards towards tact and therefore hesitancy in removing long-serving trustees should also be noted.

Board Appointments

- There is a need for trustee guidance on good practice and potential problems when appointing new trustees who have been introduced by Chief Executive Officers.

Corporate Governance

- Elements of corporate governance, especially nominations committee can be very effective for large charities.

- Development of good governance would be encouraged if accounts had to show separately the cost of governance.

- Donors are not immediately encouraged to donate by the presence of particular elements of corporate governance.

- The experiences of some charities would suggest a limited effect of nominations committees on income raising and performance.

Chapter 10

CHARITIES BITING THE HAND THAT FEEDS: RELATIONSHIPS WITH THEIR FUNDERS
Debra Morris[1] and Karen Atkinson[2]

10.1   Introduction

"Without independence there is no voluntary sector, and without an independent voluntary sector, there is no civil society, no freedom."[3]

There are many different types of funders with which a charity may have a relationship. These include statutory funders, grant-making trusts, foundations, companies, individual donors, and the Community Fund. Each may be providing a different type of funding to a charity, such as core, project or service funding[4]. The issue of appropriate funder roles is not new. But it is especially appropriate now to consider the very real power role played by funders.

There are a number of reasons why this is a particularly topical question, including: the emergence of the "contract culture" under which charities are paid to deliver services previously provided by various elements of the State; the rise

---

[1]   Debra Morris is currently lecturing at Cayman Islands Law School. She was previously Senior Lecturer at Liverpool Law School, and the Director of the Charity Law Unit from 1996-2001.

[2]   Karen Atkinson is Research Assistant to the Charity Law Unit at the University of Liverpool. She is also studying for a MSc in Applied Social and Community Research in the University's Department of Sociology, Social Policy and Social Work Studies.

[3]   Dahrendorf S. *Challenges To The Voluntary Sector* Arnold Goodman Lecture, 17 July 2001, Charities Aid Foundation (2001).

[4]   See e.g. ACEVO *Funding Our Future: Core Costs Revisited* (2001).

of "engaged grantmaking"[5]; the current interest in "venture philanthropy"[6]. So far, the main pressure on charities has come from statutory funders; there is already a growing amount of evidence to suggest that the contract culture is partly responsible for the erosion of the independence of charities[7].

But, now private donors are also beginning, once again[8], to take a more active role in directing where their money goes[9]. For example, donor advised funds that allow donors to have more input into how their contributions are spent, are becoming more common. All these factors increase the influence that a funder can have on a charity and in this paper, having first examined the importance of independence for charities, some of the legal implications of the increased role of funders, and its knock on implications for the independence of charities will be considered.

The increasing trend for local authorities to establish charities to undertake activities previously carried on as part of their statutory functions meant that, following consultation, the Charity Commission published guidelines in February 2001 summarising the Charity Commission's views about the extent to which charities are required by law to be independent of the State[10]. Importantly, from our point of view, although this publication focused upon charities' independence from the State, the effect of the legal principles concerned is to require charities to be independent of any other body, not just of governmental authorities. These

---

[5] See e.g. the report commissioned by the Community Fund: Carrington D. *The Investor Approach: A way forward for the Community Fund?* Community Fund (June 2002) which suggests that the Fund could move towards an 'investor' approach in which the funder seeks to identify what social return it is getting on its grants.

[6] See e.g. *Third Sector* (22 May 2002) p.10.

[7] See e.g. Morris D. 'Paying the Piper: The "Contract Culture" As Dependency Culture for Charities?' in Dunn A. (ed) *The Voluntary Sector, The State and The Law* Hart Publishing (2000).

[8] Large donors do not seem to have been as actively involved in the last century, but, historically, founders were very involved with charities. See e.g. Chesterman M. *Charities, Trusts and Social Welfare* Weidenfeld and Nicolson (1979) Part I.

[9] See e.g. Warburton's discussion of 'new philanthropy' in Warburton J. 'Trusts: Still Going Strong 400 Years After The Statute of Charitable Uses' in Hayton D. (ed) *Extending the Boundaries of Trusts and Similarly Ring-Fenced Funds* Kluwer (2002).

[10] RR7 *The Independence of Charities from the State* Charity Commission (2001).

guidelines, together with legal principles underpinning them, will be examined in this paper, which also draws on the findings of a year-long empirical study[11] of 15 charities in the county of Merseyside[12] that had all experienced the contract culture through funding arrangements with a range of public bodies, including local and health authorities, central government departments and agencies, and other quasi-public bodies, such as the Community Fund. There was a broad range of beneficiaries of the services provided by the sample charities, including the elderly, children, those with physical and mental disabilities and the homeless. The sort of services contracted ranged from the provision of domiciliary care to counselling, through to the provision of leisure activities. Part of the study consisted of examining clauses of contracts[13] entered into between charity providers and local and health authority purchasers, in order to ascertain the potential liabilities of the charities under the contracts. Another element involved interviewing, at some length, those responsible for negotiating and managing the contracts in the relevant charities and the purchasing authorities.

10.2 Independence

One of the charity sector's distinctive values and characteristics has always been its independence. It is the essence of a charity that it should be independent of control by the State or any other third party. The original Charity Commission publication giving the background to the Review of the Register of Charities[14] also included those characteristics that determine the charitable status of an organisation and which will inform the decisions made as part of the Review[15]. That document suggests that one of the essential characteristics of a charity is that it must be independent. It goes on to say[16]:

> *"The independence of trustees is essential. They must make their own decisions and exercise their discretions solely in the interests of the*

---

[11] Morris D. *Charities and the Contract Culture: Partners or Contractors? Law and Practice in Conflict* Charity Law Unit (1999). This research, 'the Charity Law Unit research', was funded by the Esmée Fairburn Charitable Trust.

[12] The sample consisted of a range of charities which varied in size and organisational structure, had different sources of income and varying degrees of reliance upon the contribution of volunteers.

[13] Most of the charities supplied several contracts for analysis.

[14] R1 *The Review of the Register of Charities* Charity Commission (2001).

[15] RR1 *The Review of the Register of Charities* Charity Commission (2001) Part 2, *The Essential Characteristics of a Charity*.

[16] Ibid. (b).

charity. In an ideal world those outside the trustee body would recognise this and not seek to put pressure on or otherwise influence trustees. We know that this is not always the case and are willing to help or issue guidance as appropriate, where these matters cannot be resolved within the charity. Charity trustees must not:

- *Be controlled or directed by anyone outside the charity (except where they have to comply with general legal requirements - such as health and safety - which an outside body is there to enforce);*

- *Act on the instructions of the person or body which appointed them as trustees, such as members of the charity or central or local government; or*

- *Comply with any external or internal directions if, in doing so, they would be acting outside the charity's purposes.*

The charity may, perfectly properly, have provisions that give people other than trustees influence over the way the charity operates or particular types of decisions. Such powers must be exercised in the interests of the charity. Typically these can include powers:

- *Allowing members to appoint (and in some cases remove) trustees;*

- *Over membership rights;*

- *Requiring the consent of an outside person to certain actions (for example where the charity's Founder or Settlor must be consulted about the way in which income is distributed); or*

- *Of delegation, allowing someone outside the trustee body, such as an employee, to decide how the funds of the charity should be used within policies laid down by the trustees (provided always that the trustees retain responsibility for the delegate's actions and retain the ability to rescind the delegation if necessary)."*

The Charity Commission, in its document, *Hallmarks of a Well-Run Charity*[17] pursues this theme again, saying that charity trustees should preserve their independence, neither allowing themselves to be directly controlled by others nor acting as mere representatives of others' interests. It goes on to say that the

---

17 CC60 *The Hallmarks of a Well-Run Charity* (2002).

independence of trustees is of paramount importance. No charity should allow itself to be controlled or manipulated. Sometimes a person or body has a right to appoint (or nominate) trustees for a charity, but that does not give the appointing body any right of influence over the trustees once in place.

To add further reinforcement to this theme of independence, the Government, in its Compact on Relations between Government and the Voluntary and Community Sector in England, undertakes:

> *"To recognise and support the independence of the Sector, including its right within the law, to campaign, to comment on Government policy, and to challenge that policy, irrespective of any funding relationship that might exist, and to determine and manage its own affairs[18]."*

This message is strengthened once more in the Code of Practice on the funding relationship between Government and the voluntary and community sector.[19] Whilst the Code covers central Government departments, other public bodies and local government are encouraged to adopt and adapt the Compact and its associated Codes of Good Practice. This is particularly important given that most relationships exist at the local level, with charities benefiting from funding passed down from central Government and administered by local public spending bodies.

10.3 Legal Principles

10.3.1 Charity Trustees Must Stay Within Their Objects

The increased influence exercised by funders may tempt charities to act outside their objects.

All charity trustees are obliged to use charity funds for the specific purposes set out in the charity's governing document[20] and for no other purpose[21]. With unincorporated charities, trustees are also under an obligation to use any trust

---

[18] Cm 4100 *Getting it Right Together. Compact on Relations between Government and the Voluntary and Community Sector in England* Home Office (November 1998) para.9.1.

[19] *Compact. Getting it Right Together. Funding: A Code of Good Practice* Home Office (May 2000).

[20] That is the trust deed, constitution, memorandum and articles of association, Scheme of the Charity Commission, conveyance, will or other document describing the charity's purposes and, usually, how it is to be administered.

[21] *AG v Brandreth* (1842) 1 Y & C Cas 200

powers that they may have in accordance with the terms of the trust.[22] Any powers of a charitable company can generally only be exercised in furtherance of the objects of the company[23]. Charity funding may be conditional upon a charity acting outside its objects. This might occur where a service providing charity is required to provide services for a beneficial class that is wider than the charity's objects and, thus, beyond its powers[24]. For example, a charitable housing association for the elderly of Liverpool which has acquired considerable expertise in housing management, cannot agree by contract to manage a housing development for the general public in Liverpool. Similarly, a charity with specific objects for the relief of poverty in Manchester, which has developed a very efficient and cost effective way of converting houses for the disabled, cannot, without the risk of personal liability for the trustees[25], provide a similar service in Birmingham, even though this would also be a charitable purpose.

A second and related legal problem is that compliance with the terms of a funding arrangement may mean that a charity is not providing a *public* benefit. Benefit must be made available to the public or a sufficient section of the public and must not be restricted to private individuals[26]. It follows that a charity cannot agree to supply goods or services which will not be available to the public. For example, a contract by a London mental health charity which restricts the charity to providing community care facilities to mental patients coming from one hospital, to the exclusion of other mental patients from other hospitals who have links with that city, would be problematic.

The consequences of a charity acting outside its objects in this way (either because the class of beneficiaries is wider than that stated in the charity's specific governing documents, or because the class of beneficiaries is not a section of the public, as required under general charity law) are serious and affect both the charity trustees and the charity itself. First, as regards the charity trustees, in the case of an unincorporated charity, the contract entered into in breach of trust will be enforceable by the other contracting party against the trustees in their personal

---

22   *Re Hay's Settlement Trusts* [1981] 3 All ER 786, 792 *per* Megarry VC.

23   *Rosemary Simmons Memorial Housing Association Ltd v United Dominions Trust Ltd* [1987] 1 All ER 281. See Warburton J. 'Unauthorised acts by charities' (1987) 2 *Trust L & P* 46.

24   For an unincorporated charity this would be in breach of trust and for an incorporated charity it would be *ultra vires*.

25   See below, where the consequences for a charity entering into a contract which is outside its objects are discussed.

26   *William's Trustees v IRC* [1947] AC 447.

capacity. The trustees will also be personally liable if any breach of the contract occurs. Any monies received by the trustees under the contract will be held by them on trust for the charity on the usual basis that a trustee cannot benefit from his trust[27]. If the charity is incorporated, an *ultra vires* contract will be void and unenforceable except in favour of a third party who gave full consideration and who did not know that the contract was outside the objects of the charity or who did not know at the time of entering the contract that the company was a charity[28]. Any monies received by the charity or its directors[29] will be held for the charitable objects of the company. The directors may also be liable in damages to the other contracting party for breach of warranty of authority in respect of the void contract[30].

Secondly, in relation to the charity itself, if the unauthorised contract becomes a major part of the charity's activities, the charity may be in danger of losing its charitable status, as it is no longer established for exclusively charitable purposes. If the activity outside the charity's objects remains a limited part of its overall activities, charitable status will not be affected, but the court may restrain the unauthorised activities by injunction at the request of the Attorney General or, with the consent of the Charity Commission, at the request of any person interested in the charity[31].

Thirdly, there are adverse tax consequences for a charity which enters into an unauthorised contract. The contracted activity will probably be regarded for tax purposes as a trade[32]. Any profits will be liable to income tax under Schedule D Case I as the charity will not come within the exemption for profits deriving from a trade exercised in the carrying out of a primary purpose of the charity within section 505(1)(e) of the Income and Corporation Taxes Act 1988. In addition, if any clearly identifiable income of the charity has been used to fund the contract, that income may be liable to tax as, depending upon the particular contract, it may not have been applied for charitable purposes only within section 505 of the 1988 Act. As such, the charity is in danger of losing part of its tax reliefs[33] as

---

27   *Boardman v Phipps* [1967] 2 AC 67.

28   Charities Act 1993, s.65.

29   *Regal (Hastings) Ltd v Gulliver* [1967] 2 AC 134

30   *Firbank's Executors v Humphreys* (1886) 18 QBD 54

31   Charities Act 1993, s.33. See e.g. *Baldry v Feintuck* [1972] 1 WLR 552.

32   See e.g. *Grove v Young Men's Christian Association* (1903) 4 TC 613.

33   Income and Corporation Taxes Act 1988, s.505(3).

sums expended in connection with the contract will probably be "non-qualifying" expenditure within section 506(1) of the 1988 Act.

Within the contract culture, the Charity Law Unit research found evidence of the increasing propensity for charities to become involved in the delivery of services which are not consistent with their charitable objects[34].

10.3.2 Charity Trustees Must Exercise Discretion Appropriately

Provided that the funding received by a charity does not tempt its trustees to act outside the charity's objects, the next legal hurdle is to ensure that the trustees exercise their discretion appropriately. The increased influence being exercised by funders may cause problems for trustees in relation to the exercise of discretion. First, they may be tempted to allow others (including funders) to exercise discretion on their behalf, and secondly, even when formally exercising discretion themselves, they may be persuaded by funders to take into account inappropriate factors.

10.3.2.1 Who Exercises Discretion

If the trustees are allowed a discretion about the use of the charity property, the general rule is that decisions concerning the charity must be taken by the trustees personally. The governing document will usually specify that it is the trustees who must exercise powers of appointment, by choosing who the beneficiaries of the charity will be[35].

The office of trustee is one of personal confidence, and so, in general, cannot be delegated. This is commonly expressed in the maxim, *delegatus non potest delegare*[36]. Trustees must act in person so that decisions concerning the charity are taken by them. Trustees can always invite individuals to look into particular matters and to make recommendations, but the decision whether or not to act on the recommendations is for the trustees to take. Decisions of charity trustees may be taken by majority vote and need not be unanimous[37]. In some cases the

---

34　Morris D. *Charities and the Contract Culture: Partners or Contractors? Law and Practice in Conflict* Charity Law Unit (1999).

35　Where a power to prescribe the mode of applying a charitable gift is contained in the governing document, it is a question of construction to determine who is capable of exercising the power. *Crawford v Forshaw* [1891] 2 Ch 261 at 267–268, CA, per Bowen LJ; and see the non-charity cases of *Re Smith, Eastick v Smith* [1904] 1 Ch 139; *Re Hayes' Will Trusts, Pattinson v Hayes* [1971] 2 All ER 241.

36　McGhee J. *Snell's Equity* 30th ed. (2000) Sweet & Maxwell p.301.

37　*Re Whiteley* [1910] 1 Ch 600 at 608.

governing document of a charity may permit the trustees to set up committees with limited powers to carry out particular functions. The Trustee Act 2000 sets out the powers that trustees have, in addition to any powers expressly stated within the charity's governing document and to any other statutory powers, to delegate certain functions to agents.

The functions that may be delegated under the 2000 Act[38] are:

(i)   Carrying out a decision that the trustees have taken;

(ii) The investment of assets, including land subject to the trust;

(iii) The raising of funds for the trust other than by means of profits of trade which is an integral part of carrying out the trust's charitable purpose; and

(iv) Any other function prescribed by an order made by the Secretary of State.

So, determining the selection criteria for recipients of a charity service is the responsibility of the charity trustees, in line with their governing documents. In the absence of power to delegate (for example, under the charity's governing document), trustees cannot agree to allow a third party, such as a funder, to decide who is to benefit and in what way. That would be so even if the funder's rights of selection were restricted to persons who fell within the charity's beneficiary class; in the absence of any duty to act solely in furtherance of the charitable purposes of the charity, it would be open to the funder to apply its own policies and achieve its own wishes in making its selection. Where trustees *are* authorised to delegate, the person who makes the decision has the same duty as the trustees to take into account only considerations that are relevant to the pursuit of the charity's purpose.

In some cases, under the contract culture, local authorities *are* changing the referral practices of charity providers who previously had the flexibility to respond to all potential service users in need who presented themselves. Contracts with local authorities may now dictate that services are only provided to those people who, having proven that they meet clear eligibility criteria, are referred by social services departments[39].

---

38   Trustee Act 2000, s.11(3).

39   See e.g. Lewis J. 'Voluntary Organizations in "New Partnership" with Local Authorities: The Anatomy of A Contract' (1994) 28 *Social Policy and Administration* 206 at p.212, where a prolonged battle to negotiate over client access is described.

The Charity Law Unit research has found examples of contracts where control over the selection of users is entirely with the local authority purchaser[40].

Whelan[41] gives the example of a local authority which funded the Salvation Army on the condition that all referrals had to come from the authority's housing department. This meant that service users could not be received out of hours - a reversal of the charity's long-standing practice of immediate assistance for the needy. Conversely, Russell *et al*[42] provide an example where local authority purchasers wanted to specify longer hours of opening for a playgroup, necessitating the employment of full-time staff - even though the project had been designed partly with a view to providing part-time employment for local women.

Trustees may be in breach of duty in entering into such funding agreements, if, by doing so, they are abrogating their decision-making powers concerning selection criteria for their beneficiaries. Another example, uncovered by a Charity Commission inquiry in March 2001[43], is that of charities established and then funded by (non-charitable) sporting bodies. The inquiry concerned the Rugby League Foundation, a charity set up and funded by the (non-charitable) Rugby Football League, where the latter had then effectively ran the charity without reference to or the knowledge of the charity trustees. In breach of trust, the trustees had allowed the interests of the charity to be subservient to the interests of their funder.

Although it would not be open to the trustees of an independent charity to surrender their discretion in the ways described, the Charity Commission recognises that it *is* possible for trustees to accept funding on terms that are quite prescriptive[44]. Having negotiated at arm's-length, the trustees might properly decide that the terms (relating to matters such as levels of charging, hours of opening, facilities to be provided, forms of tenancy and standards of service) coincide sufficiently with the way that they want to pursue their charitable purposes to enable them to accept funding on those terms. Here, there would be no surrender of discretion.

---

[40] Morris D. *Charities and the Contract Culture: Partners or Contractors? Law and Practice in Conflict* Charity Law Unit (1999) p.40.

[41] Whelan R. *The Corrosion of Charity. From Moral Renewal To Contract Culture* Institute of Economic Affairs (1996) p.92.

[42] Russell L. Scott D. and Wilding P. *Mixed Fortunes: The Funding of the Local Voluntary Sector* University of Manchester (1996) p.42.

[43] *The Rugby League Foundation Inquiry Report* Charity Commission (March 2001).

[44] RR7 *The Independence of Charities from the State* Charity Commission (2001) p.7.

However, in the case of continuing decisions (such as the selection of individuals for benefit), to allow the decision to be made by an individual or body with no fiduciary duty to the charity amounts to a surrender of discretion.

Another solution to this problem may be to suggest that the trustees *are* exercising their discretion by accepting the funding with its associated conditions in the first place. For example, it is common practice under the contract culture for local authorities to retain nomination rights for accommodation that has been transferred to a charitable housing association. The charity is able to decide whether to accept or reject the land and the conditions upon which it is transferred. Provided that those nominated applicants must be within the class of beneficiaries of the charity, the nomination is simply another way of finding people in housing need; those people would still have to meet the criteria which the trustees had laid down. It could be argued that anything that flows from the contract (including decisions about selection of service users) is therefore within the initial exercise of their discretion. This is a grey area not settled by law.

What is certain is that a charity should not allow anyone to be a service user if that person does not fall within the charity's class of beneficial objects. This means that charities must retain a right to veto any decisions on users that do not fall within that class. The Charity Law Unit research found, however, that, in only two of the contracts examined, the final say on service users was firmly placed with the charity[45].

Trustees must not only avoid surrendering their discretion without proper authority. They must also avoid fettering their discretion (except where the interests of the charity require them to do so). The Charity Commission therefore concludes that independent trustees are less likely to be able to agree to highly detailed conditions which are binding for lengthy periods, than conditions which set out broad principles or outcomes and allow the trustees a degree of latitude in how they achieve those outcomes[46].

10.3.2.2   How Discretion is Exercised

Trustees are required to be independent in the sense that when they exercise powers in relation to the governance of a charity they are bound to act solely in the interests of the charity. This is not just a requirement at the point when a body is registered as a charity. Charities must remain independent throughout

---

[45]   Morris D. *Charities and the Contract Culture: Partners or Contractors? Law and Practice in Conflict* Charity Law Unit (1999) p.40.

[46]   RR7 *The Independence of Charities from the State* Charity Commission (2001) p.7.

their existence. Trustees invested with discretionary powers must exercise them honestly and with a fair consideration of the subject[47]. They need not give reasons for their actions[48].

Where they state reasons which do not justify their conclusions[49], or where they have acted corruptly or improperly[50], the court will interfere.

In carrying out their responsibilities, trustees must act solely in the interests of the charity. It is not a trustee's function to represent or promote the interests of a third party, whether that third party is the appointing body, a funding body, or a body of which the trustee is a member or employee or in which he or she has some other interest. There is evidence to suggest that local authorities that hive off certain activities to a charitable body often fail to understand that the charity must be truly independent from the sponsoring local authority[51]. Local authorities need to be aware that even if they do have representation on the trustee board, they cannot exert operational control.

Within the contract culture, it is acknowledged by the Charity Commission that it would be unrealistic to expect a charity to be given an entirely free hand, given that funding authorities have a responsibility to protect the interests of taxpayers and service users[52]. Moreover, it has to be recognised that, in practice, funders generally enjoy a strong bargaining position[53]. However, simply carrying out the policies, wishes or statutory duties of a governmental authority is not the same as carrying out a charitable purpose. Hence, the Charity Commission has stated that trustees cannot agree to accept funding on terms that require them expressly:

- To implement particular policies of the local authority; or

---

[47] *Scott v National Trust for Places of Historic Interest or Natural Beauty* [1998] 2 All ER 705.

[48] *Re Beloved Wilkes' Charity* (1851) 3 Mac & G 440.

[49] *Dundee General Hospitals Board of Management v Walker* [1952] 1 All ER 896 at 905 per Lord Reid. See also *Re Hastings-Bass (deceased)* [1975] 1 Ch 25.

[50] See e.g. *AG v Glegg* (1738) Amb 584, *AG v Governors of Harrow School* (1754) 2 Ves Sen 551.

[51] See e.g. Ravenscroft S. 'The Business of Pleasure' *Charity Finance* (April 2002) p.24.

[52] RR7 *The Independence of Charities from the State* Charity Commission (2001) p.6.

[53] See in general Morris D. *Charities and the Contract Culture: Partners or Contractors? Law and Practice in Conflict* Charity Law Unit (1999).

- To comply with decisions that are made from time to time by the local authority; or

- To pursue the objectives of the local authority; or

- To discharge the statutory duties of the local authority[54].

Trustees should not pre-commit themselves to choosing beneficiaries in a particular way (thereby preventing them from exercising an independent judgment at the appropriate time) *unless* this commitment is in the interests of the charity.

An analogy can be drawn with the position in Company Law of directors, who are also regarded as fiduciaries, and who must not in general fetter their discretion by entering into an agreement with a third party as to how they will exercise their discretion. There is an established exception where directors decide that it is in the best interests of the company to enter into a contract and to carry it into effect. In this situation, they can themselves enter into any undertaking to exercise their powers in a particular way, if it is necessary for them to do so to effectuate the contracts. In *Fulham Football Club Ltd v Cabra Estates plc*[55] the Court of Appeal stated:

> "It is trite law that directors are under a duty to act bona fide in the interests of their company. However, it does not follow from that proposition that directors can never make a contract by which they bind themselves to the future exercise of their powers in a particular manner, even though the contract taken as a whole is manifestly for the benefit of the company. Such a rule could well prevent companies from entering into contracts which were commercially beneficial to them."

The Court of Appeal went on to hold[56]:

> "The true rule was stated by the High Court of Australia in Thorby v Goldberg[57]. The relevant part of the headnote reads: If, when a contract is negotiated on behalf of a company, the directors bona fide think it in the interests of the company as a whole that the transaction should be

---

54 RR7 *The Independence of Charities from the State* Charity Commission (2001) p.6.

55 [1994] 1 BCLC 363 at 392.

56 Ibid.

57 (1964) 112 CLR 597.

entered into and carried into effect they may bind themselves by the contract to do whatever is necessary to effectuate it."

The issue would appear to be whether the degree of control that a funder seeks to exercise compromises the discretion of the trustees and whether the trustees have sufficient independence to carry out the objects according to their own discretion.

10.3.3 Particular Problems of Funder-Appointed Trustees

It follows that a funding body cannot properly insist upon appointing a trustee to protect its interest as a condition of providing funding. Funders' legitimate concerns about how their money is being spent must be met by other means. This is often a concern with local authority funders. Where a funder has been given powers under a charity's governing document, it is bound to exercise those powers solely in the interests of the charity. A power to appoint trustees, for example, must be exercised so as to select the individuals best suited (in the opinion of the appointer) to act as trustees of the charity[58]. If a local authority could exercise a power in the administration of a body for its own benefit, the body in question would not be a charity, since it would exist in part for the benefit of the local authority.

Where a funder *does* have a constitutional role in the governance of a charity, (for example, a local authority may have power under a charity's governing document to appoint trustees or may have a veto over the application or investment of the charity's funds) this role must be carried out entirely in the interests of the charity, and not for its own benefit. A funder must not expect its appointee to represent its interests or carry out its wishes. Such appointees must exercise their own judgement and act solely in the best interests of the charity.

Like any other trustee, charity trustees owe fiduciary duties of loyalty and fidelity that require them never to use their position for their own personal gain:

> *"It is an inflexible rule of a Court of Equity that a person in a fiduciary position... is not, unless otherwise expressly provided, entitled to make a profit; he is not allowed to put himself in a position where his interest and duty conflict..."*[59]

---

[58] A power to appoint trustees is considered to be a fiduciary power: this means that it must be exercised in the interests of the charity, and not in the interest of the person who exercises it. For example, a body having power to appoint trustees will generally be bound to select the best people it can find for the purpose: *Re Skeats' Settlement* (1889) 42 Ch 522.

[59] *Bray v Ford* [1896] AC 44 at 51.

Where, for example, there is a contractual relationship between a charity and a local authority, a trustee who is a councillor or officer of the local authority is placed in a position of conflict between duty to the charity and loyalty to the local authority whenever the trustees discuss matters relating to that contractual relationship (for example, the proposed terms of the contract, whether the contract is being performed properly and its enforcement or termination). Both the charity and the local authority have an interest in securing the terms most favourable to itself. It may be possible to deal with a conflict of interest by requiring the trustee to withdraw from discussion and to refrain from voting upon the matter in question[60]. However, in the case of a substantial and recurring conflict of interest, it may be necessary in the interests of the charity for the trustee to resign. Where a trustee benefits personally as a result of a conflict of interest, he or she may not be allowed to retain that benefit in the absence of express authorisation in the charity's governing document or from the Charity Commission.

For a charity to function independently, the trustees must be able to discuss its business in confidence. The Charity Commission notes that provisions in a charity's governing document, or in funding agreements, that tend to inhibit confidential discussion by the trustees may show that the body is not intended to be independent.

Examples of provisions of this kind include:

- Provisions expressly permitting trustees to be present despite a conflict of interest;

- Requirements that trustees who are members or officers of the local authority must be present in order to found a quorum; and,

- Provisions entitling the local authority to send an observer to all trustee meetings[61].

Whether or not they undermine a body's claim to charitable status, provisions of this kind would certainly be inconsistent with independent governance.

---

[60] See e.g. NCVO / Local Government Association *Are you Sitting Comfortably? A Code of Practice for Local Authority Members and Officers Serving on the Boards of Voluntary Organisations* (1998).

[61] RR7 *The Independence of Charities from the State* Charity Commission (2001) p.5.

The Funding Code of Good Practice notes[62] that agreement should be reached at the outset in respect of the extent to which funders will receive copies of papers and minutes of management committee, steering group and trustee meetings, and whether and on what basis the funder will observe such meetings. Any requirement to receive copies of papers and minutes of trustee meetings, and to observe such meetings, should be limited to particular items of business concerned with the grant.

10.3.4 Influence Over Other Matters

Quite apart from influencing the exercise of discretion as to how funded activities are to be carried out, there are other areas in which funders might seek to inhibit the independence of the trustees. Trustees should not have to consult funders before making decisions on matters such as staffing[63], obtaining funds from other sources, campaigning, or carrying out other charitable activities. Trustees should be free to make their own decisions on matters outside the funding arrangement.

The funders should also not oblige charities to provide detailed information going far beyond what might reasonably be required for monitoring purposes. The Better Regulation Task Force[64] emphasises the importance of maintaining proportionality in accounting and auditing requirements, and suggests[65] that accounting and auditing thresholds for funded charities should not be any stricter than those imposed by the Charity Commission. In response, the Funding Code of Good Practice states[66] that specific funding conditions attached to government grants should be no more than are necessary to enable funders to satisfy themselves that public money is: spent for the purposes for which it was intended; will achieve a cost effective outcome; and, is not put at undue risk. Importantly, it states[67] that information and accounting requirements should reflect both the size of the grant and the size of the funded organisation, and

---

[62] *Compact. Getting it Right Together. Funding: A Code of Good Practice* Home Office (May 2000) para.17.2.

[63] The Charity Law Unit research found examples where charities were not free to employ and dismiss staff at their own discretion. Morris D. *Charities and the Contract Culture: Partners or Contractors? Law and Practice in Conflict* Charity Law Unit (1999) pp.41-42.

[64] Better Regulation Task Force *Access to Government Funding for the Voluntary Sector* Central Office of Information (1998).

[65] Ibid. p.13.

[66] *Compact. Getting it Right Together. Funding: A Code of Good Practice* Home Office (May 2000) para.17.1.

[67] Ibid. para.20.1.

Government departments should not demand more stringent accounting and auditing requirements than required by the Charities Act 1993.[68]

Many charities are accountable to several funders and they should accept charities' needs to cope with multiple accountability[69]. Charities should try to find their own means of assessing their performance and then try to persuade funders that this system should be used to report back to them, rather than complying with a new system imposed by each individual funder. This concept is supported in the Funding Code of Good Practice which states[70] that an effective framework for monitoring and evaluation should take account of the monitoring procedures already agreed by the charity's other funders and any quality assurance system introduced by the charity itself. These should be examined to see if they satisfy the funder's needs before devising any additional requirements. This approach will help to reduce the paid staff and volunteer time spent in reporting in a number of different formats and should in turn reduce the associated costs.

It is important to remember that the legal requirements for most charity accounts are contained in Part VI of the Charities Act 1993 and regulations made under it[71]. Although there are some exceptions, most registered non-company charities must:

10.3.4.1 Keep Accounting Records

Section 41 of the 1993 Act requires all registered charities to keep accounting records sufficient to show and explain all the charity's transactions. It also gives details of what these should contain. The records should be kept for six years.

---

[68] Charities Act 1993, Part VI.

[69] See e.g. Ashby J. *Towards Voluntary Sector Codes of Practice* Joseph Rowntree Foundation (1997) p.18.

[70] *Compact. Getting it Right Together. Funding: A Code of Good Practice* Home Office (May 2000) para.21.2.

[71] Charity (Accounts and Reports) Regulations 1995; Charities (Accounts and Reports) Regulations 2000.

10.3.4.2 Prepare Statements of Accounts

The requirements for preparation of the statement of accounts under section 42 of the 1993 Act vary according to the income and expenditure of the charity. Charities with gross income not over £100,000 in the relevant financial year may prepare their accounts on either a receipts and payments[72] or an accruals[73] basis. If they choose the latter, they must do so in accordance with the relevant Regulations[74]. Charities with gross income over £100,000 must prepare their accounts on an accruals basis in accordance with the Regulations. The 2000 Regulations prescribe the form and content of the statement in detail[75], and require that it is prepared in line with the Charity Commission Statement of Recommended Practice (SORP)[76].

10.3.4.3 Ensure Independent Examination / Audit of Accounts

Under section 43 of the 1993 Act, charities with gross income or total expenditure above £10,000, but with gross income not above £250,000 in the relevant financial year (or the preceding two years) must have their accounts externally examined. They can choose between independent examination[77] or audit. There is no statutory requirement for registered non-company charities with neither gross income nor total expenditure above £10,000 in the relevant financial year to have their accounts externally examined. However, the Charity Commission can require a full audit, regardless of income or expenditure, in exceptional circumstances. A full audit must also be carried out if gross income or total expenditure in the relevant year or the preceding two years is over a certain sum, currently £250,000.

10.3.4.4 Prepare and Submit Annual Reports

Section 45 of the 1993 Act requires all registered charities to prepare Annual Reports. Under the 2000 Regulations, whilst charities with income over £250,000 must prepare a full Report reviewing all their activities, charities with income of

---

[72] See CC64 *Receipts and Payments Accounts Pack 2001* (2001).

[73] See CC65 *Accruals Accounts Pack* (2001).

[74] The Charities (Accounts and Reports) Regulations 2000.

[75] Ibid. r.3.

[76] *Accounting and Reporting by Charities: Statement of Recommended Practice* Charity Commission (2000).

[77] See CC63 *Independent Examination of Charities 2001: Directions and Guidance Notes* (2001).

£250,000 or less can prepare a simplified version, briefly summarising their main activities and achievements[78]. Reports must usually be submitted to the Commission within ten months of the end of the financial year, and the Statement of Accounts and Auditor's or Examiner's reports discussed above should be attached[79].

10.3.4.5 Enable Public Inspection of Annual Reports and Accounts

Section 47 of the 1993 Act requires charities to make their annual reports available for public inspection at all reasonable times, and to provide copies of the accounts requested in writing, for which they can charge a reasonable fee.

This requirements extends to all charities, including charitable companies and exempt or excepted charities.

10.3.4.6 Submit Annual Returns

As an additional monitoring requirement, section 48 of the 1993 Act requires charities, other than those with neither gross income nor total expenditure above £10,000 in the relevant financial year, to submit an Annual Return to the Charity Commission, usually by the same date that they must submit their Annual Report.

As noted earlier, there are a number of exceptions to and variations from the general requirements contained in Part VI of the 1993 Act, which arguably involve differences in form rather than lowering of accounting standards.

Exempt charities[80] may have specific legislation governing their accounting procedures. If not, then they must prepare consecutive statements of account in a prescribed form and preserve them for six years[81].

Excepted charities[82] which have chosen to register must fulfil the same accounting and reporting requirements as other charities of the same type. If they do not register, the requirements for external examination and annual reports do not generally apply[83]. However, under section 46 of the 1993 Act the Commission

---

[78] The Charities (Accounts and Reports) Regulations 2000 r.7(3).

[79] Charities Act 1993, s.45(4).

[80] Defined in Charities Act 1993, s.3(5).

[81] S.46(1), (2).

[82] Defined in Charities Act 1993, s.3(5).

[83] S.46(3).

can request an annual report from some types[84] of excepted charities. If it does so, the report must be prepared in line with the Regulations, and the procedural provisions of section 45 will apply.

Charitable companies must produce Annual Reports and facilitate public inspection of them in the same way as other charities. However, the 1993 Act provisions regarding statements of accounts and external examination do not apply; their accounting procedures are mostly governed by the Companies Act 1985. They must prepare a Director's Report and Accounts (the accounts should be prepared on an accruals basis), and must file these with Companies House.

It should also be noted that charities may have specific provisions in their governing documents relating to the preparation of accounts. Where statutory provisions and governing document provisions cover the same accounting matters, the Commission advises that whichever provisions require the higher standard of accounting should be followed[85].

The SORP expands upon the general statutory requirements and these variations from them. It builds on the legislative framework and provides detailed procedures and a rigid accounting format, which, it states, will, if followed:

> *"not only ensure that they are in accordance with the law but also help the reader to gain a clearer understanding of the nature and extent of the charity's work* [86]*."*

and therefore:

> *"discharge the charity trustees' duty of public accountability and stewardship* [87]*."*

It is arguable that this clear aim and the detailed framework laid down to achieve it should be enough to fulfill the accounting requirements of most funders and negate the need for imposition of further complex (and possibly duplicate) procedures.

---

[84] Those excepted under s.3(5) (a) or (b).

[85] See CC61 *Charity Accounts 2001: The Framework* (2001) paras.20-21.

[86] *Accounting and Reporting by Charities: Statement of Recommended Practice* Charity Commission (2000) para.17.

[87] Ibid. para.3.

10.4 Conclusion

There is an obvious tension for trustees when entering into relationships with funders, whether it be a local authority, lottery distributor or a large grant-making trust. Clearly, charity funders require some freedom to give effect to their own policies. However, this cannot go so far as to leave the trustees with little or no discretion over the beneficiaries of the charity.

Where an instrument purporting to set up an institution as a charity gives an outside body such control that the institution is merely an extension or arm of that other body becoming, in effect, a mere conduit through which funds are channeled without the institution having any truly independent functions to carry out, then the document purporting to create the institution can be treated as a sham and the Charity Commission is entitled to reject it for registration. However, there is a considerable difference between that situation and the case where, for example, a funder merely keeps a watching brief on a charity or

requires it to act within certain policy guidelines if it is to receive funding. Clearly, there is scope between these two examples for numerous degrees of control, and it is extremely difficult to say exactly where the line should be drawn in any particular case as, on each occasion, it will be a matter of fact and degree having regard to the nature of the arrangement and control exerted.

Within the contract culture, the opportunity for governmental control of charities through the selection of beneficiaries should be avoided as trustees cannot properly accept funding on conditions that fetter their discretion. Yet, it is understandable that the organs of the State, accountable for the proper use of public funds, should wish to have at least some measure of control over how the money is spent. Having the right to appoint all or a majority of trustees is not the best way to represent a funder's interests. It should take other steps to monitor the use of its funding and to ensure that funding is used for the purposes for which it was given. While it is in order for funders to attach conditions, hopefully expressed in general terms, it is for the trustees to decide how, subject to those conditions, the funds should be distributed. In other words, the ultimate discretion of the trustees should not be compromised. If this causes local or national government difficulty then it would be better to provide the services which they wish to fund under their own aegis.

Due to the contract culture, charity trustees cannot be seen as free agents, but are linked in an on-going relationship with government, which at once constrains their behaviour. There is an extreme view[88] that charities can only be truly independent if they distance themselves entirely from State funding and rely wholly upon private philanthropy. In a debate in the House of Lords, in March 1998, on the importance of the work of charities, Lord Ponsonby commented:

> *"The single most beneficial action [the government] could take would be to reverse the trend from unrestricted funding to restricted funding, and to encourage funders to give charities whose work they value the flexibility to allocate funding where it is needed most* [89]*."*

The Charity Commission concludes that, in the case of an independent charity negotiating with a governmental authority for funding, the trustees:

- Would have a choice about whether or not they accepted funding on the terms proposed;

- Would take their own legal and financial advice;

- Would draw up their own policies and business plan;

- Would conduct arm's-length negotiations with the governmental authority;

- Would not commit themselves simply to giving effect to the policies and wishes of the governmental authority;

- Would not agree to conditions that undermined the confidentiality of their discussions (such as the presence at their meetings of an observer from the governmental authority);

- Would be free to make their own decisions on matters outside the scope of the funding arrangement;

- A trustee who was subject to a conflict of interest would not participate in discussions; and,

---

[88] See e.g. Whelan R. *The Corrosion of Charity. From Moral Renewal To Contract Culture* Institute of Economic Affairs (1996), where the author laments the decline of 'Christian values' and the reduced emphasis on spiritual renewal in some Christian welfare charities and blames this, to some extent, upon the 'contract culture'.

[89] House of Lords Debate, 4 Mar 1998, Hansard col.1236.

- The funding arrangements would preserve the trustees' fundamental discretions as to the selection of beneficiaries and the provision of services[90].

The fewer of these characteristics that a body displayed, the more likely it would be that it had been created in order to promote the local authority's interests and thus for a non-charitable purpose. Depending upon the circumstances, an alternative conclusion might be that the body had been created for exclusively charitable purposes but was not operating properly. In that event, while recognising the body's charitable status, the Charity Commission would need to take steps to secure its proper administration.

There are some who would argue that the greater regulatory control of the operations of a charity by its funders is justified as increasing its accountability. To the extent that accountability means simply being more responsive to the needs of a charity's beneficiaries, within the proper scope of a charity's objects, that is unobjectionable. Indeed, whilst care should be taken so as not to compromise the charity's independent status, there are, nevertheless, beneficial aspects that a funder may bring to a fledgling organisation (or indeed to established charities) by continuing to maintain on-going involvement with that organisation. For example, where the funder is a local authority, it may well have an informed view of the needs of the charity's beneficiaries, especially if the charity provides services similar to services provided by the authority. The authority may even be willing to subsidise the operation of the charity out of its own statutory funds, either directly, by way of grant aid, or indirectly by, for example, meeting the cost of maintaining the charity's property or providing professional services free of charge.

For such reasons, it may well be in the best interests of the charity to have a representative of the funder on the trustee board. As the rules on conflict of interest currently stand, however, at the time when such a person could have the most valuable input, they must withdraw from discussions. Whilst the rationale behind these rules are appreciated, they can impact negatively on the effectiveness of a charity board. One solution might be to suggest a graded level of trusteeship with both a core and an advisory membership. It may be beneficial if the latter, who would not have full voting rights, could nevertheless contribute to discussion in such circumstances.

Funders that offer charities financial assistance, even where this may be necessary for the charity's continued survival, should not expect to receive, in return for that assistance, the right to appoint all or a majority of the charity's trustees. However, if a funder is insistent, there may be no practicable

---

[90] RR7 *The Independence of Charities from the State* Charity Commission (2001) p.4.

alternative, if the charity's viability is to be secured. Any financial gain to the charity, however, should not be at the expense of the charity losing its independence. The fact that a funder has the power to appoint a trustee may provide a useful means of communication, but it does not carry with it the legal power to direct a trustee on how to vote.

It has been seen in this paper that, in order to comply with legal requirements, charity trustees must remain within their objects, exercise discretion appropriately and comply with detailed accounting standards. Charities should therefore use the law as an ally to prevent funders exerting undue influence. By deferring to the law when entering into funding arrangements, charity trustees have a perfect excuse for not agreeing to arrangements which allow too much interference by funders. If charity trustees were to adopt this approach, law and practice would be brought more into line. It is suggested that the law in this regard does not need to be strengthened, but rather, more widely known and applied.

Charities must retain their freedom of choice, both in the tasks that they take on and in the ways in which they perform them. Practically, charities will help themselves to retain their independence if they can:

- Ensure a mix of funding;

- Adopt a transparent style of operation; and

- Maintain clarity and purpose, by setting clear goals and sticking to them.

Chapter 11
_____

INFLUENCE OF FUNDERS
Robin Currie[1]

11.1 Introduction

Major changes have occurred in commercial and social life over the last two decades. These have had fundamental effects on the nature of organisations and the way they operate. Charities have not been immune from these changes, but that is nothing new to them.

As society has changed over the years so individual charities have either become outmoded and declined or else adapted their mission or way of working (and often both) to new situations. Some have sought to influence their environment or at least control how it impacts upon them; others have reacted more radically and adopted a social enterprise approach embracing methods more traditionally associated with business and the private sector[2].

It might be reassuring to believe that such changes in charities are dictated solely by needs or at least the ambitions of trustees, but without the means to act, even the most philanthropic aspirations have little impact. Charities need resources and for most this requires access to funds. The availability of funding is a major determinant of what charities do or do not do. In the face of this, how do trustees manage to govern independently whilst ensuring they can attract the funds to continue? How do they ensure that it is their view of the charity's mission that predominates rather than the ambitions of funders?

Like many, I come to this issue with perspectives accumulated from a variety of roles. In my case, this has been mainly over the last 25 years as a trustee, as a researcher, as a funder through government, foundations, and quangos, as a

_____

[1] Robin Currie is Chief Executive of PSS, a large social care charity operating in the north west of England, north Wales and central Scotland. He has wide experience in government, business and charities, and has undertaken research on behalf of NCVO.

[2] Conaty P. 'The Social Economy and Sufficiency' in Knight B., Smerdon M. and Pharoah C. *Building Civil Society* Charities Aid Foundation (1998) p.113.

donor, as a volunteer and as a beneficiary. However, most of my day-to-day experience has been as a charity employee, Chief Executive of PSS, a social care charity based on Merseyside[3].

11.2 Background

Much has changed in these 25 years. Almost all features of life have become more performance focused, at times to the point of obsession. Concepts such as quality assurance, objective setting, the measurement of inputs and outputs, itemising costs and benefits, "Value for Money" analysis and now "Best Value", have had profound effects on the way we think and operate.

In line with this trend, funders of charities have become ever more concerned with results. Corporate funders have responded to the pressures upon them by looking at the return they get from "donations" to charities. Rather than a philanthropic gift, companies now want to know what the donation will give back to them. Mostly, they want results in terms of positive publicity or increased sales, but sometimes also more subtle objectives such as provision of volunteering and staff development opportunities to improve the motivation or social cohesion of their workforce. Companies may feel they get a better PR return by being seen to fund large, national-known charities with strong positive brand images, rather than local or regional charities.

The decline of companies in the North West and other less prosperous parts of the UK has also adversely affected funding for charities in these regions. Many long-standing corporate supporters of charities have gone out of business; others have been taken over by national or international firms with headquarters responsible for donations based in the South East, with little knowledge or interest in local charities. When they do fund charities, they increasingly specify how the money is used. This allows them to ensure that the company itself receives some benefit in return for the donation, providing justification to shareholders and others in terms of the effect on their bottom line of profit and loss.

---

[3] See website: www.pss.org.uk

Charitable Trusts and Foundations have also been taken over by the trend. In setting their objectives and criteria for funding, they specify ever more closely what they will fund and the requirements they make of recipients, especially in relation to the achievement of outcomes. The growth of this "Investor Approach" to funding is evident across a wide range of charities, and becoming ever more refined [4].

Other non-government and quasi-government bodies, such as the Community Fund and other Lottery Boards, are also adopting this approach as they strive to achieve set objectives, typified by restrictions on the types of activities they fund and a preoccupation on outcomes and impact.

Many corporate donors have taken up a similar style. Some have moved away from the giving of direct donations to charities. For example, in Merseyside, Marks & Spencer has identified the key issues of "safer streets" and "lack of parenting skills" as major concerns of its customers. It is now appointing voluntary sector partners to help it address these issues[5].

In short funders are seeking more control and involvement in what, how and when.

Individual donors have also become more discerning, perhaps influenced by "donor fatigue" from overkill of constant charity campaigns. To successfully raise funds from individuals, charities find they not only have to specify closely how funding will be used but also restrict appeals to popular causes, often ignoring less attractive issues. This can lead trustees to feeling pressurised to change the focus of their operations.

Fund raising methods can also raise ethical dilemmas – to achieve a fundraising goal, it may be necessary to reinforce negative stereotypes, thereby undermining the charity's mission. Disabled people may need to be portrayed as helpless and deserving rather than as active and achieving. It may be more effective to raise money for Liverpool causes by emphasising poverty, disease and unemployment, rather than the city's positive achievements of recent years.

A counterbalance to some of these pressures may come from the growing interest within the voluntary sector in the Social Audit Approach[6]. Social audits provide a

---

[4] Carrington D. *The Investor Approach* Community Fund (June 2002).

[5] Pollack L. 'On Your Marks' in *Voluntary Sector* NCVO (July 2002) pp.20-23.

[6] Raynard P. and Murphy S. *Charitable Trust? Social Auditing with Voluntary Organisations* ACEVO (2000).

wide ranging assessment of the social impact and performance of an organisation by those groups and individuals affected by it, its stakeholders. In charities it would bring together the interests of service beneficiaries, supporters, volunteers, staff, donors and other funders to assess the social impact of the organisation. This would involve both setting, and testing the achievement of objectives and examining the difference the charity makes to people's lives.

11.3 The Influence of Government Funding

All these influences have put real constraints on charities and their trustees. However, they have not been the major change in recent years. This has come as the result of state funding.

> "Until 1980s the role of the voluntary sector was primarily seen as supplementing statutory provision, filling gaps, meeting special needs, trying out new forms of delivery. Mainstream services were provided by local authorities, health authorities and other statutory agencies. An important role of the voluntary sector was to monitor statutory provision and campaign for improvements when these were needed [7]."

Charities often received grants from local authorities to assist them in these functions. As Gutch argues[8], two important influences have changed this. First, successive Governments have placed an increased emphasis on the role of the independent sector in service provision. Second, a belief developed in government that open-ended grants were an unsatisfactory way of ensuring accountability for public money. This resulted in the introduction of tighter, more contractual funding agreements.

These changes have not only transformed the relationship between government and the voluntary sector but have also had a major effect on the scale and the way in which many charities operate.

> "The voluntary sector is a rising star. Since the Second World War, its role as a provider of services to disadvantaged people was all but eclipsed by the growth of the Welfare State. But now ... that is changing[9]."

---

[7] Gutch R. *Contracting Lessons from the US* NCVO (1992) p.7.

[8] Ibid.

[9] Tissier G. 'A Profitable Partnership' *Community Care* (12 July 1990) p.27.

The way in which charities have responded to these changes has been critical to their survival.

> *"Some have become more entrepreneurial, with a framework for achieving social result ... others dither and become so engrossed in the 'process' of change that they cease to produce outcomes of any value[10]."*

Commentators correctly predicted a major shift from relatively small government grants based on goodwill and generosity to closely specified service agreements and contracts based on payments by results.

> *"The voluntary sector is on the brink of massive change. There will be some who cannot cope and will harp back to the old authoritarian days of small grants and sherry with the Chair of Social Services. There will be those who cannot get into gear quick enough and will watch the private sector take over health and social care. And there will be those who are prepared to grab the trends as they occur, and steer them in the new direction[11]."*

Concerns about the potential effects of these changes in the late 1980s led the trustees of many charities, particularly in the fields of health and social care, to examine carefully their position. Fears were accentuated by reports of the adverse effects on the voluntary sector in the US, where contracting-out of services had occurred since the 1960s[12].

In particular, there were worries about how changes would distort the mission of charities. Experiences of the way specific (and plentiful) Manpower Service Commission funding in the 1980s had intruded into charities and ultimately hindered their goals was not reassuring for trustees.

Worse, experience had taught trustees that freely available government funding could not be relied upon in the long term. What appeared to be golden opportunities for charities in the mid-1980s had led many into an over-dependence on County Councils. When central government later abolished the Councils, many longstanding charities had found their traditional funding base had been eroded and their very existence threatened [13].

---

10   Heginbotham C. *Return to the Community* Bedford Square Press (1990).

11   Ibid.

12   Gutch R. op. cit.; Currie R. *Contracting: Facing up to Difficulties* NCVO (1993).

13   Williams I. *The Alms Trade* Unwin Hyman (1989) pp.184-186.

There were worries too about the expectations and dangers of subsidising Government contracts with charitable funds. This posed threats to their independence but also could adversely affect charitable income – donors may not wish to see gifts used to do things that they considered governments should do. Some also were worried about the financial gearing required in subsidising contracts and the consequent business risk[14].

There were also major concerns about the likely changes in funding methods – particularly the shift from grants usually received in advance to a system of invoicing with all the dangers of delays in payment and the consequent effects on cashflow. In the US, voluntary organisations had had to cope with major problems in this area, resulting in a much greater commercialisation and business orientation in order to survive[15].

Trustees had concerns about the effects on their campaigning role, on volunteering, on their ability to innovate, on the reaction of their traditional financial supporters, on the potential growth in the scale of their operations, and especially that what they did and, how they did it, would become increasing specified by others[16].

Given all the threats posed by these changes, how could trustees manage to govern independently?

11.4 Case Study

I would like now to describe the experiences of one charity, PSS, the one in which I have been most closely involved over the last 20 years.

PSS is a social care charity, founded in 1919 in Liverpool. It was set up by prominent individuals including social reformers and philanthropists involved in city institutions, professions and business, as well as other major organisations such as the University and the Council for Voluntary Service. These founders were the initial funders of the organisation. Its aim was to provide personal help to Liverpool people in need.

In the 1920s and 1930s much of the work of PSS focused on the considerable poverty in Merseyside and people's basic need for food and shelter. It was the

---

[14] Hind A. The Governance and Management of Charities Voluntary Sector Press (1995) p.170.

[15] Currie R. op. cit. pp.22-23.

[16] Gutch R. op. cit. p.8.

main organisation to which people turned in times of crisis. During the Second World War it opened offices in many parts of Merseyside to help people cope with the traumas of war. At the peak of the air raids in 1941, 600 people a day were visiting the Society's city centre offices. During the war almost half a million people received assistance from the organisation.

Throughout its history PSS has been at the forefront of innovation and pioneering in social services. Many forms of provision which have now become accepted features of national health and social services were started by PSS. In 1927 it formed the first Old People's Welfare Committee in Britain, the forerunner of the national Age Concern movement. In 1938 it established the country's first Citizens Advice Bureau. In 1939 it seconded its general secretary, Dorothy Keeling, to the National Council of Social Service in London in order to establish the national network of CABs based on its work in Liverpool. In the following year 1940 she established the national Old People's Welfare Committee which later changed its name to Age Concern England, again based on the experience from Liverpool.

PSS was a significant pioneer in the Marriage Guidance movement, Home Help and Legal Aid services and helped set up one of the first housing associations in the country in 1928, (Liverpool Improved Houses, now Riverside Housing Association). Its pioneering has continued in recent years, having started many services as alternatives to institutional care and traditional day centres. For example, from 1978 it pioneered Adult Placement, the placing of older people or those with disabilities or mental health difficulties with families. Similarly, in the 1990s it managed the first UK projects to respond to the needs of young carers.

After 1950, the growth of local authority services gradually took over PSS's broad social welfare role, a trend reinforced in 1971 with the formation of Social Services departments.

By 1980 PSS faced a crisis in terms of direction and finance. Deficits were fast eroding its limited reserves, whilst its overall sense of direction was confused. Few were sure what the charity was really about or where it was going.

After a major review, the trustees concluded that PSS should concentrate on the things that it was recognised as being good at and, significantly, those for which it was likely to be able to secure funding. This led to a focus on its work with volunteers and on the development of community alternatives to care in institutions.

A new strategy was adopted based on these issues which quickly turned around the financial position. Despite potential external funding crises, not least the election of a militant Labour Council in Liverpool fundamentally opposed to the voluntary sector, PSS was able to secure its financial situation and revitalise its reputation for quality and innovation. Staff numbers rose from 40 in 1981 to 85 by 1988. At this point the trustees recognised that major changes were happening in the environment in which PSS operated and began to review how they should respond.

A fundamental issue was whether the organisation should grow. It was predicted that over the following decade there would be a large growth in the community of the number of very elderly people, (a group to which PSS's services were particularly directed). It was also recognised that, with social policy trends reducing long stay hospital provision, there would be a growth in community care services (again, a central focus of PSS activities). Importantly, they recognised there was a changing scene in which health and local authorities were likely to increasingly contract out services rather than provide them themselves. The dilemma for trustees was how PSS should respond to these changes. Should it grow or should it seek to remain as it was in terms of size and purpose?

After much discussion and examination of the factors involved including the views of relevant stakeholders (service users, funders, staff, volunteers, supporters), the trustees decided that PSS should grow. They felt that, if the organisation did not take up the new opportunities for work, then other organisations would and many would do them less well. It was also thought that, as others took on new work, if PSS failed to grow it would cease to be a major social care charity in the region. This in itself might not matter, but it was feared that it would adversely affect the organisation's ability to attract funding for innovation, since corporate funders and others were likely to financially back those organisations that were perceived to be "go-ahead" and relevant to a changing world. It therefore appeared that staying the same was not a real option and attempts to do so were likely to lead to the organisation's decline.

Perhaps the most important factor that caused trustees to opt for growth was their perception that exciting opportunities lay ahead to develop health and social services, the kind that many people in PSS had fought for over the years, responding to people's individual needs and choices. They recognised what they thought could be a real chance to be in the mainstream of social care rather than at the margins.

The impact of this decision upon the organisation was huge. Turnover rose from around £1m in 1990 to £10m by 2000. Employed staff grew from 85 to almost 600.

Importantly, however, trustees were clear about why they wished the organisation to grow and decided to ensure that it was controlled and on their terms. They wanted to ensure that the organisation was not weaker and less effective as a result of growth but that it was stronger and more able to fulfill its mission. They set out a series of major points, which have been developed and adapted over the years, to provide a framework for that growth. This list included the following:

- *Not to lose sight of what we're about*

    The organisation should be clear about the things it wished to do and say "No" when it was approached, or saw opportunities, to do things that did not fit with this. This was to have important consequences for the direction in which the organisation developed. So, for example, PSS resisted the overtures made to it by local authorities on Merseyside to take on large elderly persons' homes, seeing its role as providing alternatives to them; it similarly rejected other approaches made to it to run advice services, sports facilities and mainstream youth provision.

- *Strategic Planning*

    It was recognised that in order to resist pressures from funders there was a need to grasp strategic management in order to find ways to maintain or even increase trustees independence and strategic freedom[17]. They invested in training for senior managers, and released them to gain and build experience from elsewhere.

- *Innovation*

    Having been an important part of the PSS's past, it was felt that innovation would be an important part of its future. As there was growth in its mainstream services, trustees promoted strongly the need to maintain its pioneering work.

- *Diversified Funding*

    In 1990 all government funding coming to PSS came from Liverpool City Council or Liverpool Health Authority. The trustees were anxious that, as growth occurred, dependence on any one organisation should not increase. They recognised that most growth was likely to occur through government funding and so it was decided to promote and develop services in surrounding local authority areas. Today, PSS receives

---

[17] Hudson M. *Managing Without Profit* Penguin Books (1999) p.96.

funding from 35 different health and local authorities. This has given it great strength in its negotiations over the terms of contracts as well as its ability to pick and choose which work it undertakes.

- *Quality*

   Trustees asserted the need to maintain high quality of services and resist the anticipated pressure on government officers to negotiate ever reducing prices. The trustees decided PSS was to be in the business of high quality services, not large, low quality provision at low cost. This clear position has been important in guiding PSS managers in discussions and has resulted in the organisation refusing to take on many contracts.

- *Negotiate Appropriate Contracts*

   The trustees felt it important to be clear about the sorts of contracts PSS took on and those it did not. At an early stage a check-list was produced of issues to take into account in discussions regarding both the provision of services and in the subsequent contracts.

   Trustees made an important stance in deciding that the charitable and unrestricted funds of PSS should be protected and used for specific purposes that they set out. They decided that such funds should not be used to subsidise contracts with health or local authorities. This position has been maintained in spite of considerable pressure from outside the organisation, not least from competing charities which have subsidised services in this way. The trustees' position has been considerably assisted by the guidance issued on such matters by the Charity Commission[18].

- *Management Skills: Project planning, implementation, administration and finance*

   The trustees recognised the need for the organisation to bring in new skills as well as build on those present, in order to cope with the changes of scale and nature in its operation. This involved investment in the recruitment of new personnel and training of existing staff. In particular, there has been a need for a strong and robust Finance Department to cope with the impact of the major changes to the funding of the organisation.

---

[18] CC37 *Charities and Contracts* (2001) paras.21-24.

- *Volunteering*

    Trustees recognised and wished to counter the potential reduced emphasis on volunteering as growth occurred in mainstream social care services traditionally provided by paid staff. In spite of the growth of such services, volunteering has maintained a high profile in the agency with new programmes funded by charitable sources.

- *Communication*

    Trustees recognised that as the organisation grew, there was a need to ensure good communication. In particular, the changes required a shift in culture from a grant-aided charity to one that took a much more business-like approach.

    Many staff came from social work or nursing backgrounds and were initially resistant to methods which they saw as belonging to the private sector they had previously rejected.

    If the organisation was to succeed in growing and developing in the changed world, trustees recognised that all in the organisation needed to embrace their vision. People working with and for the organisation were critical to its future. It needed to be strong in order to follow through an independent line. There needed to be an understanding of where the organisation was going, why it was going there and how everybody, individually, contributed to that.

    As a result of this determination, the trustees committed PSS to the achievement of the national recognised Investor in People standard[19]. PSS became one of the earliest organisations in the region to so commit itself and one of the first to be recognised as having achieved the standard. However, trustees made it clear that they wished to pursue this, not in order to achieve an award just for itself, but to strengthen the organisation by implementing standards of staff development and support which they saw as vital to the organisation's future.

---

[19] See website: www.investorsinpeople.co.uk

11.5 Conclusion

Charities have faced many changes over recent years. As funders of all kinds have increasingly specified their requirements, trustees can feel constrained in their ability to govern.

However, maybe this is not totally a bad thing at a time when the accountability of all institutions, including charities, is increasingly questioned. The demands of funders are undoubtedly an important stream of accountability.

Funders, who wish certain things to be done, invest in those charities able and willing to fulfill their wishes. Some funders are individuals, others companies, others public institutions or arms of government. Furthermore, the latter's responsibility to the electorate provides charities with an indirect accountability to the public in relation to funding it receives from government. Arguably, a similar indirect accountability links charities to shareholders in relation to the use of company donations. The concern arising from this is less the issue of accountability to funders but more of two questions that arise from it.

First, how can charities avoid the danger of domination, manipulation and control by any particular funder? This paper has argued the crucial role of trustees in relation to this.

Trustees need to furnish their charity with a clarity of mission and ensure that it is then translated into plans and action. This practice can maintain or even enhance independence, enabling a charity to more effectively fulfill its mission.

Second, what other streams of accountability are there or should there be?

The Social Audit approach may provide an effective way for charities to address the issue of accountability. Social Audits are a new phenomenon in the voluntary sector[20]. However, they have the potential to ensure improved communication with and involvement by different stakeholders, build greater understanding, confidence and trust in wider society and, ultimately, bring a deeper sense of accountability. These features will be vital if charities are to ensure a distinct and reputable place in a modern civil society.

---

[20] Bubb S. in Raynard P. and Murphy S. *Charitable Trust? Social Auditing with Voluntary Organizations* ACEVO (2000) p.7.

Chapter 12

MONEY OR CAUSE: HOW MUCH INFLUENCE SHOULD FUNDERS HAVE ON CHARITIES?
David Nussbaum[1]

12.1 Introduction

Among the most distinctive and valued characteristics of charity are its independence of purpose and action, its focus on beneficiaries and the public trust and confidence it engenders. These characteristics are reflected in its governance structure and regulation. Governance is usually founded on the working of an independent group of individuals who take responsibility for ensuring a charity is properly managed and focused primarily on the interests of its beneficiaries. Charity regulation is premised on the virtues of self, or at least relatively light, regulation. How charities structure their governing bodies is, I believe, central to a charity's ability to respond to some of the funding challenges charities face and I will return to this later.

The question of how charities can retain independence of governance while receiving funds from official or institutional donors goes far beyond accounting policy and practice, although accounting principles do have something to say about what qualifies as charitable income.

Some people presuppose that there is a fundamental conflict of interest between funder and funded. This may not always be the case, but over-dependence on any one source of income can cause problems for charity governance. Funding from government or institutional donors causes particular problems since it can come with stringent conditions attached and may compromise a charity's ability to

---

[1] David Nussbaum is the Managing Director of Transparency International ("TI"), the leading global anti-corruption organisation, and took up his position at its headquarters in Berlin in November 2002. He was previously the Finance Director and a Deputy Chief Executive of Oxfam, which he joined in 1997.

promote their beneficiaries' wider interests through criticism of government policy.

Charities are not alone in valuing the virtues of independence and focus on beneficiaries. Whenever government, regulators, or philanthropic institutions seek to describe the distinctive competence of the charitable sector - its added value - they do so by emphasising the virtues of independence, flexibility and community focus. I expect these virtues to be reinforced by the latest government review of the regulation of the voluntary sector[2].

So a vital issue is the extent to which conditions put on grants or contracts awarded to charities by official or private funders compromise these distinctive characteristics of charity.

In recent times perhaps the most polarised expression of concern about the potentially malignant influence of funders was the Centris report "Voluntary Action" published in 1993. This is a useful place to start. The report followed the publication by the Home Office of its Efficiency Scrutiny of the Funding of the Voluntary Sector (1987) and the introduction of competitive tendering for contracts by local authorities. Among the conclusions of this report were the following:

> *"There needs to be a radical change of mind-set in relation to voluntary action. Voluntary action needs to get back to its essentials – the harnessing of independent energy for a moral purpose. Resource factors should be supporting not leading...We should distinguish and promote two very different types of action:*
>
> *The first force: This is authentic voluntary action, prophetic, vision led, reformist, independent of government, pursuing independent energy for moral purposes...*
>
> *The third force: This is part of the wider social economy. It acts philanthropically on sub-contract from the state...The state oversees performance and pays for work done on the basis of independent evaluations to ensure quality control....*

---

[2] HM Treasury *The Role of the Voluntary and Community Sector in Service Delivery. A Cross Cutting Review* (2002); Strategy Unit, Cabinet Office *Private Action, Public Benefit. A Review of Charities and the Wider Not-For-Profit Sector* (2002).

> *It is unrealistic to combine these types of action in a single organisation. Choices must be made*[3]*."*

For the authors of the Centris report anything which compromised the independence of charities clearly violated the true spirit and purpose of voluntary action. They saw "contractual" relationships with the State not just as a threat to the independence of charity undermining its true purpose, but also as the basis for predicting the future governance and regulation of charities.

These prophesised divisions within the sector have not developed. At least not yet. It is interesting though, that one purpose of the "Review of the Legal and Regulatory Framework for Charities and the Voluntary Sector" of the Cabinet Office Strategy Unit (previously called the Performance and Innovation Unit) was to explore the appropriateness of current legal forms for voluntary action. A number of think tanks have also promoted the idea of a "public interest company" to fill the perceived gap in service provision caused by the loss of confidence in state funded and delivered services. To that extent legislators have recognised that "charity" is not the best or only legal form for a not-for-profit organisation to enter into a contractual relationship with the State.

Existing charities though, are caught in a number of dilemmas created by the demands of funders and the changing external environment. The challenges are multiple. They include issues of:

- Governance

- Management

- Accountability

In terms of *governance* the issues are not simply the "either/or" dichotomy proposed in the Centris report. Rather, they are how to plan strategically and manage complex stakeholder expectations while at the same time retaining the integrity associated with independence of purpose and action. In *management* terms the questions are ones of competence and capacity – can your charity negotiate, manage and deliver this contract? Questions of *accountability* do not only apply to meeting the terms of a specific contract, but more generally: charities depend on maintaining high levels of public trust. How to build and maintain that trust has been central to the debate about the future of the sector for many years and has spawned any number of initiatives, such as trustees' codes of

---

[3] Home Office *Voluntary Action* (1993) p.xvii.

conduct, revised financial reporting standards, detailed work on fundraising ratios, impact assessments and so on.

The pressures on charities which result from the changing relationship with funders are constantly evolving. Government is clearly intent on improving the quality of public services and views the voluntary sector as an important player in the delivery of those services. This is not without cost to the sector: those who deliver services on behalf of the State are increasingly taking on the responsibilities of the State. Although the Court of Appeal has recently decided that the Leonard Cheshire Foundation (LCF), who were providing services under contract from a local authority, was not a "public authority" under the terms of the Human Rights Act, it did state:

> *"It is not in issue that it is possible for LCF to perform some public functions and some private functions"*

And thereby be covered by the requirements of that Act[4]. Charities which contract for the State in the future may indeed find that contracts seek to ensure that they agree to be bound by the terms of the Human Rights Act. All of which will impact on the voluntary ethos and the kind of relationships involved for charities who enter into contracts with the State as a means of furthering their charitable objects. Those they seek to benefit through their activities may well become seen more as potential litigants in an adversarial framework, rather than fellow humans involved in common activity together.

Regardless of the complexities involved it is important to recognise that official and (private) trust funds form an invaluable resource for charities and our beneficiaries. The question for most of us is not whether or not we access those funds but how we respond to the changing external environment. And unless charities understand the changing environment faced by funders we are unlikely to be able to adapt or (when necessary) influence their behaviour.

In this paper I want first to establish the context for institutional income and its characteristics compared to other sources of income. Then I shall briefly describe Oxfam's experience of the changing external environment. A major section of the paper will seek to identify some of the trends in relationships with funders, and then look at the implications of these trends for governance. Finally, I will set out proposals for a "charity accountability triangle", which demands more explicit recognition of what role the funders of a specific charity should have in its governance and calls for experimentation. And I shall end with some concluding remarks.

---

[4] *R (on the application of Heather) v Leonard Cheshire Foundation* [2002] 2 All ER 936

12.2 Generic Income Types

We can distinguish four generic types of income for charities, each with its own ethos. The first is when a charity solicits donations from the general public for its charitable objects – this involves essentially a relationship of *trust*. Second, a charity can sell a product or service, for example to the public as in the case of charity shops – this is a matter of making a *profit*. The third arises when a charity accepts money from a donor on condition that the charity use the money to undertake specific activities, such as the provision of agreed services to particular beneficiaries – this is a question of *contract*. Finally, charities earn interest, dividends and capital gains on their unused funds – these investments generate a *return*.

We can summarise these:

Source of Income	Type of Income	A question of . . .
Individual donors	Donations	Trust
Shop customers	Sales	Profit
Institutional donors	Grants	Contract
Investments	Interest etc	Return

Each type of income has its own characteristics, and their fund-raising ratios and risk profiles vary greatly. For example, return on investment is the income type which is independent of the charity's reputation.

The income portfolio of many charities includes several of these income streams, which increases their financial resilience.

In this paper we will be focussing on the third of these: grant income from institutional donors under contract. The influence that such funders have over the charity as a whole will depend in particular on the strength of the other sources of income to which the charity has access.

12.3 The Oxfam Experience

Oxfam has always maintained a balance of income flows, in particular to ensure we can act independently.

Oxfam receives funding from a range of official and institutional sources. In our last financial year (2001/02) we received:

- £12.8m from DfID

- £10.4m from the EU

- £3.4m from UN agencies

- £1.6m from other governments

- £1.3m from other international agencies

This amounts to about £30 million in restricted funds out of a total gross income of £189 million.

Our experience with official and private funders in recent years has been varied but some trends are clear.

12.3.1 Trends

- Relationships with funders have become more strategic, formal and complex.

- Overall levels of funding are linked to public perception of need and political priorities.

- Increased competition and changing compliance standards are increasing costs and challenging ways of working and human resources.

- There is pressure for fewer but larger programmes, and a focus on those outcomes which are easier to measure.

12.3.2 Implications for Governance

- Corporate strategies need to be developed to respond to changes.

- Independence and innovation need sustaining.

- Organisational culture needs to change.

- Reporting and accounting issues need clarifying.

12.4 Trends

12.4.1 Relationships with funders have become more formal and complex

Oxfam has long been a recipient of UK government and European Union funds for humanitarian, development and educational work. The framework within which those funds are disbursed and accounted for has changed significantly over recent years.

There have also been interesting developments in the way that "partnerships" between funder and funded are developing. Funders are seeking to work with INGOs (International Non-Governmental Organisations – Oxfam is a BINGO: a Big International Non-Governmental Organisation) in new and different ways all of which throw up challenging questions for management and governance. All institutional donors face the same pressures to "scale up" their impact and increase their accountability. This has led to a number of changes: increased strategic use of funds; increased volume of funds; increasing pressure for transparency in donor processes; pressure for donors to reduce transaction costs; increasing decentralisation of donor decision making; the trend with some donors to become more sectoral and cross disciplinary.

In some areas change resulted from a greater strategic analysis by both funder and funded. For example, Oxfam used to receive a block grant of funds from the Overseas Development Administration (the predecessor of DfID) for community development work. The funds were allocated to Oxfam as part of a matched funding scheme. Provided certain criteria were met Oxfam could allocate the cost of projects against the grant. Oxfam made submissions twice a year and projects were subject to thematic reviews, visits and assessments by the ODA.

Things are now different. The Department for International Development ("DfID") now provides core funds to 11 UK NGOs through a Programme Partnership Agreement. These set out at a strategic level how the two partners will work together to meet agreed International Development Targets (the "Millennium" development targets set for 2015). DfID provides strategic funding linked to jointly agreed strategic objectives. Funds are agreed for a 3-4 year period.

Reporting is agreed in an "Implementation and Monitoring Plan" which builds on Oxfam's own systems of impact assessment. Progress reports provide an overview of performance assessment issues and DfID's review of the PPA includes assessment of the partnership itself, the level of contact and effectiveness of communication between Oxfam and DfID. The PPA also requires that Oxfam submit a "Management Assertion" to provide assurance that Oxfam's internal systems adequately monitor and manage risks. More conventional reporting to DfID outside the PPA system has also changed within recent years and involves a standard format using a "logical framework" specifying objectives, activities and outcomes along with measurable indicators, means of verification and key assumptions (as well as a budget, CVs of staff and so on).

The question of risk assessment and management has also arisen in recent discussions with DfID. DfID is itself required to make a risk assessment for all its programmes over a certain level by grading them as high/medium/low. DfID are now looking for more detail of major risks involved in the PPA partnership. Again there is nothing new about assessing and managing risk but having to make formal statements to DfID on risk management within Oxfam is both a spur to management and a reminder to trustees of their responsibilities and the increased level of scrutiny under which charities now operate. On the other hand, it requires additional time to be spent on administrative and compliance procedures.

Fortunately DfID are still fairly flexible about making changes to contracts where we can make a good case for doing so. However this requires Oxfam to have the management skills and organisational culture to anticipate where problems might arise in order to manage the contractual relationship. This is not always easy given the conditions under which we operate, but these new realities have forced the pace of change within Oxfam.

The situation has also changed with regard to the EU. The EU has undergone significant changes in the way it allocates funds, including grants to non-governmental bodies. These changes have inevitably led to changes in the way the EU funds development work. The EU have introduced a standard contract which requires NGOs and their partners to maintain a standard of accounting and financial control, which although reasonable for a European organisation, is not found in many grass roots organisations whom Oxfam might support[5]. This thus limits the range of southern civil society organisations that a European NGO could fund with EU co-financing.

We used to have strong formal and informal links to the relevant funding department and to EU delegates (the "in-country" representatives of the EU based within the countries where we work). This enabled us to anticipate what sorts of funds would be available and for what type of work. In its attempt to

---

[5] The Beneficiary holds accurate and systematic statements, and accounts, relating to the performation of the Action, in the form of double entry specific accounting, in the framework of or as an addition to its own accounting system. These specific accounts are operated in line with the arrangements laid down by professional usage. Separate accounts must be kept for every action, showing all the expenditure and receipts. It must give precise monthly indications of the interest paid on the funds paid by the Commission. *Vade-Mecum for Grant Management* EuropeAid (1999).

make its own processes more transparent and accountable the EU has formalised bidding and reporting procedures. It is not alone in doing so. It is a function of the external pressures on institutions to undertake initiatives to improve their accountability. Oxfam has reviewed its own grant making procedures many of which reflect the imperatives, prevailing standards and expectations of official funders and the media.

The practice now is for the EU to announce that funds are available (a "call for proposals") specifying areas and countries to be covered and a deadline for application. Any contact with an official or a delegate once a "call for proposals" has been announced could jeopardise the application as it could be seen as inappropriate lobbying, although contact is permitted with an identified "help desk" and any answers provided are placed on a web site. The application process has also become rigid. Any error in the application can mean instant rejection. Again, in theory once a contract has been agreed we can re-negotiate but in practical terms, the time scale involved makes this difficult. This can have repercussions on how financially flexible Oxfam can afford to be in underwriting a contract when faced by a changed and changing programme environment.

So the major official donors of international development work have moved away from traditional grant funding for NGOs, which allowed the NGO the "right of initiative", to contract funding where the donor defines the programme or sector for intervention and invites NGOs and/or the private sector to bid. For example, DfID is disbursing some of its funding "in-country" both to national and international "civil society" organisations and for a wide range of purposes. This provides increased opportunities for Oxfam and others to bid for funds. This has created opportunities for greater impact, as the resources involved are significantly greater, as well as an opportunity to influence donors, but contracts introduce the risk of the NGO becoming contract driven and losing its legitimacy through mission drift.

Oxfam has been pragmatic in deciding whether or not to bid for such funds. For example, Oxfam has recently bid for US$10m over five years for work on developing civil society structures and activities in Peru. If successful, Oxfam will manage a programme funded by DfID and will chair a panel who will decide which applications will be funded within the policy agreed with DfID. The panel will include representatives from the Peruvian government, the World Bank, DfID as well as local NGOs/civil society groups. This will be a challenging programme. However, where the funds support the general or specific thrust of our own programme and where we do not feel that accepting or managing funds will comprise our impartiality and independence then we will bid for such funds. This pragmatic line was the result of intense discussions within Oxfam about the impact on our image and standing and whether or not, if we bid for such funds, host governments, our partners and beneficiaries would continue to see us as independent and impartial.

12.4.2 Levels of funding are linked to public perception of need and political priorities

Funds raised by charities, and public expenditure allocated, is invariably linked to public awareness of need and sympathy with the cause. Given the huge sums of money raised for international emergencies it would be understandable to assume that even the direst emergencies were adequately funded. This is not the case.

The role of the media is critical in raising public awareness and consequent political commitment to allocate funds. Within the UK Oxfam, along with a number of other leading humanitarian agencies, work in coalition with the BBC and ITV at times of particular crisis through the Disasters Emergency Committee (DEC). One of the factors taken into consideration before a DEC appeal is launched is whether or not film footage which the broadcasters think is suitable is available, as well as the numbers affected and the nature of the crisis. Usually a DEC appeal either provokes or is in the wake of UK government funding. The picture is less rosy when the media are absent.

Globally, UN agencies, notably the World Food Programme and the UN High Commission for Refugees launch a number of appeals annually which often receive little or no media coverage. These appeals are almost universally underfunded.

In 2000 Oxfam published a report on "forgotten crises". Comparisons of per capita receipts revealed a stark picture. In response to the 1999 appeal for the Democratic Republic of Congo (DRC), funds received equalled US$8 per capita of the targeted beneficiaries. For Sierra Leone, the figure was US$16. For Angola it was $48. By contrast, the figure for the former Yugoslavia was $207 per capita. These figures are not the amounts received by each beneficiary, as offering assistance costs more in some places than others because of changing logistical constraints. However, such considerations do not account for the disparities of up to 25 to 1 described above[6].

The reality behind the statistics reflects the same stark contrast. Oxfam colleagues in Angola running a water and sanitation programme in the Central Highland cities of Huambo, Kuito and Cubal, which I visited some years ago, describe themselves as "scratching the surface" of needs. They can only afford to assist the very worst off. This requires painful choices. Like other agencies in Angola,

---

[6] *Africa's Forgotten Crisis* Oxfam (1999).

Oxfam is working below voluntary Sphere standards[7] - providing water points for every 1000 people, rather than the standard of 1:250 set out by Sphere. By contrast, colleagues working in Albania in 1999 described an apparent absence of awareness that donor resources were finite:

"There was money to do almost anything and to do it almost anywhere."

The development costs of the US Army/OFDA site known as Camp Hope have been estimated at $50m. That would have funded half of the entire 1999 appeal for Angola.

12.4.3 Increased competition and increasingly tough compliance standards are increasing costs and challenging ways of working and human resources

Although funding from DfID is still fairly predictable we are increasingly bidding "blind" to the EU. Whereas we used to be able to contact EU officials and ask preliminary questions to ascertain details of the funds available, the "fit" with Oxfam's programme and the likelihood of an Oxfam bid being accepted, the rules are now much tighter. We are now submitting more bids with less certainty of winning. This increases costs and makes overall funding levels less predictable. The rationale for these changes was pressure from Member States for the EU to become more transparent and accountable. That change was necessary was beyond doubt but the changes introduced have affected the way Oxfam bids for and receives funds.

The EU has also been under considerable pressure to ensure that funds are disbursed across NGOs large and small, and from all member states and without any favouritism. ECHO has over 200 NGO partners alone. Increased competition in bidding and limited (if not insufficient) capacity on the EU's part leads to an increased failure rate in bids to official funders.

This leads to a number of related problems. One is the limited amount any funder allows within a contract for the costs of persuading them to make grants, and the cost of servicing the number of bids which we have to submit in order to secure a predicable level of income. Under traditional "grant funding" administrative costs were based on a fixed administrative percentage. Both the EU and DFID allow project design costs to be incorporated into budgets as well as some of the costs of contract management like audits or translation of reports. They are less keen on including an allowance for the full costs of unsuccessful bids. But it is different if there is a tender. Agencies like Crown Agents recover their costs more typically through the daily charge out rates of staff.

---

[7] The Sphere Project *Humanitarian Charter and Minimum Standards in Disaster Response* The Steering Committee for Humanitarian Response (SCHR) Geneva (1998).

Another example of donors' compliance standards was when Oxfam recently applied for funding from the US Government for work in Angola. One of the conditions attached to the grant was that Oxfam should have in place policies to undertake random drug tests of its staff. This is a standard clause in such US Government contract. This was not possible in that context, and we had to negotiate an exemption, which was not easy.

Perhaps one of the major implications for increased bidding and reporting is on organisational culture and structure. We have had to bring fundraisers and programme and project managers much more closely together which has necessitated some structural changes, potentially very much for the better. We have had to change the ways of working of staff in situations of emergency and examine recruitment practices and lengths of contracts to try and ensure that staff hired to implement specific contracts have the time, support and skills to implement and account for externally funded programmes.

12.4.4 There is pressure for fewer but larger programmes, and a focus on those outcomes which are easier to measure

There are trends within the donor community to see NGOs as "partners" who will deliver donor programmes. One of the manifestations of this "partnership" is that both the EU and DfID, understandably from their perspective, see large NGOs such as Oxfam as suitable partners to manage programmes on their behalf. This has involved Oxfam getting involved in more increasingly complex programmes with multiple partners, sometimes involving funders and foreign governments at national and regional levels.

This issue goes to the heart of this paper and the importance of working strategically with funders. Both the EU and DfID see the strategic role of Northern NGOs as not only providing a response to emergencies but also as helping to build a popular base for development, engaging in decision making at global, national, regional and local levels and helping empower the poor to demand and access public services. So there could be value to our beneficiaries for Oxfam to become one of a number of partners working to implement EU or DfID funded projects. We might be able to sensitise the way governments and private sector organisations work with and relate to poor people. But equally we could become more commercial in outlook - simply delivering to the terms of a contract in a cost effective way, or lose the ability to set an agenda independent of government. Such a role might lead over time to us being less able, or less inclined, to listen to the voices of people living in poverty. Either way working as a "strategic partner" and negotiating and managing contracts presents major challenges to governance.

Then within these contracts, there is greater focus on specifying measurable outputs and outcomes. In one sense this is to be welcomed: I and others instinctively favour being able to measure what is being achieved. Relating inputs and costs to outputs and outcomes sounds like something we should all support. After all, efficiency is an economic "good". However, the consequence can be that there is more efficiency, but less effectiveness – if the effect we ultimately want is overcoming poverty. For instance, the poorest of the poor may live in remote areas, and the time it takes to reach them by four-wheel drive could have been spent working with the rather less poor who live in more convenient places.

A further concern is that those things that are measurable may be relatively incidental. How do you measure a community's vulnerability to shocks? Developing outcome indicators for livelihood production or educational achievements may be relatively straightforward; doing the same for the capacity of a village community to cope with drought (without a convenient drought occurring) is rather harder.

12.5 Implications of Trends for Governance

If charities are to retain their distinctive competence under the pressure of a changing funding environment then there are a number of actions trustees and management need to take.

12.5.1 Corporate strategies need to be developed to respond to changes

In order to ensure independence a charity ought not to be overly dependent on any one income stream. This may not be easy to achieve and indeed may not always be appropriate (if the charity is endowed, or has traditionally only existed to supply a specific form of service). Oxfam has policies on the amount of restricted income it will accept: usually no more than 10% of general income from any one institution and no more than 50% of total income from all institutions. However this does not prevent individual country programmes being almost completely dependent on donor funding. This can create tensions whichever strategic direction the trustees choose to go down. Diversifying sources of income can assist in creating and maintaining independence but it means managing a complex set of external relationships and expectations amongst a diverse range of stakeholders. Further, it means integrating a range of different internal cultures built around those different fundraising mechanisms into one organisational whole. It also means facing competition for institutional funds from organisations whose entire ethos is built around bidding and accounting for such funds.

There are also issues of structure. As official funders have diversified their funding down to country level and increasingly linked funding to specific outcomes so Oxfam has re-structured its Institutional Funding Unit, with fundraising staff being posted overseas to work more closely with internationally based finance and programme staff. This is, in my view, a development to be welcomed.

What of the human resource issues? Staff hired to work on specific donor contracts need to have the time and space available to undertake the project reporting aspect of their role. This can become an additional overhead for the charity since funders often do not recognise and cover the full costs of the reporting they require, nor the additional time this takes after the project work itself is completed. Again, these are issues of what overhead costs the funder should bear, and what skills the charity has in negotiating contracts.

There is also a question of training. Our engineers and programme management staff need to understand the basis of the funding of each of their projects – whether it is generated from internal or external sources and what the consequences are for managing the project. Funders should pay for the staff time this takes, and we should claim for these costs. Donors do sometimes pay for these costs – ECHO has recently issued a call for proposals to improve accountability – and Oxfam is applying for funds for training. The EU co-finances a European-wide network for training to improve the quality of NGO reporting. DfID has funded workshops on reporting and financial management through BOND, an umbrella group representing international NGOs. But this targeted donor money, tied to yet more bidding, contracts and reporting, again militates against the full independence of charities.

On the larger issue of improving accountability to stakeholders and involving stakeholders in governance Oxfam has undertaken two initiatives. First is a "stakeholder survey" which is independently conducted and available on our web site. Second is to hold a biennial three-day "Assembly" to which representatives of all stakeholder groups are invited. While not being part of the formal governance structure these initiatives allow Oxfam to take soundings from stakeholders within a given structure.

12.5.2 Independence and Innovation Need Sustaining

One area of concern is whether a charity's campaigning role is compromised by working under contract to the public body whose policies it is publicly campaigning to change. There are no easy answers to this question. The government's "Compact" addresses this issue positively but in practice it is difficult but not impossible for a charity to achieve this balance. This very paper has been edited in the light of colleagues' concerns about donor reactions.

There was considerable coverage of the Royal National Institute for the Deaf's success in being both a service provider and campaigner, and the synergy which can be generated in between the two activities. In summary the RNID campaigned for digital hearing aids to be made available through the NHS. Initially contracted to work on a pilot scheme, the RNID publicly campaigned for further funds to roll out the programme nationally. One of the greatest obstacles to the provision of Digital hearing aids was the cost. The RNID then challenged the procurement processes within the NHS and consequently were asked to chair a committee reviewing procurement and succeeded in negotiating a greatly reduced cost of supply. All of this has been to the benefit of their beneficiaries. However it required considerable skill and political nous to decide when to "go public" on their campaign whilst working under contract on pilot projects which could easily have been jeopardised. While celebrating their success they are also aware that they may be used by government as a private provider within the NHS, and that they are in jeopardy of endangering relationships with key professionals within the NHS on whose support their client group depend. They have moved from service provider, to campaigner, to delivering the government's agenda on modernising the public sector. All of which may be worthwhile, but spearheading the government's agenda for modernising the NHS by being the outside "private" expertise is a rather different role from campaigning for government to supply digital hearing aids. The RNID are well aware of these issues but it is a clear example of the "uncharted" territory which arises when a charity gets deeply involved with government via an initial relationship based around a service contract.

12.5.3 Organisational Culture Needs to Change

Although the Centris report seems to have exaggerated the impact of the "contract culture" on the sector, the fact that working under contract has had such an impact on the psyche of the sector is telling. Charities, like all commercial and public organisations, are under increasing pressure to be accountable to stakeholders on the issues stakeholders regard as significant. For funders the issues are around negotiating and compliance with contracts and measurement of outcomes. For the public it might be administrative and fundraising costs. For supporters it may be evidence of impact and an ability to participate. For "partners" it is about power sharing. For beneficiaries it is about whether or not their lives are improved in a way meaningful to them.

So, meeting the demands of funders is just one aspect of a wider condition. By meeting the requirements of funders we *may* also be able to satisfy demands of other stakeholders on issues of transparency, cost effectiveness and accountability.

As all stakeholders become more demanding so organisational culture needs to shift. As I mentioned earlier, Oxfam has recently introduced a "stakeholder" analysis as part of its governance structure. This can reveal clear tensions between different stakeholders.

The following is an extract from an independent consultant's review of Oxfam's programme relationships in Ethiopia, carried out as part of Oxfam's periodic "Stakeholder Survey" and is an example of some of the problems faced.

> *"Stakeholders have raised different issues during this survey. Some donors maintain that Oxfam should emphasise its areas of technical strength rather than working in many sectors. Local NGO partners argue the opposite and maintain the view that assistance should be provided to all sectors as problems in Ethiopia are multifaceted. Some donors wish to see Oxfam and other INGOs working in the areas of advocacy and capacity building alone, not in other interventions* [8]*."*

12.5.4 Reporting and Accounting Issues Need Clarifying

In 2001 the Chancellor of the Exchequer announced the establishment of a Commonwealth Education Fund ("CEF") to generate funds from government and the corporate sector to fund education projects in 17 Commonwealth Countries.

The proposal was that the fund should be managed and administered by NGOs. This was a political response to a major global campaign by northern and southern-based NGOs to get national governments and the international community to commit funds to ensuring all children get access to primary education. Such a fund was not the primary objective of the campaign. Would accepting the fund allow the government off the hook? To get the 125 million children currently not receiving education into school requires a global strategy linked to governments agreeing anti-poverty strategies linked to debt relief and increased aid. And if the fund was accepted how was it to be managed?

A question which arises for trustees when agreeing to manage funds on behalf of another is the status of the funding. Paragraphs 81 and 82 of the Charities' SORP state the following:

---

[8] *Report on the Stakeholder Survey 2001/02* Oxfam p.14. Survey results can be seen at www.oxfam.org.uk

81 *"Some incoming resources do not belong to the charity, for instance where it receives the resources in circumstances where the trustees acting as agents (and not as custodian trustees) are legally bound to pay them over to a third party and have not responsibility for their ultimate application. In these circumstances the transaction is legally a transfer of resources from the original payer (who remains the principal) to the specified third party. If the original payer retains the legal responsibility for ensuring the charitable application of the funds, the intermediary charity should not recognise the resources in the Statement of Financial Activities or the balance sheet...*

82 *"However, in some cases an intermediary charity may own the resources prior to transfer to the third party and its trustees will act as principal and have responsibility for their charitable application. For instance, where the trustees of the intermediary charity may have applied for the grant of the resources or are able to direct how the grant should be used by the third party or both. Other forms of funding arrangements involving intermediary charities may need their trustees to accept the legal responsibility for the transfer of the grant to the third party (and for its charitable application, where the third party is not a charity). In all of these circumstances the resources should then be included in the intermediary charity's Statement of Financial Activities and balance sheet..."*

In managing the CEF Action Aid has agreed to act as the lead agency to establish a separate bank account into which funds could be deposited. Participating agencies have agreed to show as income only those funds received for projects they directly manage and to pass on to Action Aid any funds they receive from other sources for the fund but not to count that funding as income. So if Oxfam receives a corporate donation for the CEF it will not be counted as Oxfam's income but transferred to the CEF account. Oxfam will report as income funds it receives from the CEF for projects it manages.

One curious feature of the Charities' SORP is how the costs of raising restricted income are reported. Increasingly, financial statements are driven by economics, and this is true of the horizontal lines in the SOFA (Statement of Financial Activities) required by the SORP. So for example, one of the lines requires disclosure of the costs of raising income. However, the columns of the SOFA are driven by legal form, not economic substance. So restricted funds are in a separate column from unrestricted funds. This legal distinction means that the restricted fund column shows how the funds provided under certain restrictions – such as donor grant funding agreements – were spent. It does not show the economic cost of securing those funds, or of completing the work that the funding was intended to cover. In particular, the "cost of generating funds" line does *not* tell you how much it actually cost to extract the funds from the institutional donors. Rather it tells you how much of the institutional grant was given to cover the costs of getting the donor to give the grant.

12.6 Reforming Charity Governance?

In the light of these trends and their associated governance challenges, I turn in this final main section of the paper to what I hope may be some provocative proposals for charity governance. This addresses head on the question of how much influence funders, or more generically donors, should have. How can a charity's governance be most appropriate to its characteristics? This question suggests, of course, that different charities might rightly have different approaches to their governance, and that the role and place of donors should vary. To think this through, we must also ask what influence other stakeholders, most especially those who benefit from the charity's activities - its beneficiaries - should have[9].

Most charities are currently governed by a group of trustees who select and appoint their own successors. Like the snake, Kaa, from the Disney film *Jungle Book*, trustees' metaphorical request is "Trust in me", but this does not chime with the mood of our times where members, beneficiaries and donors (funders) seek a greater say.

Even if management and trustees have good intentions, how can they best be held to account for their decisions, and by whom? Charities are not commercial companies but I suggest that companies (where the primary stakeholders are the shareholders who can hold directors to account) can give insights into how to hold voluntary organisations to account. Whoever calls the charity and its trustees to account is akin to shareholders. Here are two possible scenarios:

1   The *donors* are like shareholders and their wishes should come first - the "dividend" is the pleasure of funding a solution of a particular social problem. The beneficiaries are like consumers – they receive the goods or service being provided.

2   The *beneficiaries* are like shareholders and their interests should be primary – they get the "dividend" of the goods or service provided. The donors, in this view, are more like customers buying a service for others.

---

[9]   This section of the paper was developed with Guy Strafford of *buyingteam*.

Perhaps it is time to re-think the "self-perpetuating trustees" model as the main model for charities. Charities are sufficiently varied that more than one approach may be needed. Rather than prescribe an approach, I believe that experimentation is required.

So I propose that the sector explores models for governance where either the donors or the beneficiaries are given greater formal powers. Issues to be addressed in doing so include:

- How are the views of past donors to be balanced with the views of current donors?

- How are the interests of the actual beneficiaries of today to be reconciled with those of the potential beneficiaries of tomorrow?

Now, I do not advocate that charities move exclusively to one or other of the alternatives, nor do I propose the removal of trustees altogether. Rather, charities should decide where to position themselves on what I call the *charity accountability triangle*, shown below:

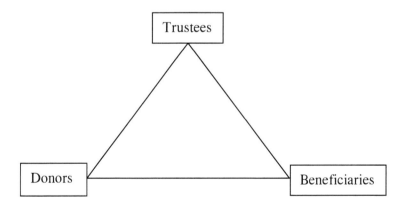

12.6.1 The "Charity Accountability Triangle"

Charities can choose their desired place on this triangle and then think how to get there. These different governance models could then compete with each other to see which proved most effective, and in what circumstances.

Charitable endeavour rightly boasts great achievement, but the prevailing current model of charitable accountability could turn out to be the weakest link. Perhaps it is time to say goodbye – and welcome a wider range of contestants in the competition for the most appropriate forms of charitable governance.

12.7 Conclusion

There have always been conflicts of interest between funder and funded, especially where public money is involved. As far back as 1863 William Gladstone challenged the unconditional right of charities to receive automatic tax reliefs without being subject to some form of government control. In his Financial Statement for the year he argued that:

> *"If we have the right to give public money, we have no right to give it in the dark. We are bound to give it with discrimination; bound to give it with supervision; bound as a constitutional Parliament, if the [charitable] hospitals are to receive a grant, to bring them within some degree f control* [10]*."*

In the short term charities defeated the motion, but bureaucracies will have their way. The Inland Revenue now has extensive powers to ensure that charitable income is expended on charitable purposes in order to qualify for tax relief.

Charities are going through another era of change and challenge. As part of this series of papers organised by the Charity Law Unit of the University of Liverpool, I was asked to comment on how charities can satisfy the competing demands of funders and retain independence of governance. If only there were such a simple solution. As discussed in the paper the challenge posed by demands made by funders, particularly major funders such as government and foundations, goes to the heart of what it is that makes "charity" a distinct and valuable asset in our society. It provokes heated debate within the charity sector and within charities. Oxfam is no exception.

Accounting policy and practice offer some valuable insights into the nature of the question and what sorts of solutions are possible. But in the end protecting the independence and autonomy of individual charities and the charity sector in general can only be answered by trustees, whose responsibility it is to ensure a sound financial basis for their charity, and policy makers who can influence funding policies and priorities.

The scenario is likely to get more complex as political parties of all colours seek to harness the energy and commitment of charities to generate more "public goods" and as pressures on all forms of fundraising increase.

I would like to end with one final thought. I have mentioned several times the importance of ethos to "charity" and how that ethos is influenced by sources of

---

[10]   Owen D. *English Philanthropy 1660-1960* London, OUP (1965) p.331.

funding. One of the most important elements of the ethos of "charity" is its voluntary nature. "Charity" can be mutual or philanthropic – it allows people to get together to do things for themselves or it allows people to support others – the "distant strangers" of charity literature. When charities become part of the means by which the State meets the legitimate claims and expectations of its citizens then they cease to be voluntary. They become an agent of the State and by so doing, inevitably take on the responsibilities of the State. This takes charity into the heart of the formal and legally enforceable relationship between citizen and State.

Charities must operate within the law, but their obligations to donors and beneficiaries are fundamentally moral and voluntary, not legal. Giving is not the same as paying tax. "Obligations" to beneficiaries are not legally binding in the same way that some of the State's obligations to its citizens are. The parable of the good Samaritan did not end with the victim of the assault suing the man who supported him for a failure to meet his care bills adequately or leaving him in the hands of an unqualified medic.

There is something at the heart of "charity" which goes beyond the formal. The purpose of "charity" has to be added value. It has to be about creating something that is new or beyond the obligation or capacity of the State to create or deliver. That is why the virtues of independence are so highly valued. So the question for all trustees is where is the added value? When a charity delivers only to contract and the contract is set by the State as a means of meeting its statutory obligations, and the charity provides no "added value", then surely it must question its status as a charity. It may have become in effect an executive branch of the State or a "public interest company". Charity must be able to demonstrate some of the qualities of the "first force" elements described in the Centris report.

The challenge for us all is to ensure that as the focus on accountability and governance increases, charities create real and additional value for their beneficiaries. If these debates are at their expense, that will entail failure for us all. Rather, let us hope and press for greater achievements from charities.

Summary 4

INFLUENCE OF FUNDERS

Diversity of Charities, Funders and their Relationships: Regulatory Issues

- A separate regulatory regime for service-providing charities has identifiable advantages, but may be impracticable given the hybrid nature of the sector and the relative scarcity of charities solely focused on service provision.

- It is notable that attention is currently focused on the role of large funding bodies, and that the rights and needs of individuals and small donors should be taken into account.

Legal Regulation of Charity/Funder Relationships: Extent and Clarity

- Consideration of the appropriate balance of power between charities and major funders such as local authorities is needed, and the role of legislation in determining the extent of funder involvement should be addressed. It should be recognised that if the law allows funders influence over charities to the extent that the former become shadow directors, consideration must be given to the creation of corresponding funder responsibility and liability.

- Clarification of the law regarding appointment of trustees by funding bodies is needed. In particular, there appears to be a lack of awareness among both funders and charities that such trustees must both be appointed and must undertake their trusteeship solely in the interests of the charity.

- A clearer statement of the law regarding the use of general charitable funds to subsidise contracts is needed.

- There is a need to consider limiting the extent of the accounting requirements that funders can impose upon charities.

Regulation of Charity/Funder Relationships: Wider Approaches

- Whilst graded trusteeship is a potential means of addressing the problems of funder-appointed trustees and negating the disadvantages of the current conflict of interest rules, it is a potentially confusing concept, the implementation of which is not supported by the current legal framework.

- Consideration should be given to the creation of a trustee licensing scheme as a means of ensuring trustee independence.

- A recurrent and important theme is the need for increased support, training and guidance for trustees. In this context there appears to be a widespread lack of awareness of the requirement of independence from funders, and clear Charity Commission guidance is needed.

- An enhanced role for clerks to trustees should be considered.

- The role of non-executives in the protection of charitable independence should be recognised and emphasized.

- A legal framework which encourages mergers (and thus a smaller number of more efficient charities) may increase charities' bargaining power and assist retention of independence. However, the implications of this for the ethos of the voluntary sector must be considered.

Accountability: The Effects of Focus on Different Interested Groups

- Charities are potentially accountable to different groups with various degrees of power to enforce this accountability. Those who can enforce it will have some power and influence over the operation of the charity. The effects of this will vary depending on the particular group and its interests.

- It is notable that distinctions between such groups are not always clear. In membership organisations, for example, members can be beneficiaries or donors.

- Although the public are an important group to which charities are accountable, they really have no power to enforce this apart from 'market' power to choose not to donate. In this respect, therefore, the Charity Commission effectively takes on the role of the public and must enforce this accountability strictly through measures such as SORP.

- Charities are accountable to both beneficiaries and donors to varying degrees. It is important to note that the level to which accountability can be enforced is dependent to some extent on whether the charity is the sole provider in its particular area, or whether there are a number of alternative sources of the particular service.

- Donors can exert pressure to encourage charities to be more efficient in terms of charitable spending. However, there is an important balance between charities being successful in commercial terms and retaining their charitable ethos.

- A shift in the balance of accountability away from beneficiaries towards donors can move charities away from their ethos, the effective implementation of their mission and their long-term goals. It can move them towards commercial efficiency and short-term goals, and can encourage trustees to take risks. A shift of balance too far in this direction and a great emphasis on value accountability can lead to conflict within charities.

Chapter 13

CHARITIES AND GOVERNANCE: THE ROLE OF THE LAW
Jean Warburton[1]

13.1 Introduction

It is the purpose of this paper to review the four seminars on charity law and governance and to try to assess the present and future role of the law in supporting good governance. The one clear message from all the seminars was that governance had raised itself in the agenda of charities and was now a topic of earnest and serious debate. This is reflected in the recent publication of a number of reports on governance including the ACEVO report on the relationship between boards and chief executives[2], the Royal Society report on corporate governance in the voluntary sector[3] and the Charity Commission Regulatory report on Trustee Recruitment, Selection and Induction[4]. Similarly, there are now moves from a number of directions to co-ordinate and clarify developments in governance[5].

---

[1] Jean Warburton is a Professor of Law in the Charity Law Unit at the University of Liverpool. From 1996 to 2001 she was a part-time Charity Commissioner.

[2] ACEVO *Leading the Organisation. The Relationship between Chair and Chief Executive* (2002).

[3] Fitzgerald P. *Corporate Governance in the Public and Voluntary Sectors* (2001).

[4] RS1 *Trustee Recruitment, Selection and Induction* Charity Commission (2002).

[5] See for example, the NCVO series of meetings on The Strategic Development of Trusteeship and Governance and the Charity Finance Directors Group development of a resource network [2000] Charity Finance June p.50. See also Dorothy Dalton's chapter (para 3.4.2.) for details of formal and informal networks of trustees.

Recent government reports have recognised the importance of good governance[6] and the need for more attention and funds to be applied to the infrastructure of charities[7]. What is also clear from both the seminars and national developments is that much of the thinking and development about governance issues is taking place with little reference to the role the law plays now and can play in the future in the support and encouragement of good governance in charities.

Although each seminar focussed on a particular aspect of charity governance, a number of general themes emerged in relation to the law as it affects governance. A common view was that in many instances, whilst the law was clear, it was not well known or easily available. In other areas the law itself was open to doubt and in need of clarification. All the seminars stressed that the law must recognise the diversity of the sector and the need for charities to retain their independence if it is to be effective and, indeed, respected. The seminars also recognised a number of areas where legal reform was needed. Each of the themes is examined in more detail below.

The participants to the seminars identified and agreed on a number of potential reforms to governance practice and those are set out below. What the participants did not come to any conclusion on was the role of the law in supporting and encouraging good governance in practice. That difficult question is considered in the light of the arguments raised by the seminars for both greater and lesser legal enforcement of particular elements of good charity governance.

13.2 Transparency

It is a statement of the obvious to say that the law can only support good governance if it is known by those involved with the governance of charities and readily understood. In a number of areas it was considered that the law was not transparent. This not only created problems in that existing trustees[8] were unsure about their duties and obligations but it also affected recruitment of new trustees; understandably, people are reluctant to buy into uncertainty.

---

[6] Strategy Unit, Cabinet Office *Private Action, Public Benefit. A Review of Charities and the Wider Not-For-Profit Sector* (2002) p.69.

[7] HM Treasury *The Role of the Voluntary and Community Sector in Service Delivery. A Cross Cutting Review* (2002) p.20.

[8] "Trustees" is used throughout this paper to mean a person having the general control and management of the administration of a charity and includes, for example, a director of a charitable company – see Charities Act 1993, s.97.

Particular concern was expressed about the lack of understanding by trustees of the extent of their personal liability[9]. It was not clear, for example, how the liability of trustees of unincorporated charities differed from that of directors of charitable companies. A related concern was confusion over the extent to which delegation was possible. This lack of understanding had two opposite effects on governance. On the one hand, some trustees assumed that they were not subject to personal liability and acted beyond their powers. On the other hand, some trustees became unduly concerned about personal liability and acted with excessive caution and they failed to delegate functions where it would be in the interests of the charity to do so.

Some of the confusion as to personal liability on the part of charity trustees may have arisen from the changes introduced by the Trustee Act 2000[10], especially those in relation to delegation. The seminars recognised that whilst a standard of care which has regard to a trustee's own experience[11] is to be welcomed, the fact that it does not apply universally[12] can give rise to confusion. The seminars noted that trustees may also have been unduly worried by some of the publicity issued by those seeking to sell trustee indemnity insurance. This may be an appropriate time for the Charity Commission to revise and reissue their guidance CC3 on the *Responsibilities of Charity Trustees* with greater prominence being given to a clear statement of the law as it affects the personal liability of charity trustees.

The other main area where it was considered that the law was not sufficiently transparent was in relation to conflict of interest. Whilst there has been much reference to conflict of interest, the emphasis has tended to be on the need to avoid conflict[13] rather than on a clear statement of the legal principle as it applies to charity trustees in particular aspects of the governance of their charity. Knowledge that the principle that, in the absence of specific authority, no trustee may place himself in a position where his duty and his interest conflict[14] applies to *all* trustees would assist many charity trustees faced with a desire by funders to become more actively involved in the decision making processes of charities[15].

---

[9] See also para 2.3; Strategy Unit, Cabinet Office *Private Action, Public Benefit. A Review of Charities and the Wider Not-For-Profit Sector* (2002) p.70.

[10] See paras 2.4, 5.11 and 7.2 above.

[11] Trustee Act 2000, s.1.

[12] For the application of the statutory duty of care see Trustee Act 2000, sch 1.

[13] See for example, CC24 *Users on Board: Beneficiaries who Become Trustees* (2000).

[14] See *Bray v Ford* [1896] AC 44.

[15] See para 10.1 above.

Knowledge that it is possible to have rules in the governing instrument to manage a potential conflict of interest would assist those charities that wish to recruit user trustees.

Closely allied to the legal requirement to avoid conflict of interest is the legal rule that a third person having power to appoint a trustee of a charity is under a fiduciary duty and must exercise that power in the best interests of the charity[16]. It was considered that many appointments, for example by local authorities, were being made either without thought as to the interests of the charity or to support exclusively the interests of the appointor. There was felt to be a need for a clear statement of the law[17] as it applied to appointors allied with a reminder that all trustees must make their decisions in the interests of the charity and no-one else[18].

Clear statements of the law as it affects personal liability of trustees, conflict of interest and duty to act in the interest of the charity would do much to reassure and educate both existing and potential new trustees. In that way recruitment of trustees may be encouraged and a more balanced approach taken to governance decisions.

13.3 Clarity

The seminars highlighted a number of areas where the law was uncertain. The view was expressed that doubt as to the legal position was causing problems for charity governance, particularly in relation to the recruitment and retention of trustees. This view is reflected in the recent Strategy Unit report[19] which stressed the need for regulation of the sector to be clear, consistent and transparent if charities were to understand their obligations and not be excessively risk averse.

Whilst the law is clear that trustees can be paid expenses[20], what is not clear is what amounts to an "expense". There is no statutory definition in the Trustee Act 2000; section 31 simply refers to *"expenses properly incurred by him when acting*

---

16   *Re Skeat's Settlement* (1889) 42 Ch 552; *Re Newen* [1894] 2 Ch 297; *IRC v Schroder* [1983] STC 480

17   There may also be scope for more detailed guidance for third parties as to relevant and irrelevant factors when appointing trustees.

18   Duke on Charitable Uses p.116.

19   Strategy Unit, Cabinet Office *Private Action, Public Benefit. A Review of Charities and the Wider Not-For-Profit Sector* (2002) p.31.

20   Trustee Act 2000, s.31.

on behalf of the trust". Similarly, it is clear that trustees cannot be paid remuneration unless there is authority in the governing instrument or authorisation by the court or the Charity Commission[21], but there is no statutory definition of remuneration. Some guidance can be gleaned from other areas of law, for example, cases which have determined that "volunteers" reimbursed more than actual out of pocket expenses are "employees"[22] and taxation cases which have determined that allowances beyond reimbursement are not expenses[23]. This lack of clarity is, in some cases, inhibiting charities from paying perfectly valid expenses such as child care costs with the resultant adverse effect on trustee recruitment. If regulations are introduced permitting remuneration for charity trustees[24] the opportunity should be taken to provide definitions of both "expenses" and "remuneration". In any event, it is considered that the Charity Commission should include more detailed guidance as to what amounts to expenses and remuneration in their guidance on trustee remuneration[25].

A related problem is the lack of definition of what amounts to a "benefit" to a trustee[26]. If additional facilities are provided for a disabled trustee, at what point do those facilities become a benefit? The problem is a serious one because without specific authority in the governing instrument or authority from the court or the Charity Commission the provision of such a benefit is a breach of trust[27]. The encouragement of user trustees and moves to diversify trusteeship have highlighted this problem. It is reasonable to say that the provision of any facility to enable a person to act effectively as a trustee will be within the powers of a charity provided that any private benefit is incidental, but judicial guidance would be very welcome.

There is lack of clarity as to what amounts to incapacity to act as a trustee[28]. This can be relevant on initial appointment, particularly for some health and social welfare charities who have user trustees. It is also relevant when an existing

---

[21] See para 5.15 above.

[22] See for example, *Migrant Advisory Service v Chaudri* Appeal Number EAT/1400/97 28 July 1998.

[23] See *Perrons v Spackman* [1981] STC 739.

[24] Under Trustee Act 2000, s.30(1). See below p. above for potential law reform.

[25] CC11 *Payment of Charity Trustees* (2000).

[26] See para 5.15 above.

[27] *Bray v Ford* [1896] AC 44; and see para 5.12 above.

[28] See para 5.8 above.

trustee, whether because of age or illness, loses capacity. It is unlikely that there will be any clarification of the law in this area until the proposals for reform in the Law Commission Report on Mental Incapacity[29] are reactivated.

The law on the extent to which a charity may, or should, use its general funds to subsidise contracts with health and local authorities is not clear. On the one hand, courts have refused to apply charitable funds cy-pres to a particular purpose on the grounds that it would have the effect of relieving the rates[30]. On the other hand, courts have specifically held purposes to be charitable because they relieved the burden on taxation and rates[31]. Despite guidance from the Charity Commission[32], charities can be subject to undue pressure when negotiating contracts and the danger of mission drift[33]. Clear judicial guidance is needed.

13.4 Legal Reforms

In a number of areas the participants to the seminars considered that legal reform was necessary if charity governance was to be supported and improved. The proposed legal reforms were largely prompted by experience of difficulty of recruiting and retaining trustees and pressure from funders.

There was a strong view that charities should have the power to provide some form of payment for trustees[34]. The lack of any power to pay was inhibiting attempts to recruit a more diverse trustee body, for example some members of minority groups found the rules against payment prohibitive. The situation was made more difficult as a number of public sector bodies, who were seeking to recruit the same people to their boards, did have power to pay[35].

---

29 (1995) Law Com No 231.

30 *Re Prison Charities* (1873) LR 16 Eq 129; *Att.-Gen. v Duke of Northumberland* (1889) 5 TLR 237

31 *IRC v Oldham Training and Enterprise Council* [1996] STC 1218; *Monds v Stackhouse* (1948) 77 CLR 232

32 CC37 *Charities and Contracts* (2001) paras.21-24.

33 See para 11.4 above.

34 Cf results of Charity Commission 1999 consultation on trustee remuneration; see Charity Commission News, Issue 12, Spring 2000.

35 See para 4.5 above.

One suggestion was the adoption of the idea of attendance allowances as used in local government[36]. An alternative suggestion was a statutory right for time off work for charity trustee duties by analogy with the rights enjoyed by magistrates and local councillors[37].

Under section 30 of the Trustee Act 2000 the Secretary of State does have power to make regulations for the remuneration of charity trustees but only if they are trust corporations or act in a professional capacity. The power is not wide enough to deal with the problem of lack of payment affecting the recruitment of lay trustees from a wide range of backgrounds. It is stressed that if legislation is introduced to permit charity trustees to be paid it should be a wide flexible power[38]. The proposal[39] to give trustees a statutory power to pay an individual trustee to provide a service to a charity, whilst helpful, does not go far enough.

It was suggested that the only real answer to concerns about personal liability on the part of trustees[40] was a new limited liability structure for charities under which any potential liability of charity trustees would be clearly spelt out. The proposal for a new corporate structure specifically for charities, the Charitable Incorporated Organisation, has now been accepted by the government[41]. The basic structure of the Charitable Incorporated Organisation has already been set out by an Advisory Group set up by the Charity Commission[42]. The relevant legislation is awaited.

A number of proposed reforms focused on the need for an effective board of trustees. As the law stands at present if a trustee becomes incapable by reason of mental disorder within the meaning of the Mental Health Act 1983 he may be

---

[36] See Local Government Housing Act 1989, s.18 and Local Authorities (Members Allowances) Regulations 1991.

[37] See Employment Rights Act 1996, s.50.

[38] See para 13.5 below for the need to recognise the diversity of the sector.

[39] Strategy Unit, Cabinet Office *Private Action, Public Benefit. A Review of Charities and the Wider Not-For-Profit Sector* (2002) p.70.

[40] See para 2.8 above.

[41] Strategy Unit, Cabinet Office *Private Action, Public Benefit. A Review of Charities and the Wider Not-For-Profit Sector* (2002) p.58.

[42] The text of the recommendations of the Advisory Group including the content of primary legislation are on the Charity Commission web site www.charity-commission.gov.uk, and see Strategy Unit, Cabinet Office *Private Action, Public Benefit: Charitable Incorporated Organisation* (2002) p.58.

removed from office by the Charity Commission[43]. This does not reflect the reality of mental incapacity and may cause the loss of a valuable trustee who merely needed a little time out to take additional treatment or otherwise address his problem. It is suggested that a sensible reform would be the introduction of a legal power to suspend a trustee for a period rather than the final step of removal.

The rule as to conflict of interest means that user trustees and trustees appointed by funders are not allowed to take part in decisions in which they have a direct interest. This can result in the loss of valuable expertise and knowledge by a board of trustees when facing crucial decisions[44]. One potential solution to this problem may simply be to accept that some trustees who are users or who are appointed by funders are representative and not independent. Such a solution would require statutory provisions setting out the duties and obligations of such representative trustees and possible permissible numbers. This would have the advantage of ensuring that the expertise of such trustees was retained by the charity but that decisions of the board of trustees as a whole were in the interests of the charity and not individual trustees.

In contrast to the proposed reforms directed at retaining trustees, it was suggested that a legal requirement be introduced limiting the length of time for which the position of trustee and, in particular, chair of a charity could be held. This suggestion was prompted by the need to avoid stagnation in the work of a charity and conflict between trustees and chief executive officers. Such time limits are imposed for boards of some public bodies[45].

Concerns about the burdens being placed on charities by individual funders[46] led to the suggestion that there should be legal limits on the extent to which a funder can influence a charity[47]. An alternative suggestion was a legal limit on the extent and type of information a funder could ask for beyond the accounting and reporting requirements imposed by Part VI of the Charities Act 1993[48]. Whilst

---

[43] Charities Act 1993, s.18(4)(c) and see para 5.8 above.

[44] See para 10.4 above.

[45] See para 4.5 above.

[46] See paras 10.3.4 and 11.2 above.

[47] For a consideration of the extent to which the law allows a funder to influence the governance of a charity see, Warburton J. 'Charitable Trusts: Still Going Strong 400 years after the Statute of Charitable Uses' in Hayton D. (ed) *Extending the Boundaries of Trusts and Similar Ring-Fenced Funds* (2002) Kluwer p.174 et seq.

[48] For details of the requirements see para 10.3.4.1 et seq.

the Funding Code of Good practice[49] states that funders should temper their demands for information and accounts[50], there is a lack of awareness and poor implementation of the Code[51]. This is an area where legal intervention may be needed if charity governance is to be supported.

13.5 Background Values

Two important characteristics of the charity sector affect the relevance and effectiveness of the law in supporting good governance: diversity and independence. The two characteristics are valued highly both by charities and the government[52] and need to be remembered in shaping any proposal for reform of the law.

The charity sector is very diverse not only in terms of size - income can range from over £10m to a few pounds a year – but also the purposes carried out[53] and the way they are carried out[54]. Charities also operate through a wide variety of legal structures, some unincorporated and some corporate[55]. It is not surprising therefore that a blanket rule, for example, that trustees should not be remunerated, causes difficulties when applied across such a broad range of organisations. The law has begun to recognise this diversity, for example, by differentiating the accounting and reporting requirements according to levels of income and expenditure[56]. It is interesting to note that the power in the Trustee Act 2000 for regulations to be made for the remuneration of professional trustees allows "different provision for different cases"[57]. The suggestion for Codes of

---

[49] Home Office *Compact. Getting it Right Together, Funding: A Code of Good Practice* (2000).

[50] See para 10.3.4

[51] HM Treasury *The Role of the Voluntary and Community Sector in Service Delivery. A Cross Cutting Review* (2002) p.29.

[52] See Strategy Unit, Cabinet Office *Private Action, Public Benefit. A Review of Charities and the Wider Not-For-Profit Sector* (2002) pp.30, 68.

[53] For a useful summary of the present state of the sector see [2001-2002] Ch. Com. Rep. p.3.

[54] See para 11.4 above.

[55] See para 2.3 above.

[56] Charities Act 1993, Part VI.

[57] Trustee Act 2000, s.30(3)(a).

Practice set out below[58] is partly driven by the need to recognise the diversity of the sector.

It is important that any proposals for reform of the law recognise the diversity of the sector if they are to have maximum effect. The proposal for a *flexible* power for trustees to be paid recognises this[59]. There is similar recognition in the Charity Commission Advisory Group's proposals for the Charitable Incorporated Organisation that the legislation should set out the basic obligations and provisions only with model governing instruments for particular types of charity to be issued by umbrella bodies[60].

Independence is a fundamental characteristic of charity[61]. Present developments in relation to the composition of trustee boards and methods of funding make the legal provisions which support independence vitally important. It is this characteristic which supports the need for greater transparency in the law and the need to keep legal provisions up to date with developments in the charity sector.

To a certain extent the two characteristics can conflict and limit the potential for proposed reform. The proposal for a separate regime for service providing charities[62] would no doubt support the independence of charities but would have serious implications for diversity and innovation. Similarly, reform of the law to make it easier for charities to merge would lead to larger charities with greater independence flowing from greater bargaining power with funders but would reduce the diversity of the sector.

13.6 Potential Solutions

A number of areas have been highlighted where the law is not transparent or is in need of clarification or reform is desirable. Whilst it may be possible for some of the problems of transparency to be dealt with by additional or revised guidance from the Charity Commission, clarification of particular areas of the law will have to await a suitable case coming before the courts and legal reform is dependent on Parliamentary time – a precious commodity. There are two possible interim solutions which can also take account of the need to recognise the diverse

---

[58] See para 13.6 below.

[59] See para 13.4 above.

[60] See footnote 42 above.

[61] See para 10.2 above.

[62] See para 12.1 above.

nature of the sector; the issuing of standard clauses for adoption into individual governing instruments and the use of Codes of Practice.

The whole area of conflict of interest would be eased if standard clauses could be agreed. Any problems caused by doubt as to the law would be solved by clear rules laid down in standard clauses in governing instruments. There are a number of precedents for this approach. As Robert Meakin points out, model governing documents have been agreed between the Charity Commission and the Charity Law Association which contain clauses dealing with the receipt of benefits by trustees[63]. The Charity Commission regularly issues standard clauses when

granting by Order powers to amend a charity's governing instrument[64]. Of even greater benefit are standard clauses specifically drafted for particular types of charity. For example, standard clauses could specify what would amount to a benefit for a user trustee[65] or could set out a workable delegation policy and procedure for charities operating in a particular area. There is considerable scope for umbrella bodies to agree either whole governing instruments[66] or particular clauses[67]. The advantage of such clauses is clarity for trustees and the ability to avoid problems before they arise.

The alternative approach to deal with areas where the law may not be clear is to agree a non-statutory Code of Practice to be followed by all trustees. The advantage is that a Code can be varied as social views as to what is acceptable change without the need to alter each individual governing instrument. There are a number of precedents in relation to governance in other areas. The Cabinet Office, for example, has issued a model code of practice for board members of advisory non-departmental public bodies which, amongst other matters, deals with handling conflict of interest[68]. There is now a Combined Code on Corporate

---

[63] See para 5.16 above and Charity Law Association *Charitable Trust. Trust Deed for a Charitable Trust* clause 6.3.

[64] See OG1 D2 Draft s.26 Order.

[65] See para 5.17 above.

[66] See for example, the model constitution for a Parent Teacher Association.

[67] See for example, the model clause for managing conflict of interest in charitable registered social landlords; Charity Commission and The Housing Corporation *Guidance for Charitable Registered Social Landlords* (2002); and see para 6.2.1 above.

[68] Cabinet Office *Model Code of Practice for Board Members of Advisory Non-Departmental Public Bodies* (2000) and Cabinet Office *Guidance on Codes of Practice for Board Members of Public Bodies* (2000).

Governance for commercial companies[69]. There are no plans to put the provisions of the Combined Code into legislation[70] as shareholder control is considered to be the most appropriate mechanism.

Although there are, at present, no Codes of Practice dealing with charity governance there are a number of Codes which govern charities' dealings with central and local government under the broad head of the 1998 Compact[71]. The subsequent history of the Compact and more detailed Codes illustrate well the potential problems of relying on Codes of Practice as a means to support charity governance. The recent HM Treasury Cross Cutting Review[72] found that there was a lack of awareness and poor implementation of the Codes with resultant problems for charities[73].

13.7 Potential Reforms to Charity Governance Practice

In the course of discussion at the seminars a number of proposals emerged for changes in charity governance practice. Some of the proposals were based on work which is already on-going.

A number of the proposals centred on the problems of recruitment and retention of trustees. There was an overwhelming call for far greater emphasis on induction, support and training for trustees[74]. This echoed the recent Charity Commission regulatory report on *Trustee Recruitment, Selection and Induction*[75] and was supported by the emphasis on induction for new members of NHS boards[76]. Whilst the need for diversity in a trustee body was recognised, it was

---

[69] *The Code of Best Practice for Corporate Governance* which incorporates the Cadbury and Greenbury Codes.

[70] See *Modernising Company Law* Cm 5553 (2002) para.3.28.

[71] *Getting it Right Together. Compact on Relation between Government and the Voluntary and Community Sector in England* Cm 4100 (1998) and see para 10.2.

[72] HM Treasury *The Role of the Voluntary and Community Sector in Service Delivery. A Cross Cutting Review* (2002).

[73] Ibid. p.29.

[74] See paras 2.8 and 3.2.1 above.

[75] RS1 *Trustee Recruitment, Selection and Induction* Charity Commission (2002).

[76] See para 4.4 above.

considered that recruitment should focus on the skills needed by the charity[77]. The recruitment of user trustees should be seen in a wider context.

In relation to general governance it was considered that publicity about the failure of trustee indemnity insurance to protect charity trustees[78] would encourage far greater focus on the adoption of best governance practice as the means of protecting charity trustees. There was a possible expanded role for the Charity Commission in setting best practice frameworks and issuing guidance. The recent Strategy Unit report[79] proposed that one of the strategic objectives of the renamed Charity Regulation Authority should be

> *"enabling and encouraging charities to maximise their economic and social potential"*

which would appear to fit with this approach.

It was considered that in a number of specific areas trustees would benefit from more detailed guidance. In particular, individual trustees needed guidance in dealing with board members who were experts and when conflict arose in a board. There was also a need for guidance when new trustees were introduced by a chief executive officer.

The seminars recognised that there were many examples of good practice in charity governance and that much work to improve governance was taking place. The developments were, however, largely uncoordinated. There was strong support for an Institute of Charity Governance to provide focus for developments on effective charity governance and to provide a forum for exchange of ideas and information[80]. Such an Institute could have a valuable role in supporting another proposal for practical reform – a permanent governance committee of the Charity Commission[81]. This would allow policies to be agreed between charities and the Charity Commission and allow greater self-regulation on the part of charities.

---

[77] See paras 2.8, 3.2.2 and 3.2.4 above.

[78] See para 2.5 above.

[79] Strategy Unit, Cabinet Office *Private Action, Public Benefit. A Review of Charities and the Wider Not-For-Profit Sector* (2002) p.73.

[80] See para 3.4.2 above et seq.

[81] See para 5.23 above.

13.8 The Role of the Law

There are many examples of best practice in charity governance, some of general application publicised by national bodies such as NCVO[82] and some of application only to charities operating in a particular area. The question remains as to how far the law should be involved in encouraging and supporting best practice in charity governance.

The seminars were generally of the view that the law should not have a major role requiring the adoption of particular forms of governance. This view was taken partly because of the diverse nature of the sector which makes the application of detailed rules inappropriate and probably unworkable across the sector as a whole and partly because of the need to be able to respond quickly to changes in practice. The view was also expressed that moves for greater accountability were destroying the ethos and richness of the charity sector and that legal rules to enforce accountability should be treated with caution. These views found support in the recent HM Treasury Cross Cutting Review of the sector where it was said:

> *"[I]n contracting with the VCS to deliver services, the Government must ensure that regulation is proportionate and the independence of the sector is recognised. The greater the regulation the greater the risk that the best features of the sector are smothered* [83]*."*

The dangers of formal prescriptive use of the law can be seen from the recent resignation of parish councillors following the requirement[84] for parish councillors to disclose their financial and other interests in a public register[85]. This example is relevant as parish councillors, like the vast majority of charity trustees, are unpaid. A recent review of penalties in company law concluded that there is a danger of over-deterrence if criminal sanctions are attached to general duties[86].

---

[82] See for example, the NCVO Trustee Services Unit Information Sheets.

[83] HM Treasury *The Role of the Voluntary and Community Sector in Service Delivery. A Cross Cutting Review* (2002) p.17. See also Strategy Unit, Cabinet Office *Private Action, Public Benefit. A Review of Charities and the Wider Not-For-Profit Sector* (2002) pp.30-31, 88.

[84] The Parish Councils (Model Code of Conduct) Order 2001.

[85] See Guardian Society May 1 2002; Times May 6 2002.

[86] See *Modern Company Law for a Competitive Economy. Completing the Structure* Company Law Review Steering Group (2000) para.13.4.

There are a number of ways in which the law can support best governance practice without directly setting out in legislation procedures or forms to be followed by charity trustees and associated penalties for non-compliance. All the ways involve development of mechanisms that are already in existence.

The Charity Commission, by section 18 of the Charities Act 1993, has power to intervene in a charity if either there has been misconduct or mismanagement or it is necessary to act to protect the property of the charity[87]. Failure to observe best practice in relation to governance could be evidence in support of the existence of either pre-condition for Charity Commission intervention. The courts have already indicated that they will have regard to whether trustees have co-operated with the reasonable requirements or requests of the Commission when determining whether to remove a trustee under section 18(2) [88]. It is a relatively small step for the court to have regard also to whether best practice in the relevant area has been complied with. If this route was taken, failure to follow best practice could only be evidence of misconduct or mismanagement if the relevant best practice was clearly agreed and set out in guidance issued by the Charity Commission[89] or, possibly, issued by an umbrella body for charities operating in a particular field.

In a number of areas the law requires trustees to act reasonably. For example, in exercising the general power of investment trustees must exercise the statutory duty of care which requires

"such care and skill as is reasonable in the circumstances"[90].

It is considered that failure to follow agreed best practice would be strong evidence that the duty of care had not been complied with. At present the courts do not appear to require a very high standard of care on the part of trustees, particularly when investing[91]. It is submitted that the courts could enforce a higher standard if there was clearly set out best practice in the relevant area that could be used as evidence of reasonable conduct. This approach of using agreed detailed best practice to support compliance with a general standard is a common

---

[87] See para 7.4 above.

[88] *Scargill v Att.-Gen* [1998] (unreported) September 4; see para 7.4 above.

[89] In this context the idea of a permanent governance committee has considerable relevance, see para 13.7 above.

[90] Trustee Act 2000, s.1 and sch 1(1)(a).

[91] See *Nestle v National Westminster Bank plc* [1994] 1 All ER 118.

one, for example, breach of the Highway Code may be used as evidence of failure to drive with due care and attention.[92]

It is now settled that the courts will intervene to upset a decision made by charity trustees if it is a decision that no reasonable body of trustees would have arrived at[93]. It is open to the courts to raise the standard of trustee decisions by referring to best practice when determining if the decision was one that no reasonable body of trustees could have arrived at.

Charity trustees have to prepare an annual report for submission to the Charity Commission[94] which is also a public document[95]. It is submitted that greater use could be made of the annual report as a means of encouraging best governance practice. Trustees of charities with gross income above £250,000 are already required to report as to whether they have considered major risks to which the charity is exposed and the systems designed to mitigate those risks[96]. It is considered that this reporting requirement could usefully be extended to other areas of charity governance. Depending on the level of enforcement considered necessary and effective, trustees could be required to detail the steps they have taken, or confirm that they have read and followed best practice or simply that they have considered a particular aspect of charity governance. A good starting point which recognises the diversity of the sector are the proposals in the Strategy Unit report for a Standard Information Return for larger charities[97] and for all charities in their annual report to include a statement on procedures for recruitment, induction and training of new trustees[98].

---

[92] Road Traffic Act 1988, s.38(7). See also Trade Union and Labour Relations (Consolidation) Act 1992, s.207(2) in relation to ACAS Codes of Practice and trade union activity.

[93] *Scott v National Trust for Places of Historic Interest or Natural Beauty* [1998] 2 All ER 705 and see para 7.5.2 above.

[94] Charities Act 1993, s.45.

[95] Ibid. s.47.

[96] The Charities (Accounts and Reports) Regulations 2000 r.7(3)(b)(ii).

[97] Strategy Unit, Cabinet Office *Private Action, Public Benefit. A Review of Charities and the Wider Not-For-Profit Sector* (2002) p.62.

[98] Ibid. p.70.

13.9 Conclusion

The law has a valuable and important role in supporting and encouraging good governance in charities but it is a role that at present is being neglected. This series of seminars has shown the importance of a cross-disciplinary approach to governance and the need for charities to be aware of what is happening in other sectors.

Charity governance will not improve across the whole of the sector until the law that underpins the operation of charities is clear and easily accessible. The seminars have shown that there are a number of steps that can be taken in the short term to make the law clearer and more transparent. Whilst reform of the law in some areas is desirable much can be done in the short term with the use of standard clauses and codes of practice.

It is the long-term approach of the law to governance which requires greater thought and co-operation from all those in the sector. This paper has suggested a number of legal mechanisms which can be developed to encourage and support the work that is being done to raise the standard of charity governance. Charity governance will only become truly effective when the law is permitted to play its full role.

INDEX

Accountability
  assessment, 9.6.2, 9.8
  costs, 12.5.1
  excessive information, 1.3
  and funder control, 10.4, 11.5
  housing associations, 6.3.1, 6.4.1.2
  rationale, 12.1
  reform, 12.6
  stakeholder surveys, 12.5.1
  tenant management organisations, 6.4.1.2
  triangle, 12.6
  trustees, 7.2
  and user trusteeship, 5.2
  weak link, 12.6
Accounts
  audits, 9.6.2, 10.3.4.3
  and governing instruments, 10.3.4.6
  policy and practice, 12.7
  public inspection, 10.3.4.5
  requirements, 10.3.4, 10.3.4.1, 13.5
  SORP, 8.4, 10.3.4.2, 10.3.4.6, 12.5.4
  statements of accounts, 10.3.4.2, 10.3.4.6
ACEVO, 3.4.2, 9.7, 13.1
Action Aid, 12.5.4
Adult placement, 11.4
Advertising, 9.4.1
Age Concern, 11.4
Age, trustees, 5.7

Agency, 5.11, 9.2, 9.4, 9.8
Agendas, 3.2.5, 3.3.3
All Saints Group, 3.4.2
Alzheimer's' disease, 5.8
Andreoni, James, 9.3
Angola, 12.4.2, 12.4.3
Annual reports, 8.4, 10.3.4.4, 10.3.4.5, 13.8
Annual returns, 10.3.4.6
Arnstein, S, 6.1
Asylum seekers, 6.3.2, 6.4.2
Asymmetric information, 9.2, 9.8
Attendance allowances, 13.4
Audit committees, 8.5, 9.5, 9.6.2, 9.7
Audits
  legal requirements, 9.6.2, 10.3.4.3
  quality, 9.6.2
  skills audits, 3.2.2
  social audits, 11.2, 11.5

Bankruptcy, trustees, 2.2
Barnado's, 8.1–7
Becker, G, 9.3
Beneficiaries
  as trustees. *See* **User trustees**
  claims against trustees, 7.5.2
  communications with trustees, 5.20
  definition, 5.5
  selection, 1.3
  status, 12.6
Bergstrom, T, 9.3

Berle, A, 9.2
Better Regulation Task Force,
   10.3.4
Board development committees,
   3.2.2
Boards of trustees
   advisory members, 5.21, 10.4
   housing associations, 6.2.1
   proportion of user trustees, 5.10
   role, 4.2
   size, 2.8, 9.5, 9.6.2, 9.7
Boateng, Paul, 1.1
BOND, 12.5.1

Cabinet Office Strategy Unit
   accountability of charities, 5.2
   charitable incorporated
      organisations, 7.3
   Private Action, Public Benefit,
      1.1, 1.3, 1.4, 7.3, 12.1, 13.3,
      13.7, 13.8
   Standard Information Return, 13.8
Cadbury Committee, 1.6, 4.1, 9.1,
   9.6.2
Cairncross, L, 6.1, 6.3.2
Carlisle Housing Association, 6.3.1
Cartel type charities, 9.3
Centris Report, 12.1, 12.5.3, 12.7
Chapman, R, 6.2.1
Charitable companies
   contractual liability, 2.6
   directors, 2.2
   governing documents, 2.3
   housing associations, 6.2.1
   personal liability of directors, 2.6
   trustees, 2.3
Charitable incorporated
   organisations, 7.3, 13.4
Charitable status, 10.2, 10.3.1
Charitable trading, 12.2
Charity Commission
   accounts and audits, 10.3.4.2,
      10.3.4.3

advice, 7.4
functions, 7.4, 7.7
funding code of practice, 1.4,
   10.2, 10.3.3, 10.3.4, 13.4
guidance, 1.1, 1.6, 7.3, 7.4, 13.8
Hallmarks of a Well-Run Charity,
   10.2
and housing associations, 6.2.1
independence of charities, 1.3,
   10.1, 10.2, 10.3.2.1,
   10.3.2.2, 10.4
interventions, 7.4
investigations, 1.3, 7.7
model governing instruments, 5.23
and parent governors, 5.16
remuneration of trustees, 3.4.1
Responsibilities of Charity
   Trustees, 2.8
SORPs. See **SORPs**
and trustee indemnity insurance,
   2.5
and trustee profits, 5.17
Trustee Recruitment, Selection and
   Induction, 1.3, 5.11, 13.1,
   13.7
and user trustees, 5.1, 5.3, 5.4,
   5.10, 5.23
website, 1.1
Charity law
   clarity, 13.3
   and funding, 10.3
   and recruitment of trustees, 2.1-8
   reform, 13.4
   role, 1.1, 1.7, 13.8-9
   and tenants' governance, 6.2.1
   transparency, 13.2
   and user trusteeship, 5.1-23
Charity Regulation Authority,
   13.7
Charity sector, diversity, 13.5,
   13.6
Charity Trustee Network, 3.4.2

Chartered Institute of Housing,
  6.2.1
Chelsea, 6.3.2
Church of England, 2.2
Citizens' advice bureaux, 11.4
Clergymen, 2.2
Codes of practice
  funding, 1.4, 10.2, 10.3.3,
    10.3.4, 13.4
  trustees, 13.6
Commercialism, 1.1, 5.12, 12.4.4
Commissioner for Public
  Appointments, 4.1
Committees
  audit committees, 8.5, 9.5, 9.6.2,
    9.7
  board development committees,
    3.2.2
  disaster emergency committees,
    12.4.2
  governance committees, 9.6.2, 9.8
  nomination committees, 9.5, 9.7,
    App D
  powers to set up, 10.3.2.1
  remuneration committees, 9.5,
    9.6.2, 9.7
Commonwealth Education Fund,
  12.5.4
Communications
  PSS, 11.4
  response to funders' pressure,
    12.5.1
  trustees and beneficiaries, 5.20
Community Fund, 11.2
Confederation of Co-operative
  Housing, 6.2
Confidentiality, and user trustees,
  5.18
Conflicts of interest
  employees as trustees, 5.15
  funder-appointed trustees, 10.3.3,
    10.4, 13.4
  funders and funded, 12.1, 12.7

  lack of clarity, 13.2
  model governing instruments, 5.16
  tenants' governance, 6.2.1, 6.3.1,
    6.4.2
  user trustees, 1.3, 5.3, 5.12–17
Congo, 12.4.2
Contracts
  conditions, 10.3.2.1, 10.3.2.2,
    12.1, 12..4.3
  contract culture, 1.1, 10.1,
    10.3.2.1, 10.4, 12.5.3
  contractual liability of trustees,
    2.6, 7.2
  government funding agreements,
    11.3
  NHS trustees, 4.5
  PSS, 11.4
  ultra vires contracts, 10.3.1
  with funders, 12.4.1
Conyon, Martin, 9.6.2
Cooper, C, 6.1
Cornes, R, 9.3
Corporate governance. *See*
  Governance
Cultural charities, 9.3

Dahrendorf, S, 10.1
Damages, *ultra vires* **contracts,**
  10.3.1
Decisions
  decision-making, 3.3.1, 7.2
  reasonableness, 7.5.2
  setting aside, 7.5
    good faith, 7.5.3
    improper considerations, 7.5.4
    informed decisions, 7.5.6
    omissions, 7.5.5
    reasonableness, 7.5.2
    ultra vires actions, 7.5.1
Delegation, 7.2, 8.7, 10.3.2.1, 13.2
Department for International
  Development, 12.4.1, 12.4.3,
    12.4.4, 12.5.1

Directors
  clergymen, 2.2
  disqualification, 2.2
  exercise of discretion, 10.3.2.2
  minimum age, 2.2
  personal liability, 2.6
Disability charities
  fundraising methods, 11.2
  and user trustees, 5.15
Disasters emergency committees, 12.4.2
Discretion, exercise by trustees, 10.3.2–4
Donations function, 9.4.1, 9.5, 9.7

East Thames Housing Group, 6.3.1
ECHO, 12.4.3, 12.5.1
Educational charities, 9.3
Educational funds, 12.5.4
Elderly, services for, 11.4
Employees
  drug tests, 12.4.3
  powers to employ, 7.2
  reporting systems, 7.6, 8.7
  role, 8.3, 8.4, 8.7
  trustees, 5.15
Environmental charities, 9.3
Equal opportunities, 4.9
Estate Action, 6.1
Estates Renewal Challenge Fund, 6.1
Ethos, 12.7
European Union, 12.3, 12.4.1, 12.4.3, 12.4.4
Exempt charities, 9.6.1, 10.3.4.6
Ex-offenders, 5.9
Expenses, trustees, 13.3

Feigenbaum, Susan, 9.4, 9.4.2
FitzGerald, Paddy, 9.6.2
Founder Syndrome, 3.3.1
Fraud, on creditors, 2.6

Fritchie, Dame Rennie, 4.1
Funders
  categories, 9.3, 10.1, 12.2
  Code of Practice, 1.4, 10.2, 10.3.3, 10.3.4, 13.4
  contracts, 12.4.1
  corporate donors, 11.2
  donations function, 9.4.1, 9.5, 9.7
  and exercise of trustee discretion, 10.3.2–4
  government grants, 9.3, 9.6.2, 11.3
  independence from, 10.1, 10.3.1–4, 10.4, 12.1, 12.5.2
  individual donors, 11.2
  influence, 1.3, 1.7
    compliance standards, 12.4.3
    contract conditions, 10.3.2.1, 10.3.2.2, 12.1, 12.4.3
    funder-appointed trustees, 10.3.3, 10.4, 13.4
    government funding, 11.3
    larger programmes, 12.4.4
    legal limits, 13.4
    measurement pressures, 12.4.4
    Oxfam experience, 12.3–5
    PSS experience, 11.4
  legal principles, 10.3
  motivation, 9.3, 11.2
  partnerships agreements, 12.4.1
  reporting to, 12.4.1
  and sham charities, 10.4
  status, 12.6
  trends, 12.3.1, 12.4, 12.5
Fundraising
  bids for funds, 12.4.1, 12.4.3
  competition, 12.4.3
  delegation, 10.3.2.1
  legacy income, 9.6.2
  and media, 12.4.2
  methods, 11.2
  performance, 9.6.2

public and political priorities, 12.4.2
sources, 9.3, 10.1, 12.2

Gladstone, William, 12.7
Glasgow, housing associations, 6.2
Glazer, Amihai, 9.3
Good faith, 7.5.3
Governance
  agency, 9.2, 9.4, 9.8
  aspects, 1.3
  CEOs' role, 8.1, 8.2, 8.3
  and charity law, 13.1-9
  codes of practice, 13.6
  corporate governance, 8.1-7
  delegation, 7.2, 8.7, 10.3.2.1, 13.2
  directors' role, 8.4, 8.5
  funding good governance, 1.4
  and funding trends, 12.3.2, 12.4.3, 12.5
  governance committees, 3.2.2, 9.6.2, 9.8
  importance, 1.1
  Institute of Charity Governance, 3.4.2, 13.7
  major policies, 8.3
  performance. *See* **Performance**
  public companies, 4.1
  public image, 8.6
  public interest in good governance, 7.4
  reform, 12.6, 13.7
  reporting systems. *See* **Reporting**
  resource deployment, 8.4
  risk management, 8.5
  and stakeholders, 12.5.3
  strategic plans, 8.1, 8.2
  structures, 12.4.3, 12.5.1, 12.5.3
  and values of charity sector, 13.5
  vision and purpose, 8.1, 11.5
Governing instruments
  accounting requirements, 10.3.4.6

  charitable trusts, 7.2
  limitation of liability, 7.3
  model instruments, 5.16, 5.23, 13.6
  nature, 2.3
  objects of charities, 8.1, 10.3.1
  review, 3.3.3
  standard clauses, 13.6
  trust deeds, 2.3
  and user trustees, 5.8, 5.10
Government
  Department for International Development, 12.4.1, 12.4.3, 12.4.4, 12.5.1
  funding, 11.3
  government v charitable role, 11.3
  role in charities, 9.3
Greenbury Report, 9.1
Guidance, Charity Commission, 1.1, 1.6, 7.3, 7.4, 13.7, 13.8
Gutch, R, 11.3

Hampel Report, 9.1
Harbaugh, William, 9.3
Hargreaves, I, 6.2
Hart, O, 9.2
Harvey Jones, Sir John, 4.1
Hawtin, M, 6.1
Headhunters, 3.2.3
Housing
  tenant management organisations, 6.2, 6.3.2
  tenant participation movement, 6.1
  tenants' governance
    case studies, 6.3
    generally, 6.2
    grants, 6.4.2
    incentives to participation, 6.4.1.3
    issues, 6.4
    legal issues, 6.2.1, 6.4.2
    model clauses, 6.4.2

transparency and accountability, 6.4.1.2
Housing associations
charitable companies, 6.2.1
group structures, 6.3.1, 6.4, 6.4.1.2
legal status, 6.2.1
local authority influence, 10.3.2.1
NHF Code of Governance, 6.2
regulation, 6.2.1
transfer of housing stock, 6.1, 6.2
Housing co-operatives, 6.1, 6.2
Housing Corporation, 1.5, 5.2, 6.1, 6.2.1, 6.3.1
Human resources
charities, 3.1.1
Investors in People, 11.4
relations with staff, 3.3.1
reporting role, 12.5.1
role of employees, 8.3, 8.4, 8.7
trends, 12.4.3
Human rights, 12.1

Independence
and charitable status, 10.2, 13.5
from funders, 1.3, 10.1, 10.4, 12.1
contract conditions, 10.3.2.1, 10..3.2.2, 12.1, 12.4.3
unrelated matters, 10.3.4
from government, 10.1
funder-appointed trustees, 10.3.3, 10.4, 13.4
sustaining, 12.5.2
Information. *See also* **Reporting**
agendas, 3.2.5
asymmetric information, 9.2, 9.8
excessive information, 1.3
Standard Information Return, 13.8
trustees, 1.4, 3.2, 3.2.1, 3.3.1, 3.3.3
Insolvency, trustees, 2.2

Institute of Charity Governance, 3.4.2, 13.7
Insurance
charitable companies, 2.6
duty of care, 5.11
trustee indemnity insurance, 2.5, 7.3, 13.7
International Students House, App C
Investment
advice to trustees, 2.4
bad decisions, 7.5.2
delegation, 10.3.2.1
duty of care, 5.11
income, 9.6.2, 12.2
Investors in People, 11.4

Jobs descriptions, 3.3.2, App B
Jungle Book, 12.6

Keeling, Dorothy, 11.4
Kensington, 6.3.2
Khanna, Jyotti, 9.3, 9.4, 9.4.1, 9.7
Konrad, Kai, 9.3

Land acquisition, duty of care, 5.11
Law. *See* **Charity law**
Legacies, 9.6.2
Legal aid services, 11.4
Leonard Cheshire Foundation, 12.1
Liverpool, 11.2, 11.4
Local authorities
consultation with tenants, 6.1
contracts, 10.3.2.1
control over charities, 10.3.2.1, 10.3.3, 10.4
relations with housing associations, 10.3.2.1
scrutiny, 4.3

Mallin, C, 9.6.2
Management
  audit committees, 8.5, 9.5, 9.6.2, 9.7
  breaches of trust, 7.4
  control mechanisms, 9.2
  division of responsibilities, 7.6
  duties of trustees, 7.6
  mismanagement, 7.4, 7.6, 13.8
  public image, 8.6
  relations with staff, 3.3.1
  reporting systems, 7.6
  risk management, 8.5
  skills, 11.4
  staff, 8.7
  or strategy, 1.6, 7.6
  top down, 5.2
Managers
  financial incentives, 9.2, 9.8
  motivation, 9.2
  remuneration, 9.6.2
  role, 8.1, 8.2, 8.3, 8.4, 8.5
Manpower Service Commission, 11.3
Marks & Spencer, 11.2
Marriage guidance, 11.4
Means, G, 9.2
Media, 12.4.2
Medical research charities, 9.4.2
Mental disability, user trustees, 5.8, 13.4
Merseyside, 10.1, 11.2, 11.4
Mills, C, 6.2
Mitchie, J, 6.2
Moral hazard, 9.2, 9.8
Mullins, David, 6.2

National Health Service
  governance, 4.1
  local government scrutiny, 4.3
  procurement for the blind, 12.5.2
  trustees
    contracts, 4.5
  equal opportunities, 4.9
  political and financial pressures, 4.8
  recruitment, 4.4
  remuneration, 4.5
  status, 4.6
  succession planning, 4.7
National Health Service Appointments Commission, 1.4, 4.1
National Housing Federation, 6.2
National Lotteries Charities Board, 5.2
National Strategy for Neighbourhood Renewal, 6.1
National Tenants Resource Centre, 6.4.2
Neighbourhood regeneration programmes, 6.2.1
New Charter Group, 6.3.1
Nolan Committee, 4.1, 9.1, App A
Nomination committees, 9.5, 9.7, App D

Objects of charities, 8.1, 10.3.1
Okten, Cagla, 9.4, 9.4.1, 9.7
Old boys networks, 4.1
Old People's Welfare Committee, 11.4
Olson, M, 9.3
Oxfam, 12.3-5

Passthrough functions, 9.4.2
Performance
  assessment, 9.4
  dataset, 9.6.1
  donations function, 9.4.1, 9.5, 9.7
  efficiency and effectiveness, 12.4.4
  empirical models, 9.5
  empirical results, 9.7
  estimation procedure, 9.5
  mechanisms, 1.6, 9.1-8

outcome indicators, 12.4.4
passthrough functions, 9.4.2, 9.6.2, 9.7
stylised facts, 9.6.2
Peru, 12.4.1
Pink, George, 9.2
Ponsonby, Lord, 10.4
Posnett, John, 9.4.1
Preyra, Colin, 9.2
Priority Estates Programme, 6.1
Professionalism, 1.1, 5.12
PSS, 11.4
Public benefit, 10.3.1
Public image, 8.6
Public interest, good governance of charities, 7.4

Quorums, 10.3.3

Reading, J, 6.3.1
Rediker, KJ, 9.2
Refugees, 6.3.2
Register of Charities, on-line, 1.1
Registered social landlords. *See* Housing associations
Relatives, meaning, 5.5
Religious orders, 5.15
Remedies, bad decisions of trustees, 7.5.6
Remuneration committees, 9.5, 9.6.2, 9.7
Remuneration, trustees, 4.5, 5.15, 13.3, 13.4
Reporting
  annual reports, 8.4, 10.3.4.4, 10.3.4.5, 13.8
  clarification of issues, 12.5.4
  cycles, 3.2.5, 3.3.3
  requirements, 12.5.4, 13.5
  SOFA, 12.5.4
  SORP, 8.4, 10.3.4.2, 10.3.4.6, 12.5.4
  staff role, 12.5.1

systems, 7.6, 8.7, 12.5.4
Riseborough, M, 6.1
Risk management, 8.5, 12.4.1
Riverside Housing, 6.3.1, 11.4
RNID, 12.5.2
Roberts, A, 9.3
Romano, Richard, 9.3
Rose-Ackerman, Susan, 9.2, 9.3
Royal Society, 13.1
RSPCA, 3.1.1
Rugby League Foundation, 10.3.2.1
Russell, L, 10.3.2.1

Salvation Army, 10.3.2.1
Samaritans, 3.1.1
Sandler, Tod, 9.3, 9.4, 9.4.1, 9.7
Schools, parent governors, 5.2, 5.16
Scotland, housing associations, 6.2
Scout Association, 3.1.1
Secret profits, 5.17
Seth, A, 9.2
Sham charities, 10.4
Sierra Leone, 12.4.2
Single Regeneration Budget, 6.1
Skills
  audits, 3.2.2
  gaps, 1.1
  identification, 3.3.3
  management, 11.4
  trustees, 1.6, 2.8
Social audits, 11.2, 11.5
Social welfare charities, 9.3, 11.4
SOFA, 12.5.4
SORPs, accounting and reporting requirements, 8.4, 10.3.4.2, 10.3.4.6, 12.5.4
Sphere Project, 12.4.2
Sport charities, 10.3.2.1
Stakeholders, 12.5.3
Strategy
  and good governance, 1.3, 1.6
  and government pressures, 12.4.4

major policies, 8.3
or management, 1.6, 7.6
PSS, 11.4
response to funding trends, 12.5.1
strategic plans, 8.1, 8.2
vision and purpose, 8.1

Structure-conduct performance, 9.4.2

Sugden, Robert, 9.3

Tax relief, 10.3.1, 12.7

Tenants
governance, 6.2, 6.3
incentives to participate, 6.4.1.3
movement, 6.1
tenant management organisations, 6.2, 6.3.2, 6.4, 6.4.1.2

Tenant's Choice, 6.1

Terence Higgins Trust, 3.2.3

Training
condition of grants, 3.2.4
and funders' requirements, 12.5.1
NHS trusts, 4.4
trustee handbooks, 3.2.4, App F
trustees, 3.1.5, 3.2.4, 3.3.1, 13.7, 13.8

Transparency
assessment, 9.6.2
charity law, 13.2
funding, 10.4
tenant management organisations, 6.4.1.2

Treasury
accounting guidance, 9.1
Cross Cutting Review, 1.1, 13.6, 13.8

Trust deeds. *See* **Governing instruments**

Trustee recruitment
advertisements, 2.8, 3.2.3
attracting, 3.3.3
board development committees, 3.2.2

and charity law, 2.1–8
competition from public sector, 3.1.2
due diligence, 3.2.1
and good governance, 1.3, 1.4
governance committees, 3.2.2
governing documents, 2.8
headhunters, 3.2.3
identification of potential trustees, 3.2.3
induction packs, App F
information, 3.2, 3.2.1
jobs descriptions, 3.3.2, App B
motivation, 2.3, 3.3.3
National Health Service, 4.4
nomination committees, 3.2.2, App D
scarcity of suitable persons, 1.3, 3.1.1
skills audits, 3.2.2

Trustees
age, 3.1.3
attendance allowances, 13.4
basic duties, 2.4
boards. *See* **Boards of trustees**
capacity, 5.6–10, 13.3, 13.4
checks on, 1.4
class, 3.1.3
codes of conduct, 3.3.2
codes of practice, 13.6
communications with beneficiaries, 5.20
confidentiality, 5.18
conflicts of interest. *See* **Conflicts of interest**
delegation, 1.1, 7.2, 8.7, 10.3.2.1, 13.2
discretion, exercise, 10.3.2–4
disqualification, 1.4, 2.2, 5.9
duty of care, 1.5, 2.4, 5.11, 7.2
employees, 5.15
expenses, 13.3
expert advice to, 2.4

fair dealing rules, 5.16
fiduciary duties, 1.3, 1.6, 1.7, 5.12, 10.3.3
funder-appointed trustees, 10.3.3, 10.4, 13.4
gender, 3.1.3
guidance, 1.1, 1.6, 7.3, 7.4, 13.7, 13.8
handbooks, 3.2.4
independence. *See* **Independence**
information, 1.4, 3.3.1, 3.3.3
insolvency, 2.2
International Students House, App C
meetings, observers, 10.3.3
misconduct, 7.4, 13.8
mismanagement, 7.4, 7.6, 13.8
mistakes, 7.4
motivation, 2.3, 3.3.3
networks, 3.4.2
no benefits rule, 5.5, 5.15, 13.3
numbers, 2.8, 9.5, 9.6.2, 9.7
personal liabilities
  contractual, 2.6
  exclusion, 2.5, 7.3
  generally, 1.4, 2.4, 7.1, 7.3, 13.2
  indemnity insurance, 2.5, 7.3, 13.7
  non compliance with objects of charities, 10.3.1
personal qualities, App A
powers, 7.2
profile, 3.1.3
recruitment. *See* **Trustee recruitment**
relations with staff, 3.3.1
removal, 2.2, 3.3.2, 7.6
remuneration, 4.5, 5.15, 13.3, 13.4
retention, 1.3, 1.4, 2.8, 3.3
  reasons for leaving, 3.3.1
  time limits, 13.4

secret profits, 5.17
self-dealing rules, 5.16
self-perpetuating, 12.6
setting decisions aside, 7.5
  good faith, 7.5.3
  improper considerations, 7.5.4
  informed decisions, 7.5.6
  omissions, 7.5.5
  reasonableness, 7.5.2
  ultra vires actions, 7.5.1
skills, 1.6, 2.8, 3.2.2
succession planning, 4.7
support and training, 3.1.5, 3.2.4, 3.3.1, 13.7, 13.8
training, 1.3
trustee handbooks, App F
ultra vires actions, 7.5.1
undertakings, App E
users. *See* **User trustees**
voluntary principle, 1.4, 2.7, 3.4.1, 5.15, 13.4
Turnbull Committee, 9.1

Ultra vires actions, 7.5.1, 10.3.1
United Response, 3.1.1
United States, 9.4.2, 12.4.3

User trustees
  alternatives, 5.19–22
  and charity law, 5.1–23
  and confidentiality, 5.18
  conflicts of interest
    direct effect, 5.13
    fair dealing rules, 5.16
    generally, 5.3, 5.12
    indirect effect, 5.14
    no benefit rule, 5.5, 5.15
    self-dealing rules, 5.16
  definitions, 5.5
  duty of care, 5.11
  and good governance, 1.3, 1.5
  and governing instruments, 5.8, 5.10

guidance, 5.4, 5.5
housing associations, 6.1–4
legal capacity, 5.6–10, 13.3
legal issues, 5.3
parent governors, 5.2, 5.16
proportion on boards, 5.10
reasons for, 5.2
representative capacity, 5.22
secret profits, 5.17
and user consultation, 6.4.2

Venture philanthropy, 10.1
Vicarious liability, 7.1
Volunteers
categories, 3.1.1
gender breakdown, 3.1.3
profile, 3.1.4
public sector support, 3.1.1
scarcity, 3.1.1
socio-economic groups, 3.1.1
voluntary ethos, 12.7

Wales, housing associations, 6.2
Walsall, 6.2
Warr, P, 9.3
WATMOS, 6.2
Weisbrod, Burton, 9.4, 9.4.1, 9.7
Wells, Sir William, 4.1

Whelan, R, 10.3.2.1, 10.4
Wrongful trading, 2.6

Yildirim, Huseyin, 9.3

Zitron, J, 6.2.1